The West Indies:
Fifty Years of
Test Cricket

TONY COZIER

The West Indies: Fifty Years of Test Cricket

FOREWORD BY
SIR GARFIELD SOBERS

ANGUS & ROBERTSON
PUBLISHERS

ANGUS & ROBERTSON . PUBLISHERS
Brighton . Sydney . Melbourne . Singapore . Manila

First published by Angus and Robertson (UK) Ltd,
16 Ship Street, Brighton, Sussex, in 1978

Copyright © Tony Cozier 1978

ISBN 0 207 95798 3

Set by Jetset Typesetters, Brighton, Sussex
Printed in Great Britain by
R. J. Acford Ltd, Terminus Road, Chichester, Sussex

Contents

PUBLISHERS NOTE

The publishers gratefully acknowledge the help of David Frith in the editing of this book, which included the onerous task of checking all facts and figures.

Foreword by Sir Garfield Sobers

THERE might be a few exceptions but it would generally be true to say that cricketers are not ones for dates and figures, even though they form such an important part of the game and its traditions. Judging by my own attitude, I would say most players felt that the statisticians are there to take care of such matters while they get on with the game.

However, I am sure that the occasion of the 50th anniversary of the West Indies' entry into Test cricket is one date that will be viewed with more than casual concern by players, old and young. It is a great landmark and one which stimulates a feeling of nostalgia.

The several exciting series which Tony Cozier recounts in this book will come to life again. I was fortunate enough to play in 93 Tests for the West Indies and the wonderful memories which they have given me will never fade, I am sure. In that time, our cricket went through good times and bad and it was a great experience to share them with so many great players—both team mates and opponents.

What I hope this book achieves above all else is to demonstrate to the modern generation (I will take the liberty of including myself in that category), that West Indian cricket was built on a very solid foundation. In these days of lucrative professional contracts and jet travel which enables players to play so much cricket in different parts of the world, it is just as well to remember what it must have been like when the West Indies were trying to bridge the gap between ordinary Saturday afternoon club cricket and Test cricket.

To me, the feats of players like George Headley, Learie Constantine, Manny Martindale, Herman Griffith, George Challenor, H. B. G. Austin, George John and the many others who carried West Indian cricket on their shoulders in the early days paved the way for the successors which followed after the end of World War II.

I am delighted that a West Indian, who himself has seen so many Tests in the past decade or so, has undertaken to write a book which recounts every series in which the West Indies have been engaged. So often I have read or heard comments about West Indies cricket—about a particular series, or a particular match, or a particular innings, or even just generally—which showed an obvious outside bias. It will be refreshing to have a West Indian interpretation on our 50 years in Test cricket.

Introduction

LEARIE CONSTANTINE, later to become Lord Constantine, Baron of Maraval and Nelson, as distinguished a West Indian as there has ever been, wrote in 1933 that "the game today needs something that West Indies cricket can give it and give it for a long time".

Constantine may have been accused of unwarranted bias for, although he himself was an all-round cricketer of immense dynamism and appeal, his team had achieved little of note since accorded full Test match status five years earlier in 1928. Yet he developed his point cogently and the following quotation from his book, *Cricket and I*, provided an expectation which he lived to see fulfilled before his death in 1971: "Conditions are such in the West Indies that we shall never be able to play cricket in the style that it is played by so many Englishmen and now a few Australians and it is my firm belief that we can learn the atmosphere of Test cricket, get together as a side in order to pull our full weight and yet, as a side, preserve the naturalness and ease which distinguish our game".

Constantine's optimism was well founded. He had been closely associated with the development of West Indies cricket (his father had played for the West Indies on tours to England in the early 1900s) and had observed its strengths and weaknesses with a keen insight into all the problems which confronted it. He knew that West Indian cricketers were, individually, as good as and, in some cases, better than those in England and Australia. He knew that, in the bounteous sunshine which they enjoyed, their cricket was bound to flourish and that their attitude was a refreshing contradiction to the dour war of attrition which the game had tended to become at international level. He also realised that there were myriad reasons for the frustrating failures which the West Indies had endured in their early days in Tests against England and Australia but that these would be overcome with the passage of time.

During the West Indies' first half-century in Test cricket, the evolution which Constantine predicted has unfolded through successive series. Yet, although they have now established themselves as a team as consistently strong as any other, they have still managed to "preserve the naturalness and ease which distinguish our game". If anything, they have become even more attractive and universally popular.

The transformation has been gradual yet pronounced. Before the Second World War, the West Indies had yet to make any great impact on the game as a whole for they had never accomplished anything of consequence against the might of England and Australia, the standards by which they were judged. George Challenor and George Headley, to be sure, had established themselves, beyond all question, as two of the finest batsmen of their time; Constantine was a quite amazing individual whose worth could not be accurately judged in terms of statistics; George John, George Francis, Herman Griffith and Manny Martindale were fast bowlers worthy of comparison with any. Yet, as a team, the West Indies seldom did justice to themselves.

It was the popular feeling that they were short of experience and that their temperament was suspect. There was, no doubt, truth in both assertions but it was not the whole truth. There were problems far more fundamental which stunted the early growth.

That of selection was probably the most compelling. Because of financial constraints and the long distances to be travelled, it was impractical in the 1930s for the best West Indies eleven to be fielded at any one time. Although the West Indies Board of Control was formed in 1927, it found its functions stymied by the reluctance of member territories to abrogate their sovereignty, even in matters relating to West Indies cricket as a whole.

There was, therefore, the divisive system of using four separate captains for the four Tests against England in 1930, when 24 players all told were chosen, and three different skippers even as late as the 1948 series against England.

Being amateurs in the strictest sense of the word, several leading players found they could not persuade employers to grant them the time off necessary to travel and take part in cricket matches, no matter what the importance may have been. In addition, inter-territorial cricket, particularly involving Jamaica, some 1,000 miles distant from its cricket-playing neighbours in the south, was spasmodic. Since the selectors did not travel around to witness them, it was not unknown for men to be chosen, especially for overseas tours, on the main basis of their performances in club cricket. When they ventured forth to England and Australia, they found this grounding inadequate against opponents hardened by a sizable, annual diet of Test and first-class cricket.

As significant as anything else was the administration's reluctance to appoint a black West Indian to the captaincy. It was historically understandable at a time when it was generally considered by the ruling classes that the black man was not ready for leadership, political, social, sporting or otherwise. Yet it generally meant that several fitting candidates for the position were eliminated and this could have done nothing for team spirit.

The war of 1939-45 marked the end of one era and the beginning of the next. During it, first-class cricket in the Caribbean was not only unaffected but actually flourished. The matches nourished a new breed of players who were well prepared for the resumption of Test cricket once hostilities ceased. Conversely, England's cricket, like everything else, suffered horribly from war and it did not refind its vigour until some years after. This gave the West Indies the opportunity to build a self-confidence which they had previously lacked as England were beaten at home and, in 1950, for the first time in England. The standard of the opposition was of little consequence; the results were. West Indies cricket had come of age and there was to be no looking back.

In the late 1940s and 1950s, new contacts were forged with other Test-playing countries—India, New Zealand and Pakistan. Almost every year, the players could anticipate a series either at home or overseas. They now gained international attention and the trickle to the professional leagues in England before the war soon developed into a flood. The game, at all levels, was, indeed had to be, better organised and administered. Instead of a handful of players of world quality, the West Indies was producing exciting new material off an unceasing assembly line—Walcott, Weekes and Worrell, the W formation which battered bowlers the world over into submission; Ramadhin and Valentine, a complementary pair of spin bowlers who became overnight sensations in 1950; Stollmeyer and Rae, the first steady opening pair the West Indies had known; Gomez, an all-rounder of stalwart reliability.

The progress continued unabated through the 1960s and into the 1970s. The greats of one decade were immediately replaced by the greats of the next—the phenomenal Sobers, who set new standards of fitness and excellence for all cricketers to be judged; Kanhai, Hunte, Nurse, Butcher of the 1960s and Lloyd, Fredericks, Kallicharran, Rowe and Richards of the 1970s, batsmen of differing styles, territories and backgrounds but all unmistakable descendants of Challenor and Headley; Hall and Griffith, Roberts and Holding, whose fast-bowling lineage started with John, Francis and Martindale; Gibbs who, in 19 years of tireless off-spin, became the most successful bowler in Test cricket history; the ebullient Collie Smith, the "mighty mouse", a cricketer supreme and a character, tragically killed when at the height of his prowess.

After the war, everywhere the struggle for political self-determination had taken on new proportions and in the Caribbean no less so. Cricket, a way of life for the people, reflected the changing times.

At last, the captaincy became open to all, with merit the only criterion. It was fortunate that a man with the qualities of leadership of Frank Worrell should have been the first black captain, for it was a crucial examination. Had he been a failure, it would have been a grave trauma. Instead, he made it such a success that the reputation of West Indian cricket never stood so high as under him. His team to Australia in 1960–61 lost the series and yet was so overwhelmingly popular that thousands lined the streets of Melbourne to acclaim it when it was leaving; that to England in 1963 caused a revision in the international schedule to allow more frequent visits to England by the West Indies. Like Constantine before him, Worrell was knighted for his services to the game before his early death at the age of 42. He handed his mantle over to Sobers, whose tenure of captaincy has, thus far, been the longest of any West Indian and who has also been knighted.

The changes in the structure of domestic and international cricket in the past decade or so have been dramatic and the present indications are that they will become even more so. In the Caribbean, as elsewhere, sponsorship has provided a welcome financial impetus which has led to a regular annual competition on a regional basis at first-class and youth level. After decades of neglect, the smaller islands of the Windwards and Leewards have been brought into the mainstream and have quickly been a nursery for new Test players. Limited-overs matches have been organised and the West Indies, their style and approach ideally suited to this new variety of the game, became the first World Cup champions in 1975.

England, worried by falling attendances, has thrown open its doors to the best players in the world and West Indians have flocked to the counties in their numbers. Most recently, Mr Kerry Packer, the Australian entrepreneur, has introduced a new dimension to the international game, the full impact of which is still to be determined.

All of this has meant an appreciable alteration in the organisation of West Indies cricket. The change, unfortunately, has caused a distinct and worrying decline in the standard and influence of club cricket, the very foundation on which the game is built.

In the early days, when Test and first-class cricket was irregular, club cricket assumed great importance. It was not uncommon for a club side to include five or six first-class players in its ranks, among whom would be a few Test men. Thousands would turn out for big matches and rivalry was intense. The scores in the club match between Pickwick and Wanderers in the Barbados Cricket Association's Division 1 Final of 1921 are worth recording as an indication of the standard that obtained. Played to a finish, the match took seven consecutive Saturdays to complete, January 8 to February 19, Wanderers scoring 590 and 489 to Pickwick's 436 and 284!

Now, the sting has gone out of club cricket. The public is satiated with an abundance of first-class and Test cricket; the opportunities for professionals in England and elsewhere has denuded the clubs of their best players, thus lowering the standard. There were, for instance, over a dozen Barbadians playing professionally in England and Holland during the summer of 1977. The counter-attractions of other activities have also reduced the numbers of those who previously took to cricket as the principal form of activity.

The young player who would have bowled to the three Ws or Stollmeyer or faced Hall, Griffith and Valentine in the 1950s has little such exposure at this level and must suffer for it. The present West Indies captain, Clive Lloyd, as an example, has played no club cricket in his native Guyana for some years. His commitments in England and Australia, in addition to those for the West Indies, have kept him too occupied for that. And this is the rule rather than the exception.

What effect such developments will have in the future only time will tell. But it does cause concern among those who care for West Indies cricket—and not merely among the pessimists.

For all the modifications down through the years, there have been several factors which have remained constant and are likely to continue so. The game's influence over the diverse people of the region remains passionate and consuming. It is the one West Indian endeavour which has endured without fragmentation although, because of its very nature, it has had to overcome its share of trials and tribulations.

It undoubtedly derives much of its strength from the fact that it is followed fervently by the people of the several races which populate the region. Men of African, Chinese, European and Indian extraction and every combination thereof have worn the West Indian colours in Test cricket—and continue to do so.

During the final Test of the 1972 series against New Zealand, only four West Indians were in the field, each of a different race. The batsmen were Roy Fredericks, a black Guyanese of African descent, and Geoffrey Greenidge, a white Barbadian of British stock; the umpires were Douglas Sang Hue, a Chinese from Jamaica, and Ralph Gosein, an East Indian from Trinidad. The composite character of the West Indies could not have been more accurately illustrated. Nor does the addiction to the game know any class divisions. The rich and the poor, the employer and the worker, the tinker, the tailor, the candlestick-maker, all follow West Indian fortunes on the field and off it with equal keenness.

And they play it, too, with unbounding verve and enthusiasm—as they have always done and, almost certainly, as they always will.

Neville Cardus prefaced Constantine's *Cricket and I* with these words: "When we see Constantine bat or bowl or field, we know he is not an English player, not an Australian player, not a South African player. We know that his cuts and drives, his whirling fast balls, his leapings and clutchings and dartings—we know they are the consequences of impulses born in the blood, a blood heated by the sun and influenced by an environment and way of life much more natural than ours; impulses not common to the psychology of the overcivilised places of the earth".

He could have been describing any one of dozens of West Indians who have followed Constantine—or, indeed, who had preceded him. The words are as applicable today to Lloyd and to Richards and to Holding as they were to Constantine back in 1933 They will ring as true, still, in 2033.

West Indies v. England

OVERALL RECORD

	Tests	Won by England	Won by W. Indies	Drawn
In England	39	14	14	11
In West Indies	32	7	8	17
TOTALS	71	21	22	28

HIGHEST TOTALS

England in the West Indies:
849 — Kingston — 1929–30
West Indies in the West Indies:
681 for 8 declared — Port-of-Spain — 1953–54
England in England:
619 for 6 declared — Nottingham — 1957
West Indies in England:
687 for 8 declared — The Oval — 1976

LOWEST TOTALS

England in West Indies:
103 — Kingston — 1934–35
West Indies in West Indies:
102 — Bridgetown — 1934–35
England in England:
71 — Manchester — 1976
West Indies in England:
86 — The Oval — 1957

MOST RUNS IN A SERIES

West Indies in West Indies:	722	G. S. Sobers	1960
England in West Indies:	693	E. H. Hendren	1930
West Indies in England:	829	I. V. A. Richards	1976
England in England:	489	P. B. H. May	1957

MOST WICKETS IN A SERIES:

West Indies in West Indies:	23	W. Ferguson	1948
	23	S. Ramadhin	1954
England in West Indies:	27	J. A. Snow	1968
West Indies in England:	33	A. L. Valentine	1950
England in England:	34	F. S. Trueman	1963

West Indies v. England

"WE have come to learn, sah", is the remark attributed by a contemporary cartoonist to a member of the first West Indies team to tour England, in 1900. By 1928, that august body, the Marylebone Cricket Club, in the manner of a discerning school-master, deemed the student had developed sufficiently and was ready for graduation to the highest class. Thus the West Indies were accorded Test match status, a standing enjoyed, at the time, only by Australia, England and South Africa.

The elevation of West Indies cricket in this manner was met with little surprise for the organisation of the game in the Caribbean and, with it, the standard, had flourished since it was first introduced by British military units early in the 19th century. No fewer than eight English teams of varying strengths had visited the region between 1895 (when R. S. Lucas led the first) and 1926 (when Freddy Calthorpe was captain of an official MCC contingent); three West Indies teams toured England in the same period and those of 1906 and 1923, both led by the celebrated H. B. G. Austin, subsequently knighted and often considered the "father" of West Indies cricket, were accorded full first-class status.

It was principally on the records of the 1923 team and of those which played against Calthorpe's side three years later that West Indian claims to full Test recognition were forcibly promoted. The former won 12 of the 26 games played (20 of them first-class), despite a summer damp and grey enough to stifle their enthusiasm. George Challenor totalled 1895 runs, including eight centuries, and Englishmen saw, at first hand, what West Indians had long claimed, that he was among the finest batsmen of the day; George Francis and George John established themselves as the first in what has been a long line of outstanding fast-bowling partnerships from the West Indies; C. R. Browne, the delightfully nicknamed "Snuffy", took 91 wickets and young Learie Constantine gave early notice that he was a cricketer and entertainer of extra-ordinary value.

Forewarned by this show of unexpected power, Calthorpe's side was, without question, the strongest ever to visit the West Indies although, it must be noted, nothing like a full England combination. The Englishmen won the only one of three matches against the West Indies to produce a definite result, it is true, but they were beaten by Barbados and generally found the opposition everywhere fully capable of holding its own.

Such advances on the field of play provided the catalyst for the formation of an umbrella organisation to administer the game in the area and the West Indies Cricket Board of Control held its first meeting on June 17 and 18, 1927. H. B. G. Austin was appointed its first president and, according to the minutes, "stressed the necessity of there being a Board of Control owing to the growing importance of West Indies cricket".

Discussion at that inaugural meeting concentrated primarily on the 1928 tour to England. It was decided that each member of the team should receive 30 shillings per week to cover out-of-pocket expenses along with one sweater, two caps, one blazer, one sash, two ties, one hat-band, six pairs of white flannel trousers, eight white flannel shirts, four suits of underwear, one warm lounge suit, four pairs of cricket socks, two pairs of cricket boots, one pair of walking shoes and one travelling overcoat ("only if necessary"). In addition, the Board sanctioned an allowance of £3 per Test match for "such professionals as may be included in the team" along with a scheme for talent money for batting and bowling feats in the other matches.

So seriously was the new Board viewing the 1928 tour that, at much expense, a series of trial matches was arranged in Barbados in the preceding December and January involving invitees from the four main territories. At the end of the exercise, 17 were chosen—one more than had been originally agreed to by the Board, under the captaincy of the Jamaican, R. K. Nunes, who was one of the six survivors from the 1923 tour. Austin, in fact, had been originally appointed as captain by the Board but, aged 52, had second thoughts, and let discretion rule.

West Indies in England 1928

The selection, for once, appears to have met with wide acceptance. No-one expected England to be beaten; that would be asking for a miracle, but it was generally agreed that the new burgundy-coloured flag of the West Indies would fly with honour. Sadly, what was an historic tour ended in acute disappointment. All three Tests were lost by an innings and the record in 30 first-class matches was five victories against 12 defeats—included among them the matches against Ireland and Wales.

Perhaps the optimism of their supporters was misplaced for the West Indies had never previously met opposition as powerful and experienced as the England team they encountered in 1928. This was Test cricket and the England selectors made no concessions to the newcomers. Hobbs, Sutcliffe, Hammond, Jardine and

Tyldesley were their main batsmen; Tate and Larwood their fast bowlers and little "Tich" Freeman and Jupp their spinners. That winter, almost the same combination, under the captaincy of A. P. F. Chapman, crushed Australia 4-1 in Australia.

For all that, the West Indies did no justice to themselves. The irrepressible Constantine, the dependable Freddie Martin, and the fast bowler Herman Griffith alone of the 17 ended the tour with their home reputations intact.

Constantine scored more runs than anyone else (1381), took more wickets (107) and more catches (70) and was seldom less than a dazzling performer. For all intents and purposes, he beat Middlesex and Northamptonshire on his own with all-round feats which have become part of the game's folklore. At Lord's in early June, the West Indies fell short of Middlesex's first-innings total by 122, Constantine scoring 86 of their 230. He then took 7 for 57 (his last six for 11 in six and a half overs) to demolish the county's second innings, clean bowling five of his victims, and, with his side 121 for five requiring 259 for victory, returned to the middle to score 103 in an hour with two sixes and 12 fours as the West Indies won by three wickets. At the end of the month, he treated Northampton to a similar display, destroying their batsmen with his pace (7 for 45 and 6 for 67 including the hat-trick) and devastating their bowlers with the power of his strokeplay, scoring 107 in 90 minutes with five sixes and 12 fours.

Inexplicably, Constantine could find no such magic in the Tests, where he managed only 89 runs in six innings and took only five wickets. Such failures simply placed too much strain on others of lesser ability and they were not up to it.

There were, of course, other failures as crucial to the West Indies' defeat as Constantine's. Challenor was only an imitation of the prolific batsman he had been five years earlier, scored no first-class century and averaged just over 16 per innings in the Tests. He was in his 41st year and this was, undoubtedly, part of the cause. Yet Constantine has attributed the decline as well to the concentration of the English bowling on his leg stump, where he was not as strong as he was on the off. Whatever the reason, the linchpin of the batting was shaky while other components, such as Maurice Fernandes and Joe Small, who had scored consistently in 1923, were also below expectations.

As if the failure of the batting was not enough to dishearten the bowlers the lack of support from the fielders, particularly in the slips and behind the wicket, was a further obstacle for the West Indies.

Ironically, the West Indian bowling and fielding brought

complimentary comments from observers for its high standard on
the opening day of the series, June 23, at Lord's. The team seemed
determined to measure up to the status accorded them and the pace
trio of Francis, Constantine and Griffith bowled particularly well,
despite an England first-innings total of 401, completed by lunch on
the second day of the three-day match. Tyldesley, batting at No. 3,
led England's scoring with 122 characterised by excellent driving
and left the West Indies with nothing else to bat for but a draw.

Challenor and Martin started soundly enough with an opening
partnership of 86 which stretched just short of two hours but,
apart from spirited hitting by Small and Browne at the tailend
of the second innings, this was the only West Indian batting of
any consequence in the match. Between lunch and close on the
second day, 16 of their wickets fell for 162 and, even though
injury prevented Larwood bowling in their second innings,
England were handsome victors by an innings and 58 runs with
time to spare.

The second Test at Old Trafford and the third and last at The
Oval brought no cheer to the West Indies either, except at the
very start when Nunes won the toss and Challenor and Roach
presented him with a stable opening. At Old Trafford, the West
Indies went to lunch on the first day 94 for one (Challenor run
out); by the end of play, England were 84 without loss replying
to 206 and never slackened their grip. With their main batsmen
scoring consistently, Jardine, Hammond, Hobbs and Sutcliffe
each getting half-centuries, England's lead climbed to 145 by the
time they were all out late on the second day. It proved enough
to save them batting a second time for the West Indies slumped
ignominiously from 71 for four at the start of the last day to 115
all out inside an hour to the combined spin of Freeman, the tiny
Kent man, and White. Freeman's 10 for 93 in the match followed
his 6 for 77 at Lord's and underscored the West Indian frailty to
leg-spin although, it must be admitted, this was no ordinary leg-
spin. Freeman at the end of the season had 304 first-class
wickets to his name.

Yet again, Challenor and Roach lifted West Indian hearts with
a spanking start to the Oval match, adding 91 in an hour and 10
minutes in Caribbean-like weather, mainly against Larwood and
Tate. Thereafter, the endeavour faded just as it had done at
Manchester and the margin of defeat was 41 runs heavier than it
was there. Four spectacular catches by Chapman, the
England captain, helped the bowlers limit the West Indies
total to 238 and Hobbs (159), Sutcliffe (63) and Tyldesley (73)
carried England's reply to 284 before the second wicket fell.

Griffith, in a spell of exemplary fast bowling with the second new ball, temporarily checked the advance by dismissing Tyldesley, Hammond, Leyland, Hendren and Chapman—a handsome haul—within an hour while only 44 were added. Once he tired, however, the late-order players carried England to a commanding 438—exactly 200 ahead. It would have been opportune had the West Indies been able to summon themselves for one final Herculean effort but they simply did not have the resolution for it and offered little resistance, all out for 129.

The West Indies team hung their heads, received a sympathetic pat on the back and were told that, despite the results, they had learned a lot. Trinidad's *Sporting Chronicle* of 1929, nevertheless, could not hide its sentiments: "The side left England with the popular feeling prevailing in the Mother Country that it was a premature step taken to initiate the West Indies into the tenseness of Test match atmosphere. This was indeed a bitter pill to swallow after such splendid feats by the side five years earlier."

MCC in the West Indies 1929–30

That "popular feeling" to which the *Chronicle* referred apparently also enveloped the England selectors for, when the time came for the next MCC team to visit the West Indies early in 1930, they chose 14 players well below full England status. Their job was complicated by the facts that they also needed to pick 15 for a simultaneous tour of Australia, with no Tests, and New Zealand, with four Tests, and that many of their principal players elected to remain at home for the winter.

Calthorpe was again the captain, as he had been in 1926, but this time he brought a side which was no stronger than it had been then, when only two of the group, Patsy Hendren and Wilfred Rhodes, had played in the Tests against Australia the previous summer and, although the great Rhodes was still in the side, he was now 52. Hendren himself was 40, George Gunn 50 and Andy Sandham 39. As a balance, there were two young men of whom a great deal was to be seen and heard in the coming years—the left-arm fast bowler Bill Voce and the wicketkeeper Les Ames, the former 20 and the latter 24.

In many respects it was a remarkable tour, England winning the second Test, the West Indies the third and the others being drawn. It was agreed that the fourth and final at Sabina Park be played to a finish, but it had to be abandoned after its ninth scheduled day because the Englishmen had to catch their boat back home. One triple, three doubles and eight single centuries were recorded in the four Tests and two batsmen on either side, with an age differential of 20 years, vied with each other for the attention of the public.

Hendren, short but powerful in build and belligerent in manner, endeared himself to everyone but opposing bowlers with stroke-play which brought him four double-centuries (including two in the Tests) and two single centuries on the tour, 1766 runs overall and averages in excess of 100 in both first-class and Test matches. This was the culmination of a great career. George Headley, a slim, dapper Jamaican not yet 21, was at the start of his and he could hardly have imprinted his name more impressively on the international game—176 in his first Test, 114 and 112 in the third, which the West Indies won, and then 223 in the second innings of the fourth with his team fighting against great odds to save the match. His 703 runs in the series was then the most by any batsmen on his first appearance in Tests.

If the England team was so only by name, not by standard, the same applied to the West Indies. The West Indies Board had still not become organised to the extent that its control could extend to such vital matters as selection of the Test team (that was done by a local panel appointed by the local association), there was little money to bring in players from other territories and put them up for long periods and, in any case, several of those players found it difficult to argue a case for the leave necessary to travel and play cricket over a period of four months.

The overall result in 1930 was that 28 players represented the West Indies in four Tests; that a new captain led them each time—Teddy Hoad, a Barbadian, in Barbados; Nelson Betan-court, a Trinidadian, in Trinidad; Maurice Fernandes, a Guianese, in British Guiana; and Karl Nunes, a Jamaican in Jamaica; and that such stalwarts as Constantine, Griffith, Francis, Browne, Martin and Scott had to miss at least a Test because they could not get time off from their jobs.

On the ideal pitch at Kensington Oval, the batsmen enjoyed themselves in the first official Test played on West Indian soil, the match ending in a draw. Bowlers toiled so unrewardingly that three on either side conceded more than 100 runs in an innings. Roach, the pugnacious Trinidad opener, set the pattern by becoming the first West Indian to score an official Test century, and Sandham, 152 in England's reply, and Headley, 176 in his first first-class match outside Jamaica, matched him later. de Caires contributed 80 and 70 to the two West Indian efforts and Derek Sealey, a Barbadian schoolboy aged 17 years 121 days, not only created a record by being the youngest Test cricketer at the time but also a very favourable impression with a first-innings half-century.

So drastic were the West Indian changes for the second Test that only five of those who played the first survived—and Tommy Scott, brought all the way from Jamaica, was not included. Instead, no doubt based on Trinidad's form in beating the tourists in one of the two colony matches, there were seven Trinidadians in the eleven, five of them for the one and only time in the series.

England lost three wickets for 12 on the first morning, conceded a lead of 46, and yet recovered to win handsomely by 167 runs. Three men were almost solely responsible for the achievement: Hendren and Ames, who staged vital partnerships in both innings, and Voce, who bowled magnificently throughout, taking 7 for 70 in the second innings and 11 for 149 overall.

Hendren and Ames came together in the first innings at 61 for four and were separated at 142, England totalling 208; in the second innings their stand, starting at 52 for three, realised 237. Hendren scored 77 and 205 not out, the first double-century in Tests between the countries, and, after only nine innings, passed his 1000 runs for the tour; Ames had 42 and 105. The West Indies were left 380 to win but they were never in it.

The Englishmen humbled British Guiana by an innings in each of two matches preceding the third Test and, knowing that it was the turn of the Guianese to choose the captain and the team, the West Indies could not have been particularly optimistic over their chances. Yet, for all the misgivings, they conclusively wiped their Trinidad defeat off the slate and put matters all square with victory by 289 runs, a signal triumph.

Four giants of West Indian cricket were principally responsible for the success—Roach and Headley as batsmen; Constantine and Francis as bowlers. Roach's is a fanciful story. After his fine batting in the first Test, he had endured such a lean patch that six subsequent innings against MCC (for Trinidad and West Indies) had brought him 24 runs, including a 'pair' in the second Test. Although invited to play in Georgetown, he felt his position might have caused embarrassment and he cabled the selectors from Port-of-Spain voluntarily offering to stand down. Perceptively, they cabled back telling him to report for duty.

Roach's answer to such confidence was a glorious 209 with three sixes and 22 fours. He and Hunte put on 144 for the first wicket and then Headley, who was to make two centuries in the game, followed to put on a further 192. The West Indies totalled 471 and England collapsed to the speed of Francis and Constantine for 145. Although ahead by 326, the new West Indian captain,

Fernandes, decided to bat again as almost three days remained in the match. England's counter-tactic was negative bowling from Rhodes and Astill, mostly wide of the off stump, and it almost worked. Headley batted like the great player he was for 112 and Browne played intelligently for an undefeated 70 but there were many who felt Fernandes erred on the side of caution by allowing the innings to run well into the fourth day to build up an unnecessary advantage of 617.

England again started shakily but Hendren took it upon himself to save his team. Calthorpe, at No. 9, supported him bravely and the home team had to wait until four minutes before the end of the match before Fernandes could breathe easily and the celebrations begin. The last wicket was that of Hendren, given out leg-before to Edwin St Hill for 123, a dubious decision for the general view seemed to have been that Hendren touched the ball.

Nevertheless, it left the final Test as the decider—and what an extraordinary match it proved. As it was to be played to a finish, the ground staff dutifully prepared a pitch to last—and last it did. Taking advantage of the conditions and the absence of Francis and Constantine from the opposing attack, England's batsmen entrenched themselves for three days to amass 849, then Test cricket's highest total and only surpassed since by England's 903 for seven at The Oval in 1938. Sandham opened and batted nearly two days for 325, Ames made 149 and added 249 with him. The fourth wicket did not fall until 667 and, no matter how long the match would last, surely England were beyond defeat. Scott's leg-spin earned him five wickets but cost 266 runs, the highest ever conceded by a West Indian bowler in a single Test innings.

The West Indian reply of 286 was puny by comparison but, inexplicably and despite local warnings that "weather" was on the way, Calthorpe did not enforce the follow-on. Instead, he allowed his batsmen to gather some more meaningless runs before declaring with nine down early on the sixth day. The academic target for the West Indies was 836 but the objective was to bat till the rains came. They—or more precisely Headley and Nunes—did precisely that. The pair put on 228 for the second wicket and Headley delighted his home crowd with an exhibition which he had saved for them. He stayed six and a half hours at the wicket for 223, spreading his 28 fours all around the ground, and when he was out the rain clouds were already banking over the Blue Mountains. It was not long before it was pouring down and it stayed that way for the next two days with the West Indies total stationary at 408 for five.

As the England players had obligations to their counties to fulfil, they gained agreement from the West Indies authorities to abandon the game so that they could take their ship back—an unusual ending to an unusual match.

West Indies in England 1933

Since gaining Test status in 1928, the West Indies had failed to cut any show on two overseas tours—to England in 1928 and to Australia in 1930–31. Their international standing had advanced none; if anything, it had declined. The tour of England of 1933 failed to provide any noticeable impetus although there were extenuating circumstances and at least two outstanding individual exceptions.

To begin with, the West Indies undertook the tour with a nucleus of only 15 players, compared with 17 in 1928, utilising the services of others who were either playing professionally or studying in England.

Among those in the latter category was Constantine, contracted to Nelson in the Lancashire League, who played a mere five matches and only in the second of the three Tests. Not everyone in the West Indies was satisfied that the Board had done enough to secure his release for all the Tests; whatever the truth, it was the first but certainly not the last time that professionals would find themselves in such a predicament. In this case, the dynamism of the individual was sorely missed.

No less telling a blow was the injury, after he had played only six matches, which prevented Martin appearing in any of the Tests. Martin's influence was the antithesis of Constantine's, calm and sobriety as opposed to action and ebullience, but it was as vital to the West Indies team as had been shown in his steady batting on tour in 1928 and 1930–31. However, he trod on a ball in the Middlesex match, wrenched an ankle and that was that.

On the other hand, England were undoubtedly weakened by the loss through injury of Larwood, the fast bowler who had so laid waste Australia's batting in the "body-line" series in the winter.

A summer of warmth and sunshine led to better batting wickets than were usually experienced in England and batsmen through the length and breadth of the land enjoyed themselves. As far as the West Indies were concerned, however, only the irrepressible Headley, on his first visit to England, prospered in the bounteous conditions. He scored seven centuries, including two undefeated doubles, and ended with a first-class aggregate of 2320 runs. It was nearly twice as many as the next-best West Indian, a statistic which accurately demonstrated the disparity in class between himself and his team-mates.

Virtually the same situation obtained among the bowlers. Manny Martindale, a new fast bowler from Barbados with a fine build, model action, speed and control, dominated both first-class and Test averages almost, if not quite, as conclusively as Headley did the batting. Aged 24 and from the same club, Empire, as Griffith, Martindale took 103 wickets all told (average 20.98) and 14 in the Tests (average 17.92)—more than any bowler on either side. Griffith, by now in his 41st year, faded by comparison with his exploits on earlier tours and, with Constantine and Francis mostly absent, Martindale lacked for support.

The record of five won and nine lost in 30 first-class matches was hardly much improvement on that of 1928 and, while the second Test was drawn, the first and third were lost by an innings, as had all been five years earlier.

In both defeats, the batting shockingly betrayed the West Indies. In the first, at Lord's, almost the entire opening day of the three-day match was lost to rain yet England won with two hours to spare.

England, batting first, proceeded steadily but no more to total 296, Ames' unbeaten 83 carrying them from the insecurity of 155 for six against the excellent fast bowling of Martindale and Griffith and the accurate left-arm spin of Ellis "Puss" Achong. The West Indies were left an hour and three-quarters' batting until the close of play and, in that time, surrendered the match by losing six for 55. Walter Robins' leg-spin claimed the remaining four wickets quickly and the West Indies total of 97 was their lowest ever against England. Following on, they needed to last out $4\frac{3}{4}$ hours to prevent defeat but once Roach had been out to the very first ball of the innings, they were always under pressure. Headley played fluently for 50, Hoad defended stoutly for 36, and the captain, Jackie Grant, who had topscored in the first innings, again batted with little trouble. But it was not enough.

Having fallen to a record low in their first innings at Lord's, the West Indies lifted themselves to their highest total against England in England, 375, when batting first at Old Trafford in the second Test, the extreme of inconsistency. Headley was at his incomparable best and, with his fellow Jamaican, Ivan Barrow, shared a second-wicket partnership of 200. Headley came in at 26 for one and was still undefeated when the innings ended after an hour's play on the second day, his 169 lasting $6\frac{3}{4}$ hours, blemished by not a single chance and including 18 fours. It was only natural that Barrow should have been overshadowed during their 205 minutes together but he never allowed this to bother him and played within his limitations, Headley only just beating him to the honour of being the first West Indian to score a Test century in England.

England, batting a man short because of injury to Macaulay, were effectively 234 for seven at one stage but Jardine, their resolute captain, and Robins staged a recovery which carried the total to within one of their opponents'. The last three wickets then fell without addition so, at least, the West Indies had the satisfaction of gaining a lead, albeit of a single run. Their second innings spluttered along so unsteadily that, at one stage, a dire collapse appeared possible but Roach and Constantine, in his only Test of the summer, scotched the threat of an England breakthrough even though James Langridge's left-arm spin brought him 7 for 56 in his first Test.

A simple draw it might have been but the match will be remembered always as the only Test in England in which the bodyline, leg-theory bowling, which caused so much acrimony in Australia in the winter of 1932-33, was utilised. Clark, in the absence of Larwood, started it for England; Martindale and Constantine responded for the West Indies and the public reaction was so severe that it was not exploited again. Hammond was hit on the chin and cut by a bouncer from Martindale but it is significant that Jardine, perpetrator of the tactic in Australia, was never ruffled and defied it for five hours while scoring an important 127.

The final Test was very much a repetition of the first. The West Indies, with Martindale claiming 5 for 93, bowled well enough to limited England to 312 after a century by the new opener, Bakewell, but were then humbled for 100 and 195. The pace of Clark caused them early reversals but, yet again, spin proved their undoing. This time C. S. Marriott's leg-breaks and googlies confused them: 5 for 37 and 6 for 59 were his figures yet he was never chosen again for England. Not only West Indian selectors have their fetishes!

Both in England and at home, doubts were cast on the West Indian temperament. *Wisden* of 1934 said the team "did not convey the impression of being fitted temperamentally for matches of such an important nature"; the *Sporting Chronicle* of Trinidad charged that they "showed a mercurial disposition that precluded any show of fighting qualities when faced with difficult situations". It was a long, long time before they could erase such slurs.

MCC in the West Indies 1934–35

Having waited more than six years and suffered the anguish of three most disappointing overseas tours since they were accorded Test status, the West Indies were not to be denied when England, under the captaincy of Bob Wyatt, played a series of four Tests in the Caribbean early in 1935. The English team was stronger than any that had been before, yet still not the strongest that could be mustered, and the West Indies, having learned from the painful lessons of the 1929–30 tour, were ready for them.

This time there was a set policy to pick the best team available. There were none of the hodge-podge elevens of five years earlier and there was one captain throughout—Jackie Grant, who had led the side in all its previous Tests for which he had been available. In addition to Grant, six others played in every Test and two others in three, maintaining a continuity which was new to West Indian cricket.

England won the first Test and the West Indies the second and the fourth handsomely and deservedly. The home team's success was based on a formula which repeatedly served them well in the years to come—batting which refused to be dominated and bowling of pace and hostility.

Headley was, once more, the heart of the batting but there were others who functioned effectively as well, notably Sealey, the schoolboy of 1930 now matured into a polished player. Martindale, Constantine and Hylton combined into a fast-bowling trio which the English captain rated the best of its kind in the world, securing 47 wickets cheaply between them and so troubling the batsmen that England only once reached 60 with fewer than three wickets down. In addition, the fielding was of a high standard, Rolph Grant, the captain's younger brother, rivalling Constantine in this department. The younger Grant, later to succeed to the captaincy, was a tremendous all-round athlete, a soccer goalkeeper of uncanny reflexes who played for England's amateur team while at Cambridge, Trinidad's heavyweight boxing champion, and an all-round cricketer who made his mark in his first series.

England took the lead at Kensington in the weirdest Test ever played in the Caribbean. The modern device of covering had not yet come into effect and unseasonal rain soaked the unprotected pitch preceding each day of the match so badly that the affair became a lottery.

In such conditions, Headley, once more, displayed his excellence by scoring 44 run out although the West Indies could muster only 102 after being sent in. Another great batsman, Hammond,

The 1933 West Indies team in England. Standing: E. A. Martindale, F. R. Martin, C. A. Merry, V. A. Valentine, I. Barrow, O. C. DaCosta, E. Achong; sitting: H. C. Griffith, E. L. G. Hoad, J. M. Kidney (manager), G. C. Grant (captain), C. A. Wiles, C. A. Roach; in front: B. J. Sealey, C. M. Christiani, G. A. Headley.

Jamaican left-hander 'Freddie' Martin, a stabilising influence in the early days of West Indies Test cricket, hits out during the 1933 touring team's match against Middlesex. Later in the innings Valentine and Griffith put on 132 in 58 minutes for the tenth wicket. The wicketkeeper is Fred Price. *Sport & General*

Ivan Barrow, the young Jamaican, hooks during his innings of 105 in the Manchester Test of 1933, when he added 200 for the second wicket with George Headley. The wicketkeeper is Les Ames. *Sport & General*

Derek Sealy, the youngest of all West Indians to have played Test cricket (17 years 122 days, Bridgetown, 1929–30), strokes leg-spinner 'Tich' Freeman through the covers during the 1939 touring team's opening match, against L. E. G. Ames's XI at Gravesend. Howard Levett keeps wicket and Frank Woolley (first) and Doug Wright are at slip. *Sport & General*

George Headley, supreme among pre-war West Indies batsmen, pulls England left-arm
spinner Hedley Verity through midwicket during the first of his two centuries in the 1939
Lord's Test match. Wally Hammond is at slip, Arthur Wood keeps wicket, and Doug
Wright is at short mid-on.   *Sport & General*

A powerful shot by Ken Weeke
Headley's Jamaican club-mate
during his memorable centur
(reached in 110 minutes) agains
England in the 1939 Oval Tes
match. *Sport & Gener*

An historic moment for West Indi
cricket as, for the first time, th
side is led by a black man: Georg
Headley tosses with Ken Cranston
England's replacement captai
('Gubby' Allen was injured), a
Bridgetown in January 1948.

using similarly fine judgment, was 43 not out at the end of the day with England 81 for 5. During the night, more rain fell and play was delayed until after tea; when it did start, Hammond and Holmes were dismissed off the first three balls bowled and Wyatt immediately declared 21 behind.

Grant retorted by reversing his batting order but this ploy failed, big Jim Smith, the massive Middlesex fast bowler, sending back Rolph Grant, Martindale and Achong with only four scored. Hylton and the wicketkeeper Cyril Christiani batted intelligently to see out the close with the West Indies 33 for three—54 ahead. Another half-inch of rain during the night delayed the resumption and guaranteed the pitch would not improve. If anything, bright sunshine from early morning on the third day conspired to make it worse, if that was possible, and the West Indies went to tea 51 for six—just 72 ahead with Roach not out and four of their major batsmen still to come.

For the second time in the match, Grant considered the odds and gambled big. Wanting to make use of the pitch while it was at its most devilish, he declared. England sent in the fast bowlers, Farnes and Smith, to deal with the situation by strong-arm tactics but Martindale, before his home crowd, soon had the innings in ruins at 48 for six. Unfortunately, at the other end, Hylton's control was wanting and Hammond, kept back until late, won the match with an innings of 29 not out worth more than many of his centuries. The last 25 runs came off only 24 balls, the winning hit being a shot over extracover for six by Hammond off Martindale and England were ahead in the series.

It was not for long. The West Indies, discounting the Bridgetown result as a freak, showed their superiority in the second Test at the Queen's Park Oval and, even though they were forced to wait until the penultimate ball for their victory (the Tests this time being four days instead of five as they were in 1930), it was massive—by 217 runs. Constantine, back home from England, rejoined the side and contributed greatly to the result: 90 and 31 with the bat, 2 for 41 and 3 for 11 with the ball.

Wyatt began by sending the West Indies in, apparently on a hunch. Certainly, there was no real evidence to influence the move but it was merely one of his many decisions in the match which were baffling. In fact, England had an encouraging start, despite the crucial absence of the injured Farnes, before Sealey and Constantine, the former with artistic polish, the latter with effective brute force, changed the fortunes. Sealey got 92, Constantine 90, and the West Indies 302 overall. When the fast bowlers routed the early part of England's batting and the board read 23 for five, a crowd of 10,000 (large in those days) was ecstatic. However, there was a resolute recovery through Iddon and Holmes and the deficit was only 44.

The West Indies built on that advantage deliberately, progressing at under three an over. Everyone batted consistently, Headley's strangely patient 93 being the best, but the declaration was not made until lunch on the final day with only 3½ hours remaining, hardly enough time realistically to expect to bowl England out. Yet bowl them out they did with not a little help from Wyatt's startling decision to shuffle his batting order, again for no clear reason. If the recognised players were hardpressed by the fast bowlers in the first innings how could the tailenders be expected to handle them? They didn't and, by tea, half the side were out for 75 and nothing that Wyatt, Hendren, Ames, Iddon, Leyland and Holmes could do at this stage could save the game. The fifth ball of the last over of the match, bowled by Constantine, found umpire Guillen favourable to a leg-before appeal against Leyland and the series was level. England's 107 was their lowest against the West Indies—but even this was lowered in the final Test at Sabina.

The third Test contained nothing of the high drama of the previous two and the cricket deserved no more than the drawn result. England batted well into the second day for 226 and the West Indies until after tea on the third, losing their last five wickets for 27 to concede a lead of 42. For the umpteenth time, a leg-spinner, the youthful Eric Hollies, created their demise by taking 7 for 50. By then, it was obvious that there was virtually no chance of a result and, even though Wyatt set the West Indies a challenge by declaring his second innings at 160 for six, the home team abandoned the task after initially making an effort.

The rubber was secured by the West Indies in the final match at Sabina Park and, in it, several records were established by the home team, both individually and collectively. For the first time they won a Test by an innings (for good measure, with 161 runs to spare), for the first time they triumphed in an overall series and for the first time they scored over 500 runs in a Test (535 for seven declared). Headley, who treated his worshipful Jamaican public to yet another Test double-century, passed his 223 of 1930 as the highest score by a West Indian in a single Test innings with 270 not out and his stands with Sealey (202 for the third wicket) and Rolph Grant (147 for the seventh) also rated as records.

It was Headley who set up England for the kill; Martindale and Constantine carried out the execution with irresistible fast bowl-

ing. Headley, coming in at five for one, held centre-stage for close
to 500 minutes, at ease at all times against an attack entrusted
mainly to the leg-spin of Hollies and Paine. Almost every shot in
the book accounted for his 30 fours. Sealey had the frustration of
being out in the 90s for the second time in the series and the
younger Grant climaxed the series with his best display.

There was immediate sensation when England went in towards
the end of the second day. Wyatt, their captain, was hit by a
bouncer from Martindale and suffered a compound fracture of
the jaw which put him in hospital for the rest of the match.
Martindale's speed was awesome and, with Hylton and Constantine at the other end, England's batsmen could offer little resistance. They were, effectively, 26 for five at one stage before the
fast bowlers temporarily ran out of steam and Ames, finally
discovering the form which he had maintained throughout the
1930 tour, lifted England's despair with a fine 126. With the ageing
Hendren, in his last Test for England, he added 68; with Iddon
158 and only a great catch by Constantine close in on the off side
ended a chanceless hand.

In ordinary circumstances, England's 271 was respectable
enough but, in this match, they found themselves 264 behind,
and followed on. This time there was no resistance to speak of
and they were swept aside in 54 overs for 103, mainly by Martindale and Constantine. The satisfaction of victory was enhanced
for the latter, who took over the captaincy during England's
innings when Grant injured an ankle fielding. He soon brought
on Sealey so that he and Martindale could change ends; Sealey
took the wicket of Errol Holmes and then Constantine
himself removed three batsmen to round off the match—half an
hour before the rain, which had been threatening throughout the
final day, began to fall.

The Jamaican crowd, as the Trinidadian had done before
them, made much of the occasion, swarming across the Sabina
outfield and calling for their heroes in front of the pavilion. They
had never before savoured the satisfaction of a win over an
England team, not by Jamaica, not by West Indies, and they
revelled in it. Little were they to know that it would be another
13 years before they saw another Test at Sabina.

It was unfortunate that Grant could not be on the field to
relish the moment for this was to be his last Test match. He had
been called from Cambridge University, as an unknown quantity,
to lead the West Indies on their arduous tour to Australia in
1930–31 and, in 12 Tests as captain, had served his team and his
men nobly. Now, only 28 years of age, he had many years of

cricket before him but, despite the fact that he was from a
prominent business family in Trinidad, he chose to undertake
missionary work in Africa. There he remained until 1976, when
he was forced to leave his post in Rhodesia because of government
pressure.

West Indies in England 1939

There was a break of over four years before the West Indies
engaged in Test cricket again, on their third official tour of
England, and this team was also led by a Grant, Rolph, two years
junior, succeeding his brother to the position.

A lot of cricket had been played at inter-territorial level in the
interim, in addition to a visit by Yorkshire to Jamaica. There
was a series between the four major colonies in Trinidad prior to
the departure for England, culminating in a match between
Jamaica and the Rest of the West Indies. The selection of the
touring squad, therefore, was somewhat baffling.

J. H. Cameron, a Jamaican who had played for Cambridge
University and Somerset, was picked on the evidence of his
bowling in England and appointed vice-captain. It was thought,
apparently, that he was still practising his googly bowling; in
fact, he was bowling off-spin. Barrow, the experienced wicket-
keeper/batsman, was also included although he had been living
in the United States. He had not played any serious cricket for
some time, but he returned to fill the gap created by the death
from malaria a year earlier of Cyril Christiani. As it turned out,
his form was well short of what was expected and Sealey was
pressed into service as wicketkeeper for the final two Tests.
Hylton, the big fast bowler from Jamaica, was not among the 15
originally chosen but joined the party as a result of a public
subscription in that island which paid his way.

In comparison with its predecessors of 1928 and 1933 this team
conveyed a slightly more favourable impression on the English
public. Several of the leading players were already well known.
Headley and Constantine were household words; Martindale, one
of the most impressive fast bowlers, and probably the fastest in
1933, was returning with no diminution of reputation; Cameron
and the skipper had played for Cambridge; Barrow, the only
West Indian apart from Headley to have scored a Test century
in England, was back. What is more, there was a group of young,
very talented newcomers—the Stollmeyer brothers, Jeff and
Victor, both batsmen, Gomez, yet another batsman, and Tyrell
Johnson, a tall, left-arm fast bowler, all from Trinidad; Bertie
Clarke, a leg-spinner from Barbados; Peter Bayley, a batsman

from Guiana; Ken Weekes, a barrel-chested Jamaican with a reputation for hitting the ball hard.

England, too, relied on a mixture of youth and experience. Hammond, the stylish batsman, Bill Bowes, the fast bowler, and Hedley Verity, the left-arm spinner, were from the old school; Len Hutton and Denis Compton were the batsmen of the new generation, the former having stunned the cricket world the previous summer with his record-breaking 364 against Australia; the leg-spinner, Doug Wright, was at the start of his long career.

The West Indies, in the Tests at least, fared better than they had ever done in England. They lost the first at Lord's in the closing minutes and might have saved it with a bit more application; rain helped them draw the second at Old Trafford, and they outbatted England in a high-scoring and inconclusive match on a benign Oval pitch.

Even so, the responsibility again rested heavily on the shoulders of too few players, notably Headley and Constantine, for years their two outstanding players.

Headley carried the batting to such an extent that he was being referred to by the press as Atlas before very long. He scored prodigiously throughout the summer, playing little heed to the war clouds that were gathering as Hitler's forces plundered one European country after another and England prepared for an inevitable war. He had two double-centuries and four singles in his 1745 runs. No other West Indian passed 1000. Constantine, now 37, bowled more overs than anyone else and took more wickets (103), although his pace had been adjusted to suit the dictates of the passing years. He could still be devastating with the bat when things went his way and his fielding was as brilliant as ever.

There were few heights left for Headley to scale yet his accomplishment at Lord's, where he registered centuries in both innings, was the zenith of his remarkable career. No other batsman has done it, before or since, in a Test at the ground regarded as cricket's Mecca.

Headley's first-innings 106 and his second-wicket partnership of 118 with the teenaged Stollmeyer allowed the West Indies to retire at tea on the first day at 226 for three, a position which deteriorated so rapidly afterwards against the fast bowling of Bowes and Copson that the total was only 277 at the end. With Cameron's off-spin accounting for three early wickets, the match was evenly balanced until three very difficult chances in the space of two overs were spilled. Thereafter, Hutton and Compton set about the bowling so effectively that they added 248 in only

140 minutes and completely transformed the match, Hutton 196, Compton 120.

England declared 127 in the lead first thing on the third day and, from the time Stollmeyer departed to a catch at gully off a lifting ball in the second over, Headley was left to fight a lone and futile struggle to save the game. He proceeded, again without blemish, to his second century but could find no batsman to remain with him for any time. Headley was eighth out for 107 during a period in which four wickets fell for 14 runs, three to Wright. Sealey's 29 was the next-highest score and England duly knocked off 100 runs for victory in the 110 minutes available to them.

Manchester's infamous weather took heavy toll of the second Test and England could not force victory, despite two declarations by Hammond. Bowlers generally held sway in helpful conditions but Grant and Headley for the West Indies and Hardstaff for England all played thrilling hands, filled with a variety of attacking shots.

Not for the first time, The Oval yielded a garrison of runs. Oddly, it began with Johnson bowling Keeton off his pads with his very first ball in Test cricket. It ended with 1216 runs scored for only 23 wickets. England batted steadily after their early setback and totalled 352, Constantine taking 5 for 75 in what was to be his last Test. Later, on the third day, when the West Indies resumed at 395 for six, he scored 79 in his most militant fashion out of 103 added in an hour. The Oval, said *The Cricketer*, "was thick with deep fielders". One of his shots was a six over mid-on off the back foot from the pace bowling of Perks. It was, in every way, a fitting epitaph to his Test career.

Before this, there had been other fine innings. Jeff Stollmeyer gathered 59 most attractively and his brother, in what was to be his only Test, atoned for running out Headley for 65 with an innings of 96 which the great man could have bettered only by going on to his century. Once these had returned to the dressing room, Ken Weekes, a club mate of Headley's at Lucas in Jamaica, launched the type of attack rarely seen in Test cricket. Throwing the bat with gay abandon and revealing a number of typically strong left-hander's shots, he raced to 137 in only two hours with a six and 18 fours, an innings to remember.

Less than five hours remained when England began their second innings and Hutton and Hammond did not waste the opportunity presented to them to bolster their respective aggregates. Hutton was 165 not out when stumps were drawn. When next he played Test cricket, a war wound would have shortened and weakened his left arm—but had no effect on his appetite for runs. Hammond scored 138 and the pair added 264 in leisurely fashion.

By now, war was certain and already shipping in the Atlantic was at peril. In the circumstances, the West Indies management hurriedly made arrangements to get the first available sailing opportunity, taking third-class accommodation (the only that was left) aboard the SS *Montrose* for Montreal. Seven remaining matches were cancelled and this caused a great deal of indignation, particularly in Sussex, which cabled to the team: "Essential to play match tomorrow. Keep the flag flying". Had they done so, the team would probably have taken the next ship of the same line to cross the Atlantic—the ill-fated *Athenia!*

By the time they reached home, Great Britain had already declared war and it was another 11 years before English crowds were to see a West Indies touring team in action again.

England in the West Indies 1948

The war years had little adverse effect on domestic cricket in the West Indies and, during them, a new stock of players emerged from the regular series of matches played, initially, between Trinidad and Barbados, and, later, involving British Guiana and Jamaica as well. The batsmen were the ones who gained the attention, the mat at Port-of-Spain and the pitches elsewhere seldom being anything less than a heartbreak for bowlers.

Frank Worrell, a young Barbadian who had first played first-class cricket as a schoolboy left-arm spinner, was involved in two massive partnerships against Trinidad—one of 502 unbroken for the fourth wicket with John Goddard and one of 574, also for the fourth, with Clyde Walcott. He, Walcott and Jeffrey Stollmeyer registered triple-centuries and there was a proliferation of double and single centuries.

Worrell and Walcott, a massively-built man, were subsequently joined in the Barbados middle order by yet another batsman whose surname began with the letter W—Everton Weekes, a ruthless accumulator of runs. In time, it became the W Formation, the most famous batting combination in West Indies cricket history. Stollmeyer and Gerry Gomez, who had been to England in 1939 as teenagers, confirmed their promise in this period. Others such as Robert Christiani, brother of Cyril, Alan Rae and J. K. Holt, Jnr, sons of famous Jamaican fathers, Ken Rickards of Jamaica, Kenny Trestrail of Trinidad all scored heavily and attractively. If bowlers suffered and there was little spin bowling of note, Prior Jones and Lance Pierre of Trinidad, Hines Johnson of Jamaica and John Trim of British Guiana all could generate a real turn of speed.

Not since 1935 had an international team visited the West Indies and players and public alike were eager to test the apparent new strength against the might of England, the first scheduled post-war visitors, in 1948. They were let down when the MCC omitted several of its leading players and adopted the condescending pre-war policy of sending an emaciated side. Compton and Bill Edrich, who had captured everyone's imagination with their batting deeds the previous summer, were out; so too were Cyril Washbrook, Hutton, Alec Bedser, Norman Yardley and Doug Wright. Instead, Gubby Allen, at the age of 45, was given the responsibility of leading a team which was patently ill-equipped for a difficult assignment.

As if its own limitations were not enough of a handicap against opponents eager to prove themselves, the MCC were also besieged by injuries to such an extent that they were forced to send for a support player mid-way in the tour. Fortunately, Hutton came and his success was evidence of how much more competitive the series would have been had the tourists been at full strength. As it was, the West Indies won two of the four Tests easily and were only thwarted in the first by rain. The MCC suffered the indignity of completing the tour without a single victory in a first-class match, a shock which English teams abroad had never previously endured.

Allen himself was the first crock, even before the side put foot on colonial soil. He tore a muscle exercising aboard the liner on the way out and he was a spectator for the first three matches, including the opening Test. Then, Cranston, the Lancashire all-rounder, took his place as captain and Headley, almost 39 years old and bridging the gap between the pre- and post-war eras, led the West Indies for the first time, a landmark in that he was the first black captain. By the odd and divisive system which had obtained before, Headley had been named captain for the Barbados and Jamaica Tests, Stollmeyer for Trinidad, and Goddard for British Guiana. Because of injury, Headley did not play again in the series and Goddard continued as captain at Sabina Park after winning at Bourda while Gomez replaced an injured Stollmeyer at the helm at the Queen's Park Oval. What a complicated tangle it was!

Both Kensington and the Queen's Park Oval witnessed drawn results but neither was dull by any means and there were some notable individual feats. At Kensington, Laker's off-spin bit into turf made soft by overnight rain and first-day figures of one for

78 were transformed, in an hour, into 7 for 103. Hardstaff scored 98 for England and was then bowled off his pads but the fates were even crueller to Robert Christiani. In his second Test innings, the bespectacled Guyanese deserved a century but was denied it by a single run, lbw to Cranston for 99. So disconsolate was he that he returned to the dressing-room and cried openly.

For sheer spectacle, nothing in the match—nor in the series, for that matter—matched the fierce hitting of "Foffie" Williams in the West Indies second innings when the match was still in the balance. He gained selection only because of the withdrawal of the indisposed Worrell yet he had bowled at fast-medium pace superbly. Now he put his name in the record books with an innings of 72 in 63 minutes, the first 50 in half-an-hour, beginning with consecutive shots of 6, 6, 4, 4 (off Laker), and 4, 4 (off Ikin) from his first six deliveries. Williams achieved little else in his four Tests for the West Indies but that innings assured him a permanent place in the memory of those who saw it.

The crowd at the Queen's Park Oval was also treated to a series of quite unexpected individual performances. With two of his three recognised opening batsmen injured, Allen was said to have settled for a replacement by picking the first man who walked through the dressing-room door after pre-match practice. It happened to be Billy Griffith, the team's reserve wicketkeeper and assistant manager, who had never gone in first in a serious match before and was to play his first Test. Very soon he had the further worry of causing Jack Robertson to be run out, all enough to disturb even the most resolute of men. Yet Griffith's adversity appeared to give him strength for he proceeded to bat for six hours for 140, his first century in first-class cricket, the backbone of a respectable England total of 362. Peculiarly it was Griffith's only Test of the series.

Even more peculiar was the experience of Andy Ganteaume. The diminutive Trinidadian opener also marked his first Test match with a dogged century which stretched $4\frac{3}{4}$ hours yet he was not only discarded for the rest of the series but never played another Test. Since he did not bat in the second innings, his one and only innings in Test cricket was 112.

George Carew for the West Indies and Robertson, in England's second innings, also scored centuries in Port-of-Spain. The former, bedecked in a felt hat, enjoyed himself by scoring 107 out of 173 for the first wicket with Ganteaume in under three hours. In his only previous Test, back in 1935, he had been dismissed first ball against England so this was sweet revenge. Robertson's defiant 133, lasting $5\frac{3}{4}$ hours, kept England safe from defeat.

The West Indies eventually broke the stalemate by winning at Bourda by seven wickets. Only in the first hour, when they took three wickets for 48, were England in the match, rain on the first night compounding their woes. The West Indian recovery from their initial peril was constructed by Worrell, the graceful right-hander, who finished 131 not out, and Christiani, who thrilled his home crowd with a masterful half-century. England were forced to bat on a pitch which spun on the second day and, after an opening partnership of 59 by Hutton, in the West Indies less than a fortnight, and Robertson, they collapsed to Goddard's slow-medium off-breaks and Wilfred Ferguson's leg-breaks to 111 all out—186 in arrears.

The pitch subsequently eased and England made a desperate effort to avoid defeat in their second innings, batting through the third day and an hour into the fourth and final day. It was not enough, however, and the West Indies won with time and wickets to spare.

Although favoured by the weather in Georgetown the West Indies had established their superiority on merit and they used the final Test to emphasise it, exposing the lack of depth in both England's batting and bowling. England's batting after Hardstaff at No. 4 had been suspect throughout and its abject failure in both innings presented the West Indies with victory by 10 wickets. Hutton and Robertson added 129 for the first wicket in the first innings yet the total could reach only 227. Hutton, Place (with his only century of the series) and Hardstaff were responsible for a lunchtime total of 312 for four (49 ahead) on the last day but then another collapse followed in which the last six wickets fell for 24 runs.

Johnson, a tall Jamaican fast bowler, caused England the most bother with his pace and accuracy, taking 5 for 41 and 5 for 55 while Stollmeyer's rarely used leg-spin helped in the post-lunch debacle on the final day. However, Everton Weekes' century was the highlight for the West Indies if for no other reason than the circumstances of his inclusion.

Headley had been the original choice but injury caused his late withdrawal and Weekes was summoned. It was not a popular choice in Jamaica, where there was great support for young J. K. Holt, the local favourite, and when Weekes took the field midway through the first day, having arrived late from Barbados, he was heckled by the crowd. Within 48 hours he was their darling after a typically dashing exhibition of strokes, including 15 fours, in 141.

It was an innings which clinched Weekes' place in the team to tour India the following season, when he plundered the bowling to add four consecutive Test centuries to this one. Perhaps if Headley had been fit, Weekes might never have gone to India, for there was a quantity of young batsmen waiting for the opportunity. Perhaps if Evans had not dropped him at the wicket early on, it would have been a temporary injunction against the pillage Weekes later wreaked on the world's bowlers.

From here on, he and the West Indies went from strength to strength—and England never again could make the mistake of sending weakened teams to the Caribbean.

West Indies in England 1950
Having disposed of the MCC so efficiently in 1948, the West Indies widened their horizons by touring India for the first time in 1948-49, a rigorous, exacting assignment which ended with the astonishing depth of the batting verified by the consistently heavy scoring of Weekes, Walcott, Rae, Stollmeyer and Christiani and even in the absence of Worrell. In addition, Gomez blossomed into an all-rounder of quality and Prior Jones enjoyed successes rare for fast bowlers on the slow pitches of the sub-continent.

Runs again flowed in profusion in the trial matches which preceded the England tour and it was plain that whatever team was chosen would carry the most powerful batting artillery ever to leave the Caribbean. The concern was over the bowling. Jones and Lance Pierre from Trinidad and Johnson from Jamaica were the three fast bowlers eventually selected, all tall well-built men who had proven their worth several times over. The West Indies had always been strong in pace and, if these were not quite in the same class as Griffith, Martindale, Constantine and others of the pre-war era, they were not to be underestimated.

But who would spin? Here the cupboard was sparse indeed and the selectors were faced with a difficult problem. Mainly on the instigation of Goddard, the captain, and Stollmeyer, the vice-captain, they indulged in a totally unexpected piece of specula-tion, including Sonny Ramadhin, a stripling of a lad from a village in south Trinidad, and Alfred Valentine, a gangling Jamaican, neither of whom had yet celebrated his 20th birthday and neither of whom had played more than two first-class matches.

Ramadhin, the first in a succeeding line of East Indians to be chosen for the West Indies, had shown distinct promise in the trials by taking 12 wickets in two matches with each-way turn delivered with no perceptible change in action. Yet he had never bowled on any surface but matting and had never travelled outside of Trinidad. Valentine, on the other hand, took only two wickets in trials but bowled well enough to earn the approval of those who mattered. The experienced leg-spinner Ferguson was left behind as a result and Goddard knew he would have to depend on all-rounders such as Worrell, C. B. "Boogles" Williams and himself to fill the breach should the gamble fail.

Far from failing, it paid handsome dividends and Ramadhin and Valentine, two unknown novices at the start of the tour, became, almost overnight, the talk of the cricketing world. They complemented each other perfectly. Ramadhin, cap on, sleeves buttoned down to the wrists, presented mysteries which no English batsman unravelled for the entire summer. The majority simply relied on the tactic of playing down the line and hoping for the best, not knowing whether the ball would turn from off, from leg, or keep straight through. Valentine, left-arm from the opposite end, pushed the ball through, tweaked it viciously and spun sharply on the easiest of pitches.

It was not long before Goddard realised his perception was, indeed, correct and he placed great faith in his two young spinners. They never let him down, each bowling over 1000 overs on tour and taking 258 wickets between them. In the Tests, Valentine sent down 422.3 overs and Ramadhin 377.5, the former claiming 33 wickets, the latter 26. "We want Ramadhin on the ball" ran one calypso line after the series. He and his partner, referred to in another calypso as "those little pals of mine, Ramadhin and Valentine", almost always were.

This surprise packet cast a spell which left the home team in psychological disarray and the staggering consistency of the West Indies batting, living up to every expectation, thoroughly capitalised on it. The three Ws were in rampant mood, Walcott and Weekes scoring seven centuries each and Worrell six. Included in Weekes' were a triple-century and four doubles. Rae and Stollmeyer almost invariably presented them with an excellent springboard and nine batsmen recorded 1000 runs for the season. Of the 31 first-class matches played, 17 were won (nine by an innings) and only three lost. After losing the first Test, they won the remaining three in succession by indisputable margins.

It is true that England, weaker than usual in any case, suffered through injuries to leading players at one time or another. Yet this was a mighty West Indies team, self-confident and intent on winning. As *Wisden* commented, "West Indies cricket firmly established itself" during this series.

It was a lesson for those who doubted the temperament of the West Indians that they rallied so spiritedly after defeat, by 202 runs, at Old Trafford. The pitch was inadequately prepared for a five-day match and it lasted scarcely an hour. Dry and dusty, it was a spinner's delight and batting was difficult throughout. Valentine had taken 8 for 26 and 5 for 41 on the same ground against Lancashire a few days before; now he claimed five wickets before lunch on his first day in Test cricket and had the first eight wickets of the England innings before Ramadhin, who had bowled equally well without reward, halted the sequence. Valentine's 8 for 104 were the best figures by a bowler in his debut Test but more pertinent to the outcome of the match was a sixth wicket partnership of 161 between Trevor Bailey and Godfrey Evans which allowed England to recover from 88 for five to 312 all out. Bailey defended in his own effective way for 82 not out, Evans was more enterprising for 104, the first of his two Test centuries and his first first-class century in England.

On such a pitch, England's total was more than adequate for their bowlers to work on and the leg-spin of Hollies (3 for 70 and 5 for 63) and the orthodox left-arm spin of Bob Berry (5 for 63 and 4 for 53) quelled any West Indian resistance. Stollmeyer defied the conditions in both innings to score 43 and 78 and Weekes was in pugnacious form first time round but the match was over within an hour of the fourth day.

The West Indies were furious at the condition of the pitch and called a press conference to let the world know their feelings. In some quarters it was construed as simply a device to excuse their loss but Goddard's men knew better and they waited for their chance. It came at Lord's in the second Test when there could be no quarrel with anything, least of all West Indian superiority. Their victory by 326 runs was their first in a Test in England, cause enough for rejoicing, but that the venue was Lord's was the icing on the cake.

The West Indies at one stage on the first day were 233 for two and Worrell and Weekes especially served up a batting feast fit to put before the King, who was among the 30,000 spectators. However, the promise of a truly large total was not kept, despite Rae's patient and commendable 106, and 326 was hardly a match-winning total, particularly as Hutton and Washbrook began with a stand of 62 for England's first wicket. Both were then stumped and the flood-gates were open. Ramadhin and Valentine caused such confusion that nine wickets fell for 60 before carefree hitting by Johnny Wardle boosted the score to 151.

The match was in the bag and the West Indies knew it. For a time, their second innings faltered but it was picked up again by Walcott and Gomez in a sixth-wicket partnership of 211 which put it beyond doubt. Walcott's power was frequently awesome, particularly off the back foot, and he hit 24 fours in 168 not out before his captain declared to allow his bowlers just over a day and a half to achieve the desired result.

This time they had to work a great deal harder. Washbrook defended with gritty determination to save his team, Gilbert Parkhouse, a Welshman in his first Test, batted well with him and the third wicket did not fall until 218. It was not before Washbrook was bowled by Ramadhin early on the fifth day after 5½ hours at the crease that England's defiance was over. 'Ram' had 6 for 86 from 72 overs and 'Val' 3 for 79 from 71 and how they were even able to walk off the field at the end was a wonder.

However, it was a grand occasion and no degree of exhaustion could curb West Indian celebrations. Impromptu calypso groups invaded the hallowed turf to sing the praises of their heroes; back home, rum shops did a thriving trade and, in many places, buildings were adorned with bunting to hail the event.

The team was now cock-a-hoop, convinced that nothing could stop them. For the third Test at Trent Bridge, England was depleted by the loss of the injured Hutton and made four changes. The West Indies made only one. As always, the Nottingham pitch was placid in the extreme yet England were all out for 223 batting first, from which point their struggle would always be uphill. Johnson, returning in place of Jones, and Worrell caused them early problems with the new ball and, in fact, Ramadhin and Valentine were called on to do comparatively little bowling.

The West Indies batsmen by now had developed an avaricious appetite for runs and, earlier in the season against Nottinghamshire, had savoured the pleasures of batting at Trent Bridge, scoring 525 for five declared. Their two highest scorers had been Weekes with 279 and Worrell with 83 and these two again helped themselves to the sweets, although the roles were reversed. It was Worrell who passed a double-century, batting for 435 minutes for 261 and hitting two sixes and 37 fours, all with precise timing and ease. Weekes, more punishing in 220 minutes, scored 129 and the fourth wicket was worth 283 when it ended, the highest partnership for any wicket in Test cricket by the West Indies. The eventual West Indian total, despite the late loss of quick wickets, was 558 and England started their second innings just before lunch on the third day 335 behind.

As he had done at Lord's, Washbrook took it upon himself to be England's saviour, scoring another century, and he received the assistance which had been lacking then, Simpson, on his home ground, sharing an opening stand of 212. Parkhouse and the left-handed Cambridge University Blue, John Dewes, continued the good work by putting on a further 106 but the effort was not maintained and the West Indies were left 102 to win, which Stollmeyer and Rae acquired without help.

Valentine (with a Test record 92 overs) and Ramadhin (81.2 overs) were put to even more toil than they had been in the second innings at Lord's but they never wavered, conceding slightly more than 1½ runs an over.

What prompted *The Times* to observe before the Oval Test that "the West Indies would sink into a slumber of insolent security" is not clear. There was no sign of slumber in an innings and 56 runs triumph against an England team under a new captain, Freddie Brown instead of Yardley, and showing no fewer than eight changes from that which played at Trent Bridge.

Another West Indian total in excess of 500 was built around centuries by Rae (109) and Worrell (138) and despite clever leg-spin bowling by the veteran Wright (5 for 141). With Hutton at his best, England then fashioned a spirited reply and the home supporters were heartened by the appearance for the first time for the summer of Compton after a knee operation. The pair added 109 for the third wicket but then unsought misfortune overtook England. Compton, not for the first time in his career, was run out, rain fell and the pitch became difficult. The last eight first-innings wickets fell for 115 runs and, following on, England could do no better than muster 103, Goddard with quick off-breaks joining his two leading spinners in causing the destruction.

Hutton stood out like a beacon in the debacle, carrying his bat throughout the first innings for 202, making no mistake in a marathon 470 minutes at the wicket. It was a prime example in the art of batsmanship but the strain took its toll and he lasted only briefly in the follow-on. Ramadhin and Valentine then made merry and the West Indies returned home in September to a great welcome. The ship docked first at Bridgetown, where huge crowds, given a public holiday for the occasion, lined the streets in a joyous welcome.

West Indian cricket had indeed come of age.

MCC in the West Indies 1953–54

England's fourth tour of the Caribbean brought modern Test cricket to the West Indian public for the first time—and accentuated all its attendant faults. Those of earlier years, while always keen, had not been accompanied by the tension and seriousness for so long associated with the Ashes encounters between England and Australia. The West Indies had been feeling their way in international cricket and were treated patronisingly by Lord's, which, invariably, sent out teams below England's best. The impression was that it was more important to create the right image than to win.

This time it was different. England was still smarting under the thrashing of 1950 and the realisation had sunk in that nothing but the best would be equal to the task. The days in which cricket was used as an extension of colonial office propaganda were over, as reflected in the 16 chosen.

Hutton, having regained the Ashes the previous summer, was reappointed captain, the first professional to take an MCC party overseas, and the names of those under him read like a Who's Who of great English cricketers—Compton, May, Graveney, and Willie Watson as batsmen; Trueman and Statham as fast bowlers; Laker, Lock and Wardle as spinners; Bailey as the all-rounder; Evans as the wicketkeeper. It is debatable whether any team of such potential has ever been to the West Indies before or since.

West Indies, their defeat against Australia in Australia two years earlier behind them, were possibly not as well balanced but carried great power in batting and spin bowling and had the advantage of playing at home where no previous England team had won the rubber.

As anticipated, two evenly-matched teams contested a close series, England staging an extraordinary recovery after losing the first two Tests to share honours 2-2. It was an effort worthy of the highest praise yet the results were almost completely overshadowed by the cantankerous friction which shrouded proceedings throughout.

The West Indian public and press became increasingly incensed over the response of English players on the field to umpiring decisions which went against them and by the reports of the several British correspondents on the spot. One writer likened the attitude of the public to the MCC team to that in Australia during the ill-starred bodyline series in 1932-33. Roy Harewood, sports editor of British Guiana's *Daily Chronicle*, called it "the worst behaved team that has ever left England's shores—at least for these parts". Dick Murray, in the *Trinidad Guardian*, wrote: "The shocking behaviour on the field of play by some of their players has left me bitterly disappointed in English cricket."

R. J. Hayter in *Wisden* explained the English attitude: "Convinced by the happenings on the field that the general standard of umpiring in the West Indies was not adequate for Test cricket, the touring team felt that the crowd atmosphere made the work of the men in the middle even harder than it should have been." The English team estimated that decisions went against them in a ratio of seven or eight to two.

The sight of players frequently remonstrating with umpires and openly showing their disgust—and English players at that—angered the crowds and frequent slow scoring and defensive tactics did nothing to placate them. It was generally accepted that the standard of umpiring did leave much to be desired but West Indians regarded this as no excuse to flout the tenets of good manners.

The crowds, of course, were not blameless and there were some unsavoury incidents. After giving out J. K. Holt leg-before-wicket at 94 in his debut Test on his home soil in Kingston, umpire Perry Burke and his family were physically molested. In Georgetown, umpire Badge Menzies, the local groundsman drafted into service after Hutton had rejected two other officials, ruled local wicketkeeper Clifford McWatt run out—a decision which led to the crowd hurling bottles and boxes onto the ground. In Barbados, schoolboys bored by England's run crawl barracked until Hutton refused to continue batting.

The West Indies won the first and second Tests, England the third and fifth, in each case a first-innings batting collapse being the main cause for defeat. At Sabina and Kensington, it was England's.

The West Indies accumulated 417 in the first innings of the series against an attack including four fast bowlers, with no batsman reaching a century, the unfortunate Holt's 94 being the highest of five half-centuries. The match was virtually decided when England fell apart for 170 to the old enemies Ramadhin and Valentine. Stollmeyer created a furore when he declined to enforce the follow-on despite his lead of 241 and he had several agonising moments before he led a triumphant team off the field victors by 140 runs.

The second-innings score stood at 119 for six before Weekes and McWatt carried it to 209 without further loss at the declaration. The left-handed Watson (116) and Hutton (56) then added 130 for England's first wicket and Watson and May (69) a further 90 for the second so that, set 457 to win, England started the final day 227 for two. With the match apparently slipping away, Stollmeyer resorted to leg theory, with his fast bowlers concentrating on the leg stump or just outside for long periods. Bailey had employed it earlier in the match and it now backfired on England.

Esmond Kentish, a well-built Jamaican far fitter than his 37

years would suggest and in only his second Test, induced May and
Graveney to tickle legside catches and then sliced through the
lengthy England tail, the last seven wickets falling for 39 runs in
the hour after lunch, 31 of them added by Bailey and Moss, the
last pair. It was, to understate the case, a most astonishing period
and immediately put England under pressure for the rest of the
series.

This match marked the end of the career of the greatest West
Indian batsman of the pre-war period, the incomparable Headley.
He was then almost 45 years old and living in England but
nostalgic Jamaicans wanted to see the master one more time. A
public subscription of £1183 0s 2d was raised and Headley
brought back. Pressure of public opinion more than anything
else forced his inclusion in the team, an embarrassment to which
the great man should never have been subjected. In his two
previous Test innings at Sabina he had taken double-centuries off
English bowling; now he managed only 16 and 1.

The no-balling of the England left-arm spinner Lock for
throwing his faster ball in the Sabina Test and then immediately
afterwards in the Barbados game was hardly surprising since his
action had been queried in England, but it all added fuel to the
fire which was, by now, flaming.

At Kensington, England's batting, so formidable on paper,
reached a new nadir. The West Indies were pulled from the
indignity of 25 for three by Walcott's massive 220, an innings he
himself rates as his best in Test cricket, and his fourth-wicket
stand of 165 with the stylish young Guyanese, Bruce Pairaudeau,
in his first Test. The score of 383, nevertheless, was hardly a
frightening one yet England approached it with a self-effacing
timidity and were all out for 181. On the third day, they scored
128 from 111 overs—and with batsmen the calibre of Hutton,
Watson, May, Compton and Graveney involved. Hutton himself
was the chief culprit and the schoolboys expressed what everyone
else felt, only more demonstratively.

The onslaught in the West Indies second innings was led by
Holt, whose 166 with a six and 26 fours is still considered by all woh
were there as some of the best batting ever seen at Kensington,
and joined by Worrell, who helped him add 222 for the second
wicket, serving to highlight the distress of England's batting. For
the second consecutive Test, Stollmeyer could declare, leaving
his opponents a daunting proposition. On this occasion, it was
495 to win or 9½ hours to survive.

Seemingly penitent for their earlier misdemeanours, England's
leading batsmen gave a display more in keeping with their

reputations, Compton leading the way with 93, Hutton, May and Graveney all passing 60 in pleasing style. At lunch on the final day, Compton and Graveney were together, only three wickets were down, and a draw was probable. Then Compton was leg-before-wicket to Stollmeyer, a decision which infuriated Compton and much of the English press, and a collapse of Sabina proportions ensued. The last six England wickets fell for 54 and the West Indies were two-up, seemingly an impregnable lead.

England, however, were far from finished. It is difficult to determine what caused the sudden metamorphosis. Hutton's men probably became more determinedly unified as a result of the criticism which had been mounting on their heads. The West Indies, possibly, became a little complacent. Whatever the reasons, England did not lose another match for the tour and miraculously pulled level in the series.

The influence of Hutton was strong in both his team's victories. At Bourda, he was intent on not squandering the advantage of winning the toss for the only time and he batted 7¾ hours for 169 around which a total of 435 was built. At Sabina, after the West Indies had been routed for 139 on a true, fast pitch on the opening day, he guaranteed a healthy lead by scoring 205, almost half the total of 414. Confronted with all the worries associated with his contentious tour, Hutton's example inspired a team which, at one stage, had been down and out.

Equally cheering to England's cause were the performances by the fast bowlers in the third and fifth Tests. In the former, Statham pressed home the advantage of his team's sizeable total by dismissing Worrell, Stollmeyer and Walcot for 16 runs at the start of the West Indies reply. Despite a brilliant 94 by Weekes and a century stand for the eighth wicket between Holt and McWatt they never recovered.

It was the end of the Holt–McWatt stand which served as the flash-point for the crowd disturbance. While such behaviour has become more commonplace among modern sporting crowds, it was the first demonstration of its kind in the West Indies and received major, and adverse, publicity. England's players remained on the field through it all and when play was restarted the West Indies found themselves following on against England for the first time at home. They did little better second time round, England winning by nine wickets with time to spare.

The fourth Test, the last to be played on the matting at the Queen's Park Oval, was drowned in a sea of runs. Weekes (206) and Worrell (167) added a record 338 for the third wicket and Walcott (124) joined them in three-figure scores, the only time all three Ws scored centuries in the same Test innings. May and Compton responded with hundreds for England and altogether only 25 wickets fell for 1528 runs.

The contrast could not have been greater than on the first day at Sabina. On a seemingly perfect pitch, Bailey tumbled out the West Indies for 139, taking 7 for 34 with a colossal piece of fast-medium bowling, and nothing that the home team could do after that could prevent England levelling the series after Hutton's masterful batting. Walcott's 116 was his third century of the series and Holt, Atkinson, Gomez and a teenaged left-hander from Barbados by the name of Garfield Sobers in his first of 93 Tests also fought doggedly to protect their team's lead. But it proved in vain and victory was England's by nine wickets with a day remaining.

For the West Indies, it was a disappointing end to a rubber which they had firmly in their grasp and the augury for trying times ahead. Another eight years and two series passed before they could win another Test against England.

West Indies in England 1957
The West Indies returned to England in 1957 with several key players who had immortalised their tour seven years earlier. John Goddard, aged 38, was reinstated as captain, a surprising choice even if it was accepted that the Board was reluctant to hand the leadership over to a professional. Atkinson, who had been captain in three Tests against Australia in 1955 and for the four-Tests tour of New Zealand a year later, was included but given no official capacity.

Under Goddard were the three Ws and Ramadhin and Valentine so that the captain, the principal batsmen and the mystifying spin bowlers of 1950 were back to the scene of their historic triumph. The fact that they were supported by several new very promising players gave the squad a weighty look on paper and led to optimistic forecasts at home.

Such optimism proved misplaced and England won three of the five Tests by an innings and had much the better of the two that were drawn. A subjective assessment of the situation would have provided forewarning of the true nature of the assignment. England were much stronger and more confident than they were in 1950; 'Ram and Val' were not descending unawares upon unsuspecting batsmen as they were then; there was no opening pair to match the solidity of Rae and Stollmeyer; none of the young players, for all their potential, had yet established themselves at international level. All these handicaps materialised during the summer while others arose quite unexpectedly. Illness and injury afflicted both Walcott and Weekes and diminished their ability; the policy of omitting the only specialist wicket-keeper for the first three Tests was ludicrous, as was that which offered Roy Gilchrist's extreme pace no adequate support; the loss of the toss in the final Test condemned the West Indies to defeat on a shocking pitch at The Oval.

Misfortune heaped upon misfortune and, according to several of the players, the team divided into factions. Perhaps it would have been beaten in any case, but as Worrell observed later: "We had the sort of team that should never have been beaten in three days. The kind of fight we put up was shabby."

Worrell was one of the notable exceptions to this condemnation. So, too, was Collie Smith, who demonstrated immense all-round talent and with an ebullient outlook never seemed bothered by the hardships confronting his team.

For all the other reasons mentioned, none was as crippling to the West Indies as the tactics used in the first Test to stymie Ramadhin. In the four matches he played before the opening of the series at Edgbaston, the only noticeable change in the cheerful Trinidadian of 1950 was around the waistline. Otherwise, he was still casting the same old spell over the batsmen and had a phenomenal 38 wickets in his bag when Goddard handed him the ball after an hour's play in the Test. Unlike 1950, he had no Valentine at the other end, for his old pal had been omitted from the eleven; yet it did not phase him. In 31 overs, he took 7 for 49 (his best figures in Tests) as England scratched their way to 186.

The batsmen then carefully built a lead of 288. Smith was the main scorer with 161, repeating his century in his first match against Australia in 1955, in his first appearance against England and adding 190 with Worrell, who batted throughout the five hours of the partnership with a runner. Walcott had set the stage earlier with a glorious 90 but in the middle of it he badly tore a leg muscle and never regained his form for the rest of the summer.

When England ended the third day 102 for two in their second innings (both to Ramadhin) and were quickly 113 for three on the third, the game appeared all over. However, the rest day, Sunday, had intervened and the England camp used it to discuss a plan to counter Ramadhin. It is said that the advice of Bill Bowes, the old Test player, to treat the bogeyman as an off-spinner and play him off the front foot was that heeded. May, the England captain, and Cowdrey employed the policy to the letter. The ball repeatedly beat the forward defensive stroke and hit the front leg, thrust forward as a shield. Soon throats became sore from appealing for lbw decisions to umpires, as customary in England, reluctant to give them with the point of contact far from the stumps.

On and on May and Cowdrey went from Monday morning till after lunch Tuesday, the West Indies hamstrung by injuries to Gilchrist and Worrell, which left Goddard without reasonable recourse to the new ball. There were, Goddard estimates, a hundred appeals in that period, none of which found favour, and by the time Cowdrey (154) was caught off Smith in the deep with England safe, his stand with May (285 not out) worth 411, the visiting team was a tired frustrated bunch.

This reflected in their batting over the final 2½ hours, in which they lost seven wickets for 72. They would, in all probability, have lost the match had not Goddard and Smith, convinced the umpires could not rule them lbw for pad-play either, repeatedly kicked Laker and Lock. Smith, after an hour and five minutes for 5, was, finally, given out leg-before, but Goddard was still not out 0 at the end—after 40 minutes in which he made maximum use of his legs.

Ramadhin, whose 98 overs still stand as the most ever bowled in a single first-class innings, was severely put out by the entire episode. To him, the tactics employed by May and Cowdrey were a negation of the spirit of the game; to England, it surely meant the difference between victory and defeat in the series.

The remaining Tests were a sad tale for the West Indies. Only Smith and Worrell did themselves full justice and it was not only Ramadhin who was left shaken by the events at Edgbaston.

At Lord's, where England won by an innings and 36 runs, the West Indies were undone by lethal fast bowling by Bailey, supported by Trueman and Statham, on a lively pitch and by their own atrocious catching. Bailey took 7 for 44 in a first-innings total of 127 but when Gilchrist threatened to reply in kind a spate of chances allowed England's chief scorers to prosper. Cowdrey hit 152, the left-handed Peter Richardson 76, and Evans, dropped five times, 82 in an overall 424. Weekes mounted a counter-attack brilliant even by his own standards and Sobers helped him add 100 in 95 minutes for the fifth wicket but once Weekes was caught behind off Bailey for 90 the resistance disintegrated.

Graveney's monumental 258 and smaller centuries by Richardson and May took fullest advantage of Trent Bridge's featherbed pitch to register England's highest total against the West Indies at home in the third Test—619 for six declared. The West Indies then barely held on for a draw in which Worrell played a martyr's role. Pressed into the No. 1 position, he batted for 9½ hours and was not out 191 at the end of the first innings of 372. He went back out when the follow-on was enforced but, not unnaturally, was soon out. Since he fielded throughout England's long grind and bowled 21 overs besides, he had been on the field from 11.30 a.m. Thursday to 3.00 p.m. Monday. In the second innings, Smith, aided by Atkinson and Goddard, saved the day after the first five wickets had gone for 89. Smith's defiance lasted seven hours and earned him 168 runs, Atkinson 2½ hours and 46 and Goddard 3¾ hours and 61.

There was no such daring in the final two Tests. At Leeds, the West Indies totalled 142 and 132 and their highpoint was Worrell's left-arm medium-paced bowling, which earned him 7 for 70. Surrey fast bowler Peter Loader's first innings hat-trick was only the second by an England bowler in England. At The Oval, the batting fared even worse against two more Surrey bowlers, Laker and Lock, on a home pitch made to order for their complementary spin: 89 and 86 were the totals, Lock 5 for 28 and 6 for 20, Laker 3 for 39 and 2 for 38.

There was, even in this, one small crumb of comfort for the West Indies. Sobers disregarded the dreadful conditions to score 39 and 42, with the skill only vouchsafed to those of extraordinary talent. The 21-year-old colt was finally maturing. Bowlers in the future would suffer at his hands.

MCC in the West Indies 1959–60

England were subjected to a crushing 4-0 loss in Australia in the season of 1958–59. With it, a glorious era ended and the team which Peter May brought to the Caribbean a year later contained a number of fresh names. There was no Graveney, no Watson, no Bailey, no Laker and Lock, no Evans, no Tyson—all of whom had been to Australia a year earlier—and a new generation, in time to serve England equally as well, took their places. Ken Barrington, Mike Smith, Geoff Pullar, Raman Subba Row, David Allen and Ray Illingworth were on their first official tour; May, the captain, Trueman and Statham were the only survivors from the disagreeable 1953–54 series.

Simply to have done well would have satisfied those following the fortunes of May's team at home, to have won the series, 1-0, as was the case, was hailed as a major coup since the WestIndies possessed the makings of a highly talented side which earned quite comfortable successes over Pakistan at home in 1958 and India away the following season. After the drubbing in England in 1957, Sobers, Kanhai, Hunte, Butcher and Solomon had quickly and effectively filled the void left by the absence of the

Ws. Hall and Gilchrist had, quite literally, scared their opponents with their great pace and Alexander not only proved a top-class wicketkeeper but a fine captain as well. If Gilchrist's alleged misdemeanours on tour had led to his banishment, Hall's new partner, Watson, was only slightly less menacing while Worrell was back to lend his talents and authority and Ramadhin was still around. On the debit side, Collie Smith's tragic death in a car crash the previous summer was a staggering loss in every sense.

If the cricket was uninspiring throughout, the captains and groundsmen had to share most of the blame. With the Tests scheduled for six days, pitches were overprepared to last so that, generally, they assisted no bowler and allowed no batsman complete freedom of strokeplay. Confronted by such conditions, the tactics, adopted by both sides, were to wear the patience and resilience of the opposing batsmen down by a steady diet of fast bowling, much of it shortpitched, interspersed with nagging spin to defensive fields. Seldom was there any urgency to the play, the scoring rates of both teams rarely climbed over three an over, and the overs generally went by at an average of 14 an hour.

Still, there was none of the rancour associated with Hutton's tour six years earlier and, even though another crowd disturbance marred one Test, the MCC team enjoyed wide popularity. For this, Walter Robins, the manager, May, the original captain, and Cowdrey, his successor when ill-health forced him to return home, deserved much credit.

Nowhere during the tour was the pitch more favourable to the accumulation of runs than it was at Kensington Oval for the first Test. Barrington and Dexter made the most of it after England had won the toss, the former's first Test innings outside England being 128, the latter 136 not out when the innings closed at 482. But even greater things were to come for, after the West Indies lost three for 102, Sobers and Worrell batted together from Friday afternoon until Tuesday morning in adding 399 for the fourth wicket, by a long way the highest for the wicket in Tests against England. The graceful left-hander treated the crowd to his first Test hundred on Barbadian soil and had been going 10¾ hours when he was bowled by Trueman for 226. Worrell, back home after self-exile in Manchester since 1955, was even longer—11 hours 20 minutes—for an undefeated 197 not out of 563 for eight declared but, as a match, the Test was dead by as early as the fourth day. The only batsman with a genuine grouse was McMorris—run out for 0 off a no-ball at the non-striker's end in his first Test.

The second Test at Port-of-Spain—or, to be more exact, the third day of it—decided the series. England's first innings had no head and no tail but the middle was substantial (Barrington 121, Dexter 77 and Smith 108) and they were all out for 382 just before the close of the second day. The West Indies started the third day, a Saturday, 22 for 0, before a capacity crowd of nearly 30,000 packed into the ground in expectation of a glittering performance from their stars. Instead, they suffered acute disappointment with wickets tumbling to Trueman and Statham.

When the eighth went down at 98, the local boy Charran Singh run out in his debut Test, the crowd's shattered emotions got the better of them, bottles and other missiles rained onto the field, spectators invaded the ground, and eventually the riot police were called to quell the trouble. No more play was possibly that day and the 75 minutes lost were subsequently made up on the succeeding days.

The outburst was the cause of considerable local embarrassment and the Trinidad Premier, Eric Williams, despatched a cable of apology to the MCC. It was repeatedly stressed that there was no animosity towards the visitors.

When play resumed, the West Indies found it impossible to slip out of the noose tied around their necks. Despite a lead of 270, May batted again and the West Indies were left 10 hours to save the match or, conversely but not realistically, 501 to win. They did neither, Kanhai's dogged $6\frac{1}{4}$-hours 110 being the only innings of the type needed, and England were one-up.

The third Test at Sabina was the best of the series, a match of constantly changing situations and stirring individual performances. In the last innings, the West Indies required 230 in 245 minutes and, at the end, both teams were within sight of victory.

England's modest first-innings 277 featured two outstanding accomplishments—one on either side, Cowdrey for England, Hall for the West Indies.

Cowdrey alone withstood a vigorous assault from the great fast bowler (7 for 69) to be ninth out for 114. With Sobers in sparkling form, supported by the solid McMorris and the more dashing Nurse, in his first Test, the West Indies ended the third day 291 for two and poised for a match-winning lead. Yet they achieved one of only 76, for once Sobers had been lbw to Trueman for 147 the batting became paralysed and then confused, the last seven wickets falling for 24. The first four had contributed 329.

Cowdrey, again batting superbly for 97, and the left-handed Pullar put England right back in the match with an opening partnership of 177 second time round but there followed another batting failure and an outright decision was just possible all the way through the final day. The West Indies did make an attempt to chase the runs on a pitch which had become somewhat unpredictable in bounce but Kanhai was handicapped by a strained muscle and wrongly refused a runner by May, so they gave it up when five fell for 140.

West Indian efforts to eliminate England's lead were once more dominated by Hall and Sobers at Bourda in the fourth Test but, in the end, the pitch thwarted them. Hall's 6 for 90 was mainly responsible for dismissing England for 295 and Sobers' 145 for a West Indian advantage of 107, but time was a factor which the batsmen had not considered seriously enough. Just over a day and a half remained when England batted a second time and, with the pitch as comfortable then as it was at the start, centuries by Subba Row and Dexter confirmed the certainty of a draw.

With May having returned home after Jamaica, England were short of batting, so it was decided to draft Jim Parks, the Sussex batsman/wicketkeeper, then coaching in Trinidad, into the eleven for the final Test, a shrewd move. Parks, with scores of 43 and 101 not out, contributed greatly to England's securing a draw and maintaining their hold on the series.

There was little difference in the first-innings scores. Alexander deliberately conceding a lead of 55 with a declaration. Cowdrey and Sobers, perhaps inevitably, led their teams' scoring, the former with 119 and the latter with 92. When six England wickets were down for 148 just before tea on the fifth day, their lead was only 203 with the last recognised batsmen at the wicket and their standing in the series was in jeopardy. It was here that Parks, with Smith an equally resilient partner, stood firm.

Not until after lunch on the final day was the association eventually broken, Alexander catching Smith for his 23rd victim of the series. He—and everyone else—know by then that England were safe. Cowdrey continued long enough for Parks to complete a well-deserved century and then made a token declaration which at least allowed the crowd to see their batsmen in more relaxed mood than they had been all series.

The glory, however, belonged to an unheralded England team which was the first to clinch a Test rubber in the Caribbean.

West Indies in England 1963

The magnificent series in Australia in 1960–61 had elevated the prestige of West Indian cricket to new heights and the sweeping victory in all five Tests over India in the Caribbean in 1962 was proof that a great side was in the making. Worrell's leadership had been the major factor in moulding the team into a happy and effective unit and his success, after the concerted campaign on behalf of him being appointed in the first place, must have given him immense satisfaction. He was coming towards the end of his playing days and his knees were crying out against the strain of continuous cricket but he set himself one more goal before he quit—to carry to England the same joyful spirit which had so enraptured Australia.

When he arrived with his team for the 1963 tour he was under no illusions about the magnitude of this task. In the early weeks, he must have been dreading the possibility of an anti-climax, for a lot was expected of the West Indies now—not least from the hundreds and thousands of their countrymen who, at the time, were emigrating to new lives in England and who would be on hand to follow their fortunes.

He need not have worried. The flame which had been lit in Australia did not flicker once; if anything, it grew brighter and the series was a colossal success from every point of view. To mark the 100th anniversary of its first publication, *Wisden* donated a trophy for West Indies–England Tests and that was won 3-1 by Worrell and his men. The Lord's Test was every bit as exciting, down to the last ball, as that which was tied at Brisbane, the crowds were huge and *Wisden* itself noted that "no more popular side has ever toured the old country"

There could have been no stronger West Indian team to England, either. It was perfectly balanced and strong in every department under the leadership of a man who knew the game and for whom his team had the greatest admiration and trust. Although it was a comparatively low-scoring series, four of the first five in the West Indies order—Hunte, Kanhai, Butcher and Sobers—scored over 300 runs and averaged over 40 per innings. The bowling lacked for nothing. Hall was now partnered by Charlie Griffith, just as fast and, if anything, more accurate with a devastating bouncer and yorker; Gibbs' credentials as the game's best off-spinner could not be challenged; Sobers was three left-arm bowlers in one, each of high quality.

Two positions were unsettled before the series began—wicket-keeper and opening batsman. Deryck Murray, a 20-year-old straight from Queen's Royal College, Trinidad, filled the former so efficiently that he finished with a record 24 victims in his very first series; the one defect, however, was in the matter of Hunte's opening partner and this was the only change which Worrell was forced to make in an otherwise set eleven.

By comparison, England possessed only three players who batted with any consistency—the captain, the flamboyant Dexter, Sharpe, who was brought in for the last three Tests, and the dogged left-hander Close—and only one penetrative bowler, the evergreen Trueman.

Worrell gained a decided advantage by winning the toss in the first Test for the pitch did not last and favoured spin from the third day onwards, Gibbs delighting in his good fortune by taking 5 for 59 in the first innings and 6 for 98 in the second. Yet a virtual innings victory (England managed to save it by just one run) would not have been possible without the massive stability established by the batsmen in amassing 501 for six declared.

Hunte was the pillar of the innings, going eight hours for 182 and paving the way for others to bat with natural ease. Kanhai was run out for 90 and Sobers scored 64, both assisting in century stands, while Worrell rolled back the years with an undefeated 74.

Dexter's 73 in the first innings of 205 and Micky Stewart's gritty 87 in the second of 296 were the only individual scores over 40 for England.

The Lord's match, with over 20,000 in the ground for every day except the dramatic fifth, produced a monumental struggle in which no team gained the ascendency at any stage. Hunte began it with a flurry which delighted his countrymen in the crowd—three fours off Trueman's first three deliveries—but this was a deceptive beginning. Only rarely after that did the bat dominate the ball. Kanhai topscored with 73 but even he had to fight for them against Trueman's controlled speed and Shackleton's nagging medium-pace, and the West Indies were bowled out for 301.

Griffith, who had taken only one wicket at Old Trafford, swiftly eliminated Stewart and Edrich in England's reply and he and Hall bowled at terrific pace. It was the setting for a thrilling duel with Dexter, who met fire with fire and launched such a counter-offensive that he sped to 70 in 81 minutes off 73 balls before Sobers brought one back to have him lbw. That was the end of the fireworks and the bowlers regained the initiative. Griffith took 5 for 91, the West Indies gained a negligible lead of four runs and then had their backs pinned to the wall by Trueman and Shackleton, who claimed four of the first five second-innings wickets which fell for 104.

For the briefest of periods, England were poised for a decisive break-through only to meet the broad bat and unruffled temperament of Basil Butcher. Before a capacity Saturday crowd (the gates were closed 10 minutes before the start), the Guianese

right-hander, with a succession of wristy strokes, despatched the
bad ball where it belonged and, at the close of the day, was 129
not out. His equally phlegmatic captain had helped him add 110;
by then the West Indies were 214 for five. The pair progressed
no further and the last five wickets fell on the Monday resumption
for 15 runs, Butcher leg-before to Shackleton for 133 (two sixes,
17 fours).

The last innings of the match was one of unremitting tension.
Stewart and Edrich were out to Hall, Dexter to Gibbs and it was
31 for three. The West Indies had taken an early initiative.
Barrington and Cowdrey then checked the advance until Cowdrey
was struck on the left forearm by a really fast ball from Hall and
had to retire with a broken bone. Close took his place and, at
stumps on the fourth day, England required 118 more with
seven wickets standing (Cowdrey's included).

To dramatise the situation even further, rain and poor light
delayed the start on the last day until twenty past two, by which
time thousands of those who had intended watching the final
chapters of the epic unfold had returned home. A mere 7000
remained to see Hall bowl the first ball of the day—and as many
of those who could stand the strain watched him bowl the last.
He operated unchanged through the three hours 20 minutes
without losing speed or accuracy; apart from five overs from
Gibbs, Griffith was his partner at the other end.

Barrington, the hero of the previous day, added only five and
Close, the thick-set left-hander, was to be England's hero, taking
several blows about the body without flinching in three hours 50
minutes of sheer courage. He made 70 but then, quite suddenly,
decided to charge the fast bowlers and touched a legside catch to
Murray off Griffith.

At his fall, with 20 minutes remaining, 15 were required and
Allen and Shackleton were the last effective pair with Cowdrey—
not expected to bat. When Hall began the last, and his 40th,
over of the innings, eight were needed. A single off the second
ball and another off the third brought Shackleton into the strike.
When he missed the fourth ball, he charged down the pitch for a
bye. Murray's throw, wide of the stumps, was picked up by
Worrell, who kept possession, sprinted to the other end and beat
Shackleton in a veterans' race by a vital few inches to run him
out. So six were needed off the last two balls, with Allen to face.
Cowdrey, to great cheers, strode to the wicket, arm in plaster,
and stood helpless as Allen defended against the last two balls to
save the match for England. It was, all things considered, the
most equitable result.

As in Australia after the tied Test, it was feared that nothing to follow could match such sensation. Yet, as in Australia, the teams never allowed the momentum to flag.

England levelled the series at Edgbaston by winning by the considerable leeway of 217 runs in a low-scoring match. The first-innings contest was neck-and-neck, England leading by 30 (216 to 186). Close's 55 was the only half-century on either side and bowling of medium-pace or more did the damage on a pitch kept fresh by intermittent rain. Sobers took 5 for 60; Trueman 5 for 75 and Dexter 4 for 38.

England started hesitantly a second time but went from 69 for four to 278 for nine declared through Sharpe'su ndefeated 85—a knock full typical Yorkshire character—and his stands of 101 with Dexter and 89 with Lock, whose 56 was his first half-century in Tests. Under leaden skies, the West Indies capitulated for 91 against some magnificent seam bowling by Trueman, whose last spell brought him 6 for 4 off 24 balls. His 7 for 44 in the innings made his match return 12 for 119.

The West Indies regained the lead at Leeds and extended it at The Oval. At Leeds, Sobers and Kanhai were involved in one of their rare partnerships of any substance, 143 for the fourth wicket, which was the backbone of a total of 397. Sobers, had he taken the doctor's advice, would not have played at all for he was nursing a septic finger, yet he batted over four hours for 102, his only century of the series. England, in their turn, were routed by Griffith, who took 6 for 36 and whose action was, for the first time on tour, openly questioned in some quarters. Many, notably Norman Yardley and Keith Miller, wrote that the allegation was unfounded but the cloud which he was to have over the rest of his career was forming. Although the West Indies scored only 229 in their second innings, it left England too many to win, 453, and too long to think of a draw (more than a day and a half). Sobers, Griffith and Gibbs combined to dismiss them for 231, victory by 221 runs.

At Lord's and at Edgbaston the teams had fought tooth-and-nail for early supremacy without achieving it and so it was at The Oval. England mustered 275 batting first, with Sharpe's 63 the best individual effort against Griffith, who again took six wickets in an innings. Hunte's 80 and Butcher's 53 carried the West Indies to 152 before the third wicket fell but Butcher and Sobers were run out and Trueman and Statham, the old pair, went through the tail with the new ball to gain a lead of 29 for the home team.

The respective second innings would decide the issue and England failed to make enough of theirs, shackled by the superb quick bowling of Hall, Griffith and Sobers, who claimed all the wickets between them. Sharpe's 83, yet another fine innings, stood out among other meagre contributions and England's 223 left the West Indies needing 253 to secure their third triumph of the series and thus emulate the 1950 side. England suffered a telling blow with an ankle injury which allowed Trueman only one over and the ever-reliable Hunte and the Trinidadian all-rounder Rodriguez, opening the batting as a desperate measure, set a steady course by putting on 78. However, it was Kanhai, scintillatingly aggressive in his strokeplay, who clinched the issue in no-nonsense fashion, blazing away for 77 in 70 minutes, a hand which left the West Indians in the crowd delirious and the result beyond doubt.

Hunte calmly collected his second century of the series and when Butcher struck the winning boundary, the ground was engulfed in a stampede of some 10,000 jubilant spectators, the majority of them West Indian.

One victory on the field led to another for the West Indies off it, at the International Cricket Conference meeting at Lord's. There, the West Indian delegates (John Dare and Worrell himself) put forward a plan by which all countries would visit England more regularly and thus the shared-tour system was born. For one thing, it meant the West Indies would be back in 1966 and 1969—instead of as far ahead as 1971 as scheduled.

It was Worrell's last Test series and a happier Swan Song could not be imagined. At the end of the season, he wrote: "I have had a great run and, as I have satisfied by greatest ambition in the last two years, I have no complaints. My aim was always to see West Indies moulded from a rabble of brilliant island individualists into a real team—and I've done it."

West Indies in England 1966

So the West Indies were back in England within three years, no longer under Worrell but, all the same, with the bulk of the players who had wrecked England in 1963. Sobers was the new captain and his exceptional all-round record, more than any other single factor, was responsible for victory in three of the first four Tests and the avoidance of defeat in the second at Lord's. When he was out first ball in the second innings at The Oval his team collapsed to its only loss.

He scored centuries in the first, second and fourth Tests and 94 in the third and finished with 722 runs at an average of 103.14 in the series, higher in both respects than any West Indian previously on tour in England; he took 20 wickets in all three left-handed styles; he caught brilliantly; he even called the toss correctly all five times. For five months he possessed the Midas touch.

If the other principals of 1963 were not as consistently out-standing, each played a part at some stage. In addition, two of those not involved three years earlier, the batting stylist Nurse, and Sobers' all-rounder cousin David Holford, filled breaches left by Solomon and Worrell more than capably. In fact, the only major deficiency remained that of an opening partner for Hunte, McMorris and Carew returning and being again unable to come to grips with the conditions.

Nor was this team as popular as Worrell's, even though there was no reduction in the gates at the Tests. There were several reasons. An over-abundance of cricket and several sub-standard pitches in a generally wet summer left the players less than enthusiastic about county matches. In addition, the feeling was held by most West Indians that there was a witch-hunt after Griffith by press and umpires. It was a common sight for umpires to observe his action from point although only once was he called (in a county match and even that was not noticed by anyone until a week after the event) and once warned, by umpire Charlie Elliott, in the fourth Test. In the public's view, he became the "big bad boy" of cricket and several poisoned-pen letters, the majority with racial overtones, were directed towards him and the team. Griffith himself found it difficult to keep his equanimity under the strain and, at the conclusion of the tour, had his bonus withheld by the West Indies Board.

England, having recently returned from a most heartening tour of Australia, entered the series with high hopes but they were so panic-stricken after an innings defeat at Old Trafford that their selectors deposed Mike Smith as captain and put Cowdrey in his place, at the same time removing several of those who had done well in Australia. When Cowdrey failed to deliver the required results, he too was dismissed and the tough Yorkshireman, Brian Close, given the job. With a gathering of different players under him and against a West Indian team which seemed to care little about the result, Close restored a measure of pride for his team with an innings victory in the final Test. England's soccer team had captured the World Cup earlier that summer and now English cricket had, at least, some achievement to point to.

The Old Trafford Test was decided, as it had been in 1950 and 1963, by the pitch. This one was freshly prepared and favoured batting for the first day and a half, during which the West Indies helped themselves to a total of 484. Hunte, 135 this time, repeated

The famous 1950 West Indies side which toured England, pictured at Eastbourne. Standing: C. B. Williams, R. E. Marshall, A. L. Valentine, L. R. Pierre, C. L. Walcott, H. H. Johnson, A. F. Rae, K. B. Trestrail, W. Ferguson (scorer); seated: S. Ramadhin, P. E. Jones, F. M. Worrell, Rev P. Palmer (assistant manager), J. D. C. Goddard (captain), G. E. Gomez, J. B. Stollmeyer, R. J. Christiani, E. D. Weekes.   *Paul Popper*

The excitement at Lord's moun[t] as Alf Valentine claims one of th[e] more distinguished of his 33 wicke[ts] in the 1950 series—Len Hutton f[or] 10—and West Indies move clos[e] to their first ever victory [in] England. *Sport & Gener[al]*

Two of the great three Ws, Fran[k] Worrell (left) and Everton Weeke[s] resume their devastating fourt[h] wicket stand of 283 at Trent Brid[ge] in the third of the 1950 Te[st] matches. Worrell made 261, Week[es] 129, and West Indies won by [an] innings. *Central Pre[ss]*

Jubilation at Lord's after West Indies had beaten England on her own soil for the first time: 'Lord Kitchener', guitar in hand, carries his song and his friends onto the hallowed St John's Wood turf.

Sport & General

One of the most successful of West Indian opening partnerships: Jeff Stollmeyer, of Trinidad, and Allan Rae, of Jamaica, pictured as they go out to start the fourth Test, at The Oval, in 1950. Rae made a century and shared a big stand with Worrell.

Central Press

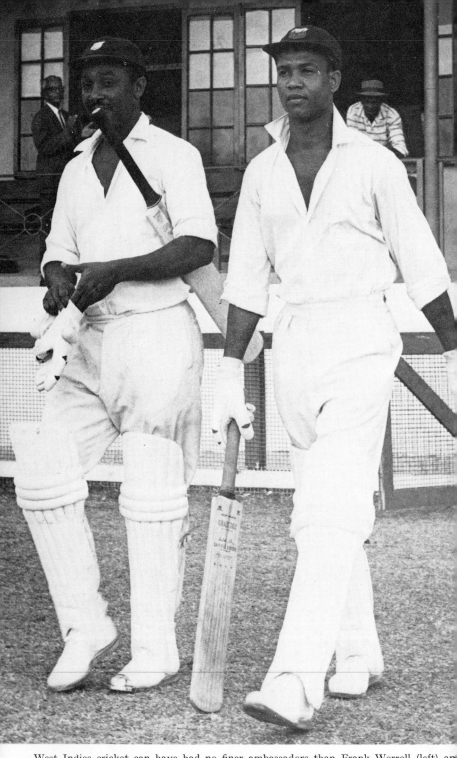

West Indies cricket can have had no finer ambassadors than Frank Worrell (left) and Garry Sobers, each a Test captain in his time and knighted for services to the game. Here they resume their record partnership of 399 for the fourth wicket against England at Bridgetown in the 1959–60 series.

End of a long, long innings: Garry Sobers is bowled by Fred Trueman for 226 at Bridgetown in the first Test of the 1959–60 series. Roy Swetman is the wicketkeeper and Worrell the non-striker.

David Allan Photo

The ugly side of West Indian cricket: firemen and officials tackle the mess after the bottle-throwing at Port-of-Spain on the third day of the 1960 Test match against England.

The famous tumbling sweep shot
Rohan Kanhai, the brillia
Guyanese batsman, here bringi
him six runs off Tony Loc
bowling during the Oval Te
match of 1963. His **77** and Conr
Hunte's century ensured We
Indian victory. Wicketkeeper is J
Parks, with Phil Sharpe at slip.

Central P

The controversial fast bow
Charlie Griffith leads the team fr
the field at Leeds during the 19
Test match, in which he took 6
36 and 3 for 35. *Sport & Gene*

A triumphant motorcade through the streets of Bridgetown gives the adoring public the chance to show their appreciation of the highly successful 1966 West Indies team upon their return from the tour of England. Captain Garry Sobers and manager Jeff Stollmeyer lead the procession.

Barbados Daily News

A new generation of bats
emerged in the early 1970s. Am
them was Alvin Kallicharrar
diminutive left-hander f
Guyana, here hooking John S
in the 1973 Oval Test match.

Patrick E

Garry Sobers' wicket was invaria
the one most sought-after. Here
the final Test of the 1973–74 se
against England, he is bowled
Underwood for 20—the key wic
and Sobers' final Test innings.

Trinidad Exp

his century of three years earlier and Sobers revealed the form he was to maintain all season with 161. When it came England's turn to bat, they found the spin of Gibbs (5 for 37 and 5 for 69), Holford and Sobers biting, and lost by the end of the third day. A swashbuckling innings by Colin Milburn in his first Test was the home team's only solace. A large, rotund man with a jolly approach to the game, Milburn hit lustily for 94 before Gibbs bowled him. But he did not have to wait long for his first Test century.

It came in the Lord's Test but was dwarfed, as was all else in that game, by a record sixth-wicket partnership between Sobers and Holford which pulled the West Indies from the jaws of defeat. Higgs' 6 for 91, peerless batting by Graveney (96 in his first Test for three years) and Parks' 91 earned England a first-innings lead of 86 which soon became a winning one with the West Indies 95 for five (Hunte, Carew, Kanhai, Butcher and Nurse) in their second innings 40 minutes before lunch on the fourth day. Sobers was still there but his habit of batting at No. 6 had surely left him powerless to do anything about his team's plight this time.

Incredibly, Holford, in his second Test, reassured by the presence of his illustrious cousin at the other end, chose this moment to play the innings of his life. Typically, Sobers made no effort to shield him in the early stages even though he knew him to be an uncertain starter. Cowdrey spread the field for Sobers, invited him to take the singles and the West Indian captain duly picked up several unearned runs. Holford, growing in confidence, gradually dispersed the close men Cowdrey had around him and, by the end of the day, the pair had added 193 and the West Indies were 288 for five, 202 ahead.

The next day, Sobers allowed Holford to pass his century and then declared at 369 for five with the stand worth 274, impudently challenging England to score 284 in the remaining four hours. He himself was 163 not out, Holford 105. With Boycott, Barrington, Cowdrey and Parks out for 67, the fortunes had swung full circle in 24 hours but Milburn's refreshing aggression in hitting three sixes and 17 fours and Graveney's calm supporting role, despite a bruised thumb, saw England through.

The West Indians demonstrated their resilience in the third Test as well. Nurse's polished 93 was matched by no other bats-man and a first-innings total of 235 was clearly inadequate on the Trent Bridge featherbed. England lost three for 13 but Graveney and Cowdrey, two of the most elegant post-war batsmen, put conditions in their true perspective with a fourth-wicket partner-

ship of 169 before both were magnificently caught, the former for
109 by Holford in the gully, the latter by the wicketkeeper
Hendriks for 96. D'Oliveira attacked purposefully for 76 and then
dismissed Hunte and Lashley with his medium-pace swing to
enhance England's lead of 90.

From that moment, a great West Indian effort first checked
England, then put them on the defensive and, finally, destroyed
them. Kanhai and Butcher provoked the anger of a huge
Saturday crowd with their careful tactics but, when settled, both
opened out. Butcher, lucky it is true, was 209 (7¾ hours, 22 fours)
when Sobers declared yet again at 482 for five, having helped
with a quickfire 94. England struggled in vain to keep the varied
West Indies attack at bay and lost by 139 runs.

By now, it seemed that Sobers had worked some sort of obeah
on his dumbfounded opponents and he proceeded to bewitch
them totally at Headingley. First, he numbed them with a
glorious innings of 174 which included a century between lunch
and tea on the first day; then he struck them down with his
bowling, 5 for 41 and 3 for 39, some with pace, some with spin.
Nurse's 137, in a fifth-wicket stand of 265 with his captain, Hall's
great opening spell in England's first innings and Gibbs' 6 for 39
in the second helped earn an innings and 55 runs verdict which
ensured the Wisden Trophy. Only D'Oliveira's militant 88, including four sixes, one straight off Hall, saved some face for
England.

Desperate problems called for desperate measures and England's
selectors went back to the drawing-board for the Oval Test. They
bowed to mounting press pressure and recalled Close as skipper,
one of five changes in all. Of those who played in the first Test,
only Higgs, the hard-working Lancashire medium-pacer, remained. The transformation did the trick, England winning by
an innings and 34 runs in a match of unusual happenings.

Kanhai (104) and Sobers (81) strove to outdo each other to the
delight of the crowd in a stand of 122 which was just about the
extent of the West Indian batting, all out 268, Kanhai's being
his first Test century in 15 Tests in England. England's response
was tottering at 166 for seven when Graveney and the new
wicketkeeper J. T. Murray, a most underrated batsman,
fashioned an astounding recovery that was continued by the last
pair, Higgs and Snow. The last three wickets advanced England's
total by 361—Graveney (165) and Murray (112) responsible for
217 together; the opening bowlers, Higgs and Snow, for 128.
Graveney's last innings of the series marked a wonderful return
to the Test arena for him, just as England's win did for Close.

For both, now at the veteran stage, it was a new lease of life.

For the West Indies, in spite of the result, the first cracks were beginning to show in their formidable team.

MCC in the West Indies 1967–68

They had widened considerably when the MCC toured the West Indies early in 1968.

Hunte, whose value in the earlier successes could not be overemphasised, announced his retirement in late 1967. Moral Re-Armament's gain was West Indies cricket's loss. More crippling to the overall balance was the deterioration of Hall and Griffith, whose fast bowling had carried such menace when at the peak of their careers.

Hall was injured in a motor accident the previous August and, not fully recovered, was as much as 25 pounds over his fighting weight and several miles an hour under his pace of earlier years. Griffith, too, lacked the speed and aggression of old and a muscle injury limited him to three overs in the fourth Test and eliminated him entirely from the fifth. Between them, they claimed only 19 English wickets, in comparison with 48 in 1963, and only once did either of them secure the first wicket of the innings. Holford, the find of 1966, appeared debilitated by a serious illness while in India the previous year and did nothing; Murray, back in the side after completing university studies, was in shocking form.

Such handicaps threw even more responsibility than usual on Sobers, the superman. As always, he shouldered it bravely, scoring 545 runs and taking 13 wickets. Yet it was he who took all the blame for a declaration which has become one of the most disputed in the game's history and which led to the only outright result—in England's favour.

England arrived seemingly disunited and underrated. The selectors had recommended Close as captain; the MCC overruled them because it was alleged he used time-wasting tactics in a county match towards the end of the English season. Cowdrey was appointed instead and, as he had done eight years before, he displayed a reassuring approach, both as captain and batsman, generating a vibrant team spirit among his men. He himself was the outstanding batsman in a team which batted consistently while Snow, David Brown and the awkward left-hander Jeff Jones, three young, zestful fast bowlers, provided him with an unexpected striking force.

Snow, with his high action, extracted bounce and movement from pitches which had often proved the graveyards of fast bowlers and his 27 wickets in only four Tests was a new record for an England bowler in a West Indian series. In Alan Knott, on his first tour, England discovered a wicketkeeper/batsman of the great Kent tradition.

Although there was only one decision, four out of the five Tests ended in high drama and nerve-wracking tension. In the first two, England made all the early running but were not strong, or lucky, enough to deliver the final thrust.

In the first, at the Queen's Park Oval, the visitors so dominated play that the West Indies were forced to follow on and, in the end, rely on a ninth wicket partnership between Sobers and Hall to save the match. England's form up until then had been far from convincing yet they raised a massive 568 after Cowdrey won the toss, batting into the third day. Barrington blunted the attack with 143 stretching 6½ hours, the elegant Graveney decimated it with 118 highlighted by 20 glorious fours and it was 432 for four when Gibbs finally separated the two after a stand of 188. Griffith then took the last four wickets to finish with 5 for 69.

Lloyd, in his first Test innings in the West Indies, hammered a powerful 118 and Kanhai matched Graveney's grace with 85 but an all-out 363 could not avert the follow-on for the home team.

Although a downpour on the fourth day reduced the West Indies' task by two hours, six wickets fell in one sensational spell for 16 runs on the final afternoon and left them 180 for eight at tea with an hour and a half to go. Defeat was inevitable but for the fact that Sobers, having lowered himself to No. 7 in the order, was one of the not-out batsmen. He and Hall, dropped before he had scored, defied everything Cowdrey could pit against them, amidst great excitement, and not another wicket fell.

England had lost their best chance of winning. A similar opportunity would not come again. So it was said. Yet, in the very next Test at Sabina the West Indies were again following on and in trouble when the crowd erupted into a bottle-throwing riot, stopping play until police used teargas to quell the disturbance. From that point the entire fortunes changed with startling completeness.

The crowd, as it had done in 1954 in Georgetown and 1960 in Port-of-Spain, was giving vent to its immense disappointment in its team's performance and an otherwise acceptable umpiring decision sparked them into regrettable action.

England's 376, the groundwork of which had been laid by Cowdrey's 101 and Edrich's 96, was followed by a shocking West Indian collapse for 143 on a new and treacherous pitch against Snow, whose 7 for 49 included Sobers lbw first ball. When Parks caught Butcher down the leg side in the follow-on to make the

West Indies 204 for five (still 29 in arrears), some of the spectators apparently interpreted the fact that the wicketkeeper's glove touched the ground as illegal. Thus yet another bottle-throwing incident began and it was not halted until an hour and a quarter later, the police compounding the chaos by firing their teargas into the breeze. The upshot was that it wafted away from the section of the ground mainly responsible into those sections not, including the players' pavilion.

The West Indies Board readily agreed to tack the lost time onto the end of the match if necessary but this eventuality was considered far-fetched. To all, that is, but Sobers. He was convinced, and said so to myself and others at the time, that the match was far from lost. It might have been sheer bravado but he had performed miracles so often in the past that who was to doubt him now. When play continued so it proved and yet another chapter in the Sobers Saga unfolded. The West Indies captain, ignoring the odds, the pitch and the bowling, scored 113 not out (after being dropped at slip when 7) and, with the help of Holford, Murray and Griffith, established a lead of 158. He then cheekily declared, took the new ball himself and dismissed Boycott and Cowdrey before a run had been scored.

England, 19 for four when the fifth day ended, were fighting for survival and would now have gladly foregone the additional 75 minutes they had pressed for following the crowd troubles. On a pitch jigsawed with a mosaic of gaping cracks, the ball did strange things. Parks suffered a terrible blow on his Adam's apple from one which stood up straight from Hall and England, incredibly, were 68 for eight when time ran out. One excuse on their behalf was that they had been upset by the commotion, yet those of 1954 and 1960 had not prevented those teams clinching wins.

The Barbados Test provided welcome relief for nerves fraught from the first two and, with rain playing its part, was a lack-lustre draw. Edrich scored a century for England and Lloyd one for the West Indies but neither was as hard-earned as Snow's eight wickets on a perfect pitch.

Throughout the first four days and into the fifth, the fourth Test also headed towards a high-scoring draw. Steve Camacho, the young bespectacled opener who had moved into Hunte's position, stroked the ball magnificently in 87, Nurse (136) and Kanhai (153) put on 273 for the third wicket in five hours and England were left with nothing to play for but a draw after the West Indies reached 526 for seven declared. This they endeavoured to do with understandable care. Cowdrey led the way with 148 but only when Knott, in his first Test of the series, helped him add 113 for the sixth wicket was the threat of the follow-on averted.

Butcher's little-used leg-spin wrapped up the tail and earned him the flattering figures of 5 for 34 but, even then, there was nothing in the match.

Sobers' declaration, which came like a bolt from the blue, changed all that. It left England 215 to get in 164 minutes and the crowd dumbfounded. It was variously described at the time as sporting, stupid, shrewd, foolish, mad, reckless and a gift. When England, through Boycott and Cowdrey, made it with seven wickets and eight balls to spare, the comments were somewhat stronger. Sobers had clearly miscalculated, particularly since Griffith's injury deprived him of the one bowler who could put a brake on the over rate. He was left with Gibbs of all people to open the bowling.

Why did he do it? Simply, according to Sobers, because he wanted to break the stalemate in the series. He felt his team had a chance of winning and he took that chance. Some say he was infuriated by England's negative tactics in the pre-lunch session in which they dilly-dallied to such an extent that they bowled only 22 overs in the two hours. Whatever the reasons, Sobers, the folk hero extraordinary, was suddenly the public whipping-boy. In Port-of-Spain that night, a Sobers effigy hung in Independence Square.

It says volumes for the man's temperament that the acute disappointment he must have felt did not deflate him. In fact, it had the opposite effect and he and his team summoned themselves for such an effort in the final Test at Bourda that they came within one wicket of levelling matters.

Sobers scored 152 and 95 not out and took 3 for 72 and 3 for 53. Kanhai, scored 150. In England's long and desperate pull to save the match and the series, Gibbs bowled his heart and his fingers out for 40 overs in which he took 6 for 60.

England were delivered from defeat by the doggedness of Boycott, Cowdrey, Lock and Pocock in the first innings; Cowdrey and Knott in the second. Boycott climaxed a grand series for him with his only century, 116 in over $4\frac{1}{2}$ hours, and he and Cowdrey put on 172 for the second wicket. When the middle order capitulated and eight were down for 259, the balding veteran Lock, recalled from a professional contract in Australia after a boating accident in Barbados cost Titmus four toes, hit about him for 89 while Pocock dropped anchor as 109 were added.

On the final day, after Gibbs had scythed through the middle, the West Indies were blocked by Cowdrey, using front pad with exasperating effect and gaining precious minutes by changing his thigh-protector, and Knott. Even so, the odds must have been on the West Indies as Gibbs bowled the last over. The No. 11, Jones, had managed only four runs in six previous visits to the crease—yet somehow he saw out the six deliveries and England regained the Wisden Trophy.

The West Indies in England 1969

The West Indies were back in England again in 1969 for the third time in the 1960s, a direct consequence of their attractiveness in 1963 and 1966. This time, they shared the summer with New Zealand and brought a team which the selectors had almost completely reshaped after the catastrophic happenings in Australia and New Zealand immediately before.

All four fast bowlers, including the legendary Hall and Griffith, were discarded, as was Holford. Nurse, doubtless disenchanted with the course of events, retired at the very prime of his career and Kanhai was unavailable because of injury. Sobers remained captain and Gibbs was appointed his deputy but these two, along with Butcher and Carew, were the only ones returning from 1963 and 1966. In all, seven were on their first tour.

More than ever the established players were needed to carry the load, but Butcher, in his last Test series, was the only one to do so effectively. Sobers, mentally and physically jaded, and Gibbs, who had been forced into the defensive role of stock bowler in Australia, could not produce their best form. Sobers reached 50 only once in six Test innings and Gibbs secured a mere six expensive wickets. Had they produced what had been expected of them, the West Indies might well have shared—or even won—a series in which they lost two of the three Tests.

They were well and truly beaten, by 10 wickets, in the first match at Old Trafford, following on and just averting an innings loss. A cold, wet May had frequently kept them indoors swaddled in sweaters, their new players missing the opportunity to acclimatise themselves to English conditions. England's first-innings total of 413 was carefully compiled over 10 hours by Boycott's century and half-centuries from Edrich, Graveney and D'Oliveira. John Shepherd, a Barbadian medium-pacer who had learned fast since joining Kent in 1965, bowled 58.5 overs and took 5 for 104 but it was, almost literally, back-breaking work. Before the series was over, he was suffering from vertebrae problems so badly he could take no real part in the closing stages of the keen third Test.

The West Indies slumped to 147 in their first innings to the pace of Snow and Brown and, even though they batted more consistently a second time, their 275 could not extend England beyond the fifth morning.

Their batsmen put up a far more confident show in the Lord's Test, which ended in an exciting draw with honours absolutely even. For the West Indies, the match was significant for the inclusion of Mike Findlay, the wicketkeeper from St Vincent, and Grayson Shillingford, an enthusiastic fast bowler from Dominica —the first time players from the "smaller" islands had earned selection in a major Test. It was the start of an inevitable and welcome flow.

The West Indies were given a wonderful send-off with a century opening stand between the two Guyanese, the left-handed Fredericks and the right-handed Camacho, which was resolutely capitalised on by Charlie Davis, a slim Trinidadian who had been making runs galore in inter-territorial cricket since he was a schoolboy. Subjected to the mortification of being Sobers' partner when his captain was run out for 29, he took it upon himself to atone for the error, crawling to 103 in 6½ hours with a mere six fours. Again, the fast bowlers Snow and Brown shared the majority of wickets for England.

Shepherd, Vanburn Holder and Sobers himself combined to create chaos at the start of England's innings, dismissing half the side for 61, but John Hampshire of Yorkshire met the crisis calmly in his debut Test and, with Knott and his captain, Illingworth, pulled his team's total to within 36 of the West Indies'. Hampshire's 107 was only the second instance of a batsman scoring a century at Lord's in his first Test innings, while Illingworth's 113 was his first century in 32 Tests.

The struggle for a winning position did not slacken over the final two days. Lloyd assailed the bowling for 70 in 100 minutes, Fredericks again played with assurance for 60 and Sobers, batting with a runner, was 50 not out when he declared on the final morning with nine wickets down. He gave his bowlers five hours to win the game and defied England to score 332 in that time. England's initial approach was so negative that Boycott took 2½ hours over the first 50 of an eventual 106 and Parfitt two hours for 39, despite the fact that the over rate was 21 an hour. When Sharpe came in, Boycott followed the example of his fellow-Yorkshireman to add 126 in an hour and a half. But the acceleration had been left far too late, the West Indies claimed several quick wickets after removing Boycott and, when stumps were drawn, England were 37 short with three wickets left.

The final Test of the short tour was as closely contested as that at Lord's. The pitch, as usual at Headingley, favoured seam bowling and Sobers, Holder, Shepherd and Shillingford for the West Indies and Snow, Brown, Knight and D'Oliveira for England utilised it ideally. Edrich's 79 was the only score over 50 in any of the first three innings, and when the West Indies found themselves faced with 303 to win they appeared to have little chance, particularly as Fredericks fell to a slip catch with only eight scored.

However, the pitch was at its best on the fourth day after the Sunday rest day and Camacho, Davis and the veteran Butcher batted so positively that 200 was passed with only three wickets down, Butcher and Lloyd in occupation and Sobers to come next. The odds, if anything, had shifted towards the West Indies. Then Butcher was given out caught-behind off Underwood, and, even more decisively, Sobers was bowled by the medium-pacer Barry Knight for a duck. Four wickets fell in the space of nine runs and England duly won by 30 runs.

Had Butcher gained the benefit of what appeared a close decision, had Sobers scored only half his overall Test average, had Shepherd been fully fit. Yes, a quite ordinary West Indies team had come mightily close to what would have been a quite unexpected victory.

They did not return to England again until 1973, for another truncated series, and, in the interim, they had to bear the suffering of playing 15 consecutive home Tests without a single win to show.

West Indies in England 1973

If was unthinkable, in headier days, that New Zealand and India could seriously have extended the West Indies, particularly on home soil. These, however, had been testing years and West Indian cricket was seen to slip to new depths in 1971 by conceding, for the first time, a series to India. Failure to conclude a single result against New Zealand the following year did nothing to restore the public's confidence and the encounter against Australia in the early months of 1973 not only ended in a 2-0 defeat but left West Indian cricket rejected by its own depressed followers.

The wheel turned full circle in three short months in England in 1973 when Kanhai, a greying warrior at the age of 37, led his team to handsome victories in two of the three Tests with the other drawn. The thousands of immigrant West Indians who joyfully acknowledged the end of a discouraging era and the start of a bright new one at the end of the final Test at Lord's were in sharp contrast to the few hundred who sadly watched Lady Worrell present the trophy named after her late husband to Australian captain Ian Chappell in Port-of-Spain four months earlier.

This was an almost unrecognisable West Indian team from those which had been beset by so many problems in the preceding three years. Eleven of the team, by now, had become regular county players and knew the conditions and their opponents well. Away from the pressures of parochially prejudiced publics at home and grandly and noisily supported by large contingents of West Indians (as distinct from purely Jamaicans or Barbadians or Trinidadians or Guyanese as in the Caribbean), they were mentally at ease. With only 16 players from whom to choose instead of 50-odd as in the West Indies there was not the competition for places which proved so decisive against India, New Zealand and Australia.

This team, in contrast to its immediate predecessors, was convinced of its strength and its ability to win and totally committed to the task at hand. Kanhai led it with authority and imagination and every single member made a distinct contribution to its success against an England team with obvious weaknesses. With the wily Gibbs as his vice-captain and a refreshed Sobers, his batteries recharged by his enforced rest against Australia, back in the side, Kanhai did not lack for knowledgeable support.

The West Indies achieved their first Test victory since 1969 with a flourish, winning by 158 runs at The Oval. There were many heroes but Keith Boyce, a latter-day Learie Constantine who had repeatedly shown his worth for Essex, was the principal one. At No. 9 in the order, he flayed the England bowling with Constantine-like abandon in a first-innings 72; he then bowled at devastating speed to take 5 for 70 and 6 for 77, more wickets in a Test than any West Indian had hitherto collected.

After an uncertain start the West Indies were given the kiss of life by the left-handed brilliance of Lloyd and Kallicharran, who converted 64 for three into 272 for four in $3\frac{1}{2}$ hours. The former's fifth Test century (132) included two sixes and 15 fours. Only Boycott, England's Rock of Gibraltar, stood firm against Boyce and the left-handed Sobers and Julien in the first-innings 257 with a typically steady 97. Kallicharran, with another 80, and Sobers, with an indication of things to come, presented the West Indies an ample lead of 413 and more than enough time to complete the victory. Only a sparkling 104 not out by Frank Hayes, an athletic Lancastrian in his first Test, did England any justice as Gibbs' immaculate off-spin accounted for three of the first four wickets and Boyce swept aside the tail.

Birmingham, unfortunately, was subjected to a most disagreeable match. The cricket matched the dullness of the weather and neither team made any great effort to win. The West Indies first-innings 327, in which Fredericks took 8½ hours over 150, progressed at 2.1 runs an over; England's 305 at less than two an over. There was more panache about the West Indies' batting a second time as Kanhai found his touch. Lloyd's mood was punishing in 94 and Sobers was Sobers but there was too much leeway to be made up and the game drifted to a dreary conclusion.

It was not the cricket, however, which attracted most attention but "incidents" connected to it. Umpire Arthur Fagg was so displeased with alleged West Indian reaction to his refusal of an appeal for caught-behind against Boycott in the first innings that he declined to take the field on the third morning in protest. The former England player Alan Oakman replaced him for an over before Fagg was coaxed by officials of both teams to resume. There was further controversy at lunch when the umpires warned Kanhai about the dilatory over rate in the first two hours when 26 overs and eight no-balls had been delivered.

There was plenty of incident, too, at Lord's, where a telephone threat that a bomb had been planted in one of the stands led to the cricket being suspended and the ground being cleared of spectators. Nothing was found and the only explosions were detonated by the West Indian batsmen, who accumulated 652 for eight declared. All five England bowlers used had a century against their names. Kanhai led the way with his highest Test score in England, 157; Sobers was not far behind with 150 not out. For both, it was their last Test hundred and it was fitting that Lord's, glorious throughout in bright sunshine, should have been the setting. Julien, matching Sobers stroke for stroke, added 155 in two hours with his mentor for the seventh wicket before a stomach complaint led to Sobers' temporary retirement. Julien had problems with neither his gastric system nor the bowlers and continued to plunder 121. When he was seventh out at 604, Sobers returned to continue!

England obviously had no inclination to fight back and they folded for 233 and 193 against the varied West Indian bowling. Fletcher alone did his reputation any good with scores of 68 and 86 not out but even the usually dependable Boycott lost his wicket in the second innings in the most irresponsible manner, hooking a catch to fine leg in the last over of the third day off

Boyce, who took four wickets in each innings.

Just to gilt the edge of a grand finale to Test cricket in England, Sobers followed his tremendous innings by showing his 37 years had not dulled his reflexes, holding six catches close to the wicket to add yet another record to his bulging collection. It was his fifth tour of England with the West Indies and he had experienced all the curious ups and downs that have marked West Indian cricket through the years. Now, unquestionably, the graph was on a steep incline.

MCC in the West Indies 1974

Less than six months later the contest was resumed in the Caribbean and the teams, with one important exception in each case, carried basically the same nucleus of players that had served them in England in the summer. For England, there was a new captain, Mike Denness, a Scotsman who had led Kent with some success, replacing Illingworth, an appointment which did not meet with universal approval. For the West Indies, Lawrence Rowe, the young Jamaican with a touch of genius about his batting, returned having recovered from an ankle injury in the previous season's Tests against Australia.

When Denness left London, he said, hopefully, that his team intended to return "with our heads held high". Three and a half months later, as a result of a narrow, hard-fought victory which levelled the series one match each, Denness could boast that he had achieved his objective. For England, a share in the rubber was a worthy achievement. For the West Indies it was frustrating and disappointing in the extreme for they failed to exploit fully an enormous superiority, both actual and psychological, which they established in the first three Tests. They won the first but allowed the second and third to escape them. By then, the bird had flown the coop and England, as they had done so admirably on the 1953-54 tour, regained their shaken self-confidence. Their win in the last Test at the Queen's Park Oval was a tribute to their fighting qualities.

England's effort revolved around a few individuals. Their star was Greig, the tall, blond charismatic South African, who was always in the game, batting, bowling and fielding, either needling the crowds with his aggressive attitude or captivating them with his personality. He was second in the batting averages and topped the bowling, having a major part in the sole victory by claiming 13 wickets with his little-used off-spin. The consistent batting of the opener Dennis Amiss was a key factor in keeping the team together when it was at its lowest ebb, while Boycott, on a generally sub-standard tour, applied himself to contribute two match-winning innings in the final Test.

Rowe, classic in style and ravenous in appetite for runs, was the dominant West Indian. Chosen as Fredericks' partner in the absence of any other reputable candidate, he accumulated a mammoth 302 in Barbados, plus single centuries at his native Sabina and at the Queen's Park Oval second time round. With Fredericks also in fine form, the West Indies had the benefit of century opening partnerships in three of the Tests and if Kallicharran was the only other batsman to score over 200 runs in the series, only once was there a total breakdown of the batting. Unfortunately for the West Indies that was when it mattered most, in the final innings of the series. Certainly Kanhai, Sobers and Lloyd were all disappointing and, for the first two, a signal to the end of their long and distinguished careers for the West Indies. Julien's all-round strength compensated in some measure for Sobers' fatigue.

While their one batting failure led to defeat, the inability of their bowlers to make the decisive final thrust prevented them concluding victories which had appeared theirs all the way through the second and third Tests. None of the bowlers could strike fire out of the docile pitches and Boyce, the spearhead in England, strained himself trying to do so. If Gibbs' off-spin gained him more wickets than anyone else (18) it was difficult to imagine England's lower order holding out against a Gibbs 10 years younger as they did at Sabina and Kensington.

Still, Boyce and Gibbs were vital figures in the positive seven-wickets result in the first Test. It was Boyce who started a steady England collapse to 131 all out on the opening day after Kanhai had sent them in. The weather was damp and sullen and the pitch fresh enough for the ball to bounce and move off it. When Boyce rattled Boycott with a third-ball bouncer and then had him caught later in the same over at long leg in exactly the same manner as he had been at Lord's the previous August, the cornerstone of England's batting had been removed and the entire structure crumbled.

England's bowlers struck back manfully so that, just after tea on the second day, they claimed the sixth wicket with the total at 196. All the principal batsmen with the exception of Kallicharran were among them but the little left-hander swung the course of the match back in his team's favour with a wonderful innings. At the end of the second day he was 142 out of 274 for seven—and Murray's 23 was the next-best score. Or was it 274 for eight, Kallicharran 142 run out? For a long time nobody knew following an unusual incident which led to the reversal of the umpire's decision.

The confusion and controversy followed the last ball of the day. Julien, facing Underwood, played it quietly to Greig at silly point, Knott obligingly removed the stumps at the batsman's end for the umpire, and the players began to troop off the field. All, that is, except Greig, who picked up the ball and, with Kallicharran quarter-way down the pitch on the way to the pavilion, pegged the middle stump at the bowler's end. Umpire Douglas San Hue had no option but to uphold his solitary appeal for run out. The crowd was, at first, bemused by the affair but those that remained became angry when they realised the position.

For three hours the matter was debated until an official statement declared Kallicharran would resume. It stated: "Whilst appreciating that this is not strictly within the laws of cricket, the England manager and captain have, in the interests of cricket as a whole and the future of this tour in particular, requested that the appeal be withdrawn". The umpires agreed and a potentially explosive situation was averted.

On resumption, Kallicharran was not the same player and was soon caught for 158, but the all-rounders, Julien (86) and Boyce (26 off 10 balls), carried the West Indies lead to 261. England now set about saving the game with great determination through Boycott and Amiss, who occupied 4¼ hours all told before Boycott was caught at short leg for 93 early on the fourth morning. Amiss and Denness then stayed together another two hours, pushing England ahead and causing genuine concern among West Indian supporters.

It was 328 before the second wicket fell, Denness run out, but this was the crack which broke the dam. Gibbs (6 for 108) and Sobers (3 for 54 with his orthodox left-arm spin) scuttled the rest of the innings, Amiss finally yielding to Sobers for 174 after six hours 40 minutes' defiance. The West Indies needed 132 to win and, after a few early alarms, duly got them.

If this was an epic effort by Amiss, that at Sabina in the second Test was even more so. England's first-innings 353 was belittled by the West Indies reply of 583, built around a record opening partnership of 206 by Fredericks (94) and Rowe (120) and the consistency of scoring which followed from Kallicharran (93), Lloyd (49), Kanhai (39), Sobers (57) and Julien (66). When the final day began, England 218 for five, Amiss was already 123 but there was little left by way of support if he was to save the match. Yet it was saved, Amiss remaining fittingly undefeated at the end after 9½ hours of immense concentration and stamina in which he scored 262, hitting a six and 40 fours. The assistance he needed was provided by Underwood, Old and Pocock, who each stayed with him for over an hour.

Amiss, almost singlehandedly, had kept England's interest in the series alive but when they returned to Barbados their stocks dived to a new low with a shameful defeat by 10 wickets against the island team. The resultant dejection was reflected in all but a few in the Test which followed. Boycott, remarkably, was shifted to No. 4 in the order, Denness opened in his place and, in the field, there appeared to be many leaders. It took a century from Greig and 87 from Knott to lift the first innings from the gloom of 130 for five to a respectable 395. Even that was soon being dwarfed by the majesty of Rowe, whose magnetism swelled the stands to bursting point on the Saturday when he moved from one century to another. On the Sunday, he passed his third hundred and, finally, after 10¼ hours with a six and 34 fours, he was caught in the deep for 302, the first Test triple-century on the ground, and his own first first-class century outside Jamaica. Kallicharran (119) shared a record second-wicket stand of 249 with him and the only disappointment among the crowd was that their idol Sobers, in what was obviously his last Test on home ground, failed to score.

With a leeway of 201 to make up, England entered the last day 72 for four, among them Amiss, the saviour of Sabina. This time, Fletcher and Knott filled the roles which Amiss and others had carried out so ably in the previous Test, Fletcher batting throughout the day for an undefeated 129 and Knott falling when the match was safe for 67.

England were now convinced that the worst was behind them and, in the rain-ruined Bourda Test, they had somewhat better of the exchanges, with centuries from Amiss and Greig securing their highest total of the series. They were, undoubtedly, in a better frame of mind entering the final Test than they had been for the entire tour. All along there had been the feeling in the English camp that the Queen's Park Oval pitch provided their bowlers with their best—and perhaps only—opportunity of dismissing the powerful West Indies batting twice.

So it proved. In a match extended to six days England fought desperately to make fullest use of batting first but 267 was hardly what they were aiming for. Boycott provided a worthy example by batting 6½ hours for 99 before he was caught by the wicketkeeper down the leg side but none of his team-mates emulated him. The West Indies were completely on top when

Fredericks and Rowe added 110 for the first wicket and Rowe and Lloyd a further 102 for the third.

They were 43 in arrears when the third wicket fell and yet managed a lead of only 38. Rowe dispelled all doubts about his ability to bat on a turning pitch with a flawless 123 in $7\frac{1}{4}$ hours but his work was undone by Greig, who took the last eight West Indian wickets for 38 runs in 14.1 overs of off-spin made awkward by his high delivery.

Once more, England's second innings revolved around Boycott, who did complete his century this time, his first for the series, but a winning target of 226 seemed insufficient against a team which had not been bowled out for under 300 in the series. Rowe and Fredericks provided another solid start, adding 63, but the later batsmen again had no answer to the spin of Greig, from one end, and Underwood, Pocock and Birkenshaw from the other. At 166 for eight, England's victory appeared not far away but stout resistance from Boyce and Inshan Ali caused some excitement until Denness claimed the new ball and that proved enough.

An English record of not losing a series in the West Indies since 1948 had been kept intact and Denness' team indeed returned home with heads held high.

West Indies in England 1976

The tenth and latest West Indies tour of England proved, at least in terms of results, to be the most successful. It was their first full tour since 1966 and, in a summer of sweltering heat and parched drought, they swept all before them. In retaining the Wisden Trophy by 3—0, they became the first West Indies team to conclude a rubber in England without a single defeat; their first-class record of 18 victories was one better than that of the 1950 side, which played five more matches.

West Indian partiality to English conditions had been long established and this team, under the captaincy of Lloyd, had much in its favour in this regard. The great majority had been contract professionals to county or league clubs; eight of the 17 had toured England previously with the West Indies and only one, the lithe Jamaican fast bowler Michael Holding, had never played cricket of any kind in England. As usual, they were feverishly encouraged by thousands of their compatriots resident in Britain and, to complete the formula, the unceasing sunshine resulted in hard, true pitches and a minimum of injuries.

Like so many of their predecessors, Lloyd's side based its prosperity on a simple by irrepressible formula—a long line of aggressive batsmen and a staff of very fast bowlers. If there was

one criticism that could be levelled at the combination it was that
it lacked a stabilising influence in its batting and carried virtually
no spin. Yet if this was a weakness it did not show and the resources were more than adequate for the job at hand.

Every batsman turned the conditions to his advantage and
there were no fewer than 37 three-figure innings on the tour. Six
topped 1000 runs and the striking rate was frequently an
astounding five runs an over and above. Even in such abundance,
Vivian Richards, a strongly-built, self-assured Antiguan, was
outstanding. In four Tests (he missed the second through illness),
he treated the bowlers almost as he pleased, accumulating 829
runs in seven innings, including two double-centuries. No West
Indian has scored as many in one series. If Richards had no
equal, the openers, Gordon Greenidge, born in Barbados, schooled
in Berkshire and discovered by Hampshire, and the veteran
Fredericks, either individually or in partnership, often hammered
the attack into submission for the benefit of those to follow.
Greenidge collected nine centuries in the season, including two in
the third Test and one in 69 minutes against Nottinghamshire,
and both he and Fredericks topped 500 runs in the Tests.

Lloyd's tactics were heavily reliant on aggression, both from
his batsmen and his bowlers, and he used his fast bowlers as his
shock troops. He had three of vastly contrasting physiques and
styles but with one vital element in common—real speed. Holding,
who had made his Test debut only a few months earlier in Australia, and Andy Roberts, who had already taken 75 Test wickets
at the start of the series, each took 28 wickets and Holding's 14
wickets in the final Test on a dead Oval pitch was a match-
winning effort. Daniel, a heavily-set, 21-year-old Barbadian, was
the least experienced of the lot, accordingly the wildest but, on
occasion, the fastest. Holder, by comparison a military medium,
provided relief with his unerring accuracy and movement off the
pitch. The four shared 84 wickets between them in the Tests;
other bowlers managed eight.

As the tour progressed, the West Indies quickly regained the
spirit which had appeared crushed by a shattering 5–1 defeat by
Australia the previous winter. After securing drawn results in the
first two Tests, England, now led by Greig, found their opponents
playing to the best of their ability with a joyous enthusiasm and
proved no match. Greig's undiplomatic braggadocio approach
before the series when he said he intended to make them "grovel"
rankled the West Indies and their supporters and haunted him
all season.

Both teams approached the first two Tests with a caution

which suggested neither was prepared to take a chance before assessing the other's strengths and weaknesses. In each, the West Indies were without a key player—Holding, down with mild glandular fever, missed the first at Trent Bridge; Richards, with influenza, the second at Lord's.

At Trent Bridge, the West Indies spent 11 hours putting together a first-innings total of 494 which was completely dominated by Richards' 232. After passing through troubled waters against some testing swing bowling early in his innings, Richards shared a third-wicket partnership of 303 with Kallicharran, whose share was 97. He offered no chance in 465 minutes in which he hit four sixes and 31 fours. Kallicharran, confined by fibrositis in the right shoulder which necessitated an operation after the third Test, spent six hours at the crease.

The dogged David Steele, hero of the series against Australia in 1975, recorded his first Test century and Bob Woolmer, in a style patently based on Cowdrey's, a pleasant 82 but England were hard-pressed to save the follow-on. Once they had done so, there was no feasible result other than a draw.

Lord's would probably have witnessed the first decision of the series but for the only rain in months which completely obliterated Saturday's play. Who would have won is impossible to say for the contest was close all the way through. England batted solidly but without enterprise to score 250, then gained a lead of 68 as Snow and Underwood swept through the West Indian lower order, converting 139 for four into 182 all out. Greenidge, 84, and Lloyd, 50, added 99 for the fourth wicket but that was all and euphoric England supporters under the Tavern greeted their team's position by singing *Rule Britannia* and *God Save the Queen*.

The players, however, did not appear to share the optimism and the approach to the second innings was similar to the first, with no aim except that to avoid defeat. Steele and the plucky old man Close, recalled by the selectors at Trent Bridge at the age of 45 some 27 years after his first Test, held the bowlers at bay longest although Roberts for the second time in the match claimed five wickets to finish with 10 for 123.

Set 323 to win in five hours, the West Indies left their effort too late, and although the game did not end without some excitement, no team won because neither deserved to. Fredericks' 138 was his first century at Lord's in three Test appearances.

Only briefly thereafter did England enter the picture. Their best period in the final three Tests was the opening overs of the third at Old Trafford, when Mike Selvey of Middlesex, in the team only because of injuries to several fast bowlers, created early havoc with his medium-pace swing. Fredericks, Richards and Kallicharran were his victims at 26 for four but Greenidge and his exciting fellow-Barbadian Collis King, in his maiden Test, checked England with a partnership of 111. The home team was never in it after that.

Greenidge's disciplined 134 was the body of an eventual 211, a notable, almost solo performance. Yet it was a modest enough total on a fast true pitch. England did suffer the loss of two early wickets before close in reply but it was the second morning which decided the match and, probably, the series. England's batsmen were unceremoniously skittled by Roberts, Holding and Daniel, bowling together for the first time in the Tests, and were all out for their lowest total against the West Indies, 71, eight wickets falling for 25 runs in an hour. Three were bowled and the others snicked catches to the wicketkeeper or slips. The pace was just too much.

Greenidge's second century in the match emulated Headley's feat of 1939—and with Richards atoning for his first innings failure with 135, the total reached 411 for five before Lloyd humanely declared, leaving England 13½ hours to survive or make 552. Edrich and Close, with 84 years between them, were subjected to a barrage of short-pitched bowling in the closing stages of the third day but, later, the pace trio kept the ball up to the bat and England slumped again, this time to 126 to lose by a monstrous 425 runs. Roberts took nine wickets in the match and was denied the hat-trick by a dropped catch, Holding seven and Daniel four.

Headingley was the best match of the series for it produced a feast of dazzling batting on the first day, a gritty recovery by England and a good finish. The West Indies started with an unceasing volley of punishing strokes which took the score to an incredible 330 for two at tea. Fredericks and Greenidge both scored hundreds in adding 192 for the first wicket, the latter becoming only the third batsman to register three successive centuries in Tests against England. Richards and Rowe (replacing Kallicharran in the eleven) carried on the attack but there was a final slump and the innings subsided to 450.

England were labouring at 169 for five in response before Greig and Knott put them right with a diligent partnership of 152, made almost entirely in the absence of an injured Holding. Both scored 116 and the deficit was only 63. The West Indian approach to their second innings was all carefree abandon although wickets fell frequently and they were all out for 196. King, with top score of 58 in an hour off 58 deliveries, characterised the spirit but England, needing 260 for victory, were back in with a chance. Roberts minimised it by taking three quick wickets but the result was still in doubt until Daniel finally settled the issue with three wickets in his first three overs on the final day.

While the Wisden Trophy was decided by then, both teams had an interest in the Oval match. The West Indies viewed it as an opportunity to emphasise their strength, England as a final chance to regain some prestige. Logically, the only benefactors should have been the batsmen, so passive was the pitch. No bowler could coax the ball higher than stump-high, there was no spin and the pace was slow.

This time Greenidge did not score but Richards' final innings of the series was to be the biggest by a West Indian in England, 291 in just under eight hours with 38 fours and without a blemish, his seventh three-figure innings in Tests for the year. Fredericks, Rowe, Lloyd and King all assisted in mounting a total of 687 for eight declared, more than the West Indies had managed in any of their previous 70 Tests against England.

Two great personal performances, one from Amiss, the other from Holding, marked the rest of the match.

Amiss, returning to Test cricket after his traumas against the Australian fast bowlers, made it an occasion to remember by scoring 203 in seven hours 25 minutes and was largely responsible for an England total of 435. Even so, Lloyd could have enforced the follow-on had he chosen to; instead, with Daniel injured and in extreme heat, he allowed Fredericks and Greenidge to drive the nails further into the England coffin, the pair putting together 182 in a mere 32 overs before the declaration.

That and the stirring bowling of Holding sped England to their defeat. Holding had taken 8 for 92 in the first innings; he followed with 6 for 57 in the second as England were bowled out for 203. Twelve of his 14 victims were either bowled or leg-before-wicket, a tribute to his unerring accuracy and unremitting pace. Statistically it was the most incisive piece of bowling by any West Indian in Test cricket. Given the conditions, he had come close to doing the impossible.

That victory brought the two teams exactly even on their record of Tests in England—14 wins apiece with 11 drawn. In the West Indies, the home team holds a narrow 8–7 advantage with 17 drawn and, in the 71 Tests overall, the register reads 21 to England, 22 to the West Indies, 28 drawn. There are statistics which, for once, do not lie. Test cricket between England and the West Indies has always been keenly fought.

West Indies in England 1928

AT Lord's. June 23 *to* 26. England won by an innings and 58 runs. England 401 (E. Tyldesley 122, A. P. F. Chapman 50, H. Sutcliffe 48, W. R. Hammond 45, L. N. Constantine 4 for 82). West Indies 177 (F. R. Martin 44, V. W. C. Jupp 4 for 37) and 166 (J. A. Small 52, C. R. Browne 44, A. P. Freeman 4 for 37).

AT Old Trafford. July 21 *to* 24. England won by an innings and 30 runs. West Indies 206 (C. A. Roach 50, Freeman 5 for 54) and 115 (Freeman 5 for 39). England 351 (D. R. Jardine 83, Hammond 63, Sutcliffe 54, J. B. Hobbs 53).

AT The Oval. August 11 *to* 14. England won by an innings and 71 runs. West Indies 238 (Roach 53, G. Challenor 46, M. W. Tate 4 for 59) and 129 (Martin 41, Freeman 4 for 47). England 438 (Hobbs 159, Sutcliffe 63, Tyldesley 73, Tate 54, H. C. Griffith 6 for 103, G. N. Francis 4 for 112).

England in West Indies 1929–30

AT Kensington. January 11 *to* 16. Match drawn. West Indies 369 (C. A. Roach 122, F. I. deCaires 80, J. E. D. Sealy 58, G. T. S. Stevens 5 for 105) and 384 (G. A. Headley 176, Roach 77, deCaires 70, Stevens 5 for 90). England 467 (A. Sandham 152, E. H. Hendren 80, N. E. Haig 47, F. S. G. Calthorpe 40) and 167 for three (Sandham 51, L. E. G. Ames 44 not out).

AT Queen's Park. February 1 *to* 6. England won by 167 runs. England 208 (Hendren 77, Ames 42, H. C. Griffith 5 for 63) and 425 for eight declared (Hendren 205 not out, Ames 105, L. N. Constantine 4 for 165). West Indies 254 (R. L. Hunte 58, Constantine 58, W. E. Astill 4 for 58, W. Voce 4 for 79) and 212 (deCaires 45, Voce 7 for 70).

AT Bourda. February 21 *to* 26. West Indies won by 289 runs. West Indies 471 (Roach 209, Headley 114, E. A. C. Hunte 53) and 290 (Headley 112, C. R. Browne 70 not out, Astill 4 for 70). England 145 (Hendren 56, Constantine 4 for 35, G. N. Francis 4 for 40) and 327 (Hendren 123, Calthorpe 49, G. Gunn 45, Constantine 5 for 87).

AT Sabina. April 3 *to* 12. Match drawn. England 849 (Sandham 325, Ames 149, Gunn 85, Hendren 61, R. E. S. Wyatt 58, J. O'Connor 51, O. C. Scott 5 for 266) and 272 for nine declared (Hendren 55, Sandham 50, Gunn 47, Scott 4 for 108). West Indies 286 (R. K. Nunes 66, C. C. Passailaigue 44) and 408 for five (Headley 223, Nunes 92).

West Indies in England 1933

AT Lord's. June 24 *to* 27. England won by an innings and 27 runs. England 296 (L. E. G. Ames 83 not out, C. F. Walters 51, E. A. Martindale 4 for 85). West Indies 97 (R. W. V. Robins 6 for 32) and 172 (G. A. Headley 50, H. Verity 4 for 45, G. G. Macaulay 4 for 57). *AT Old Trafford. July* 22 *to* 25. Match drawn. West Indies 375 (Headley 169 not out, I. Barrow 105, E. W. Clark 4 for 99) and 225 (C. A. Roach 64, L. N. Constantine 64, Jas Langridge 7 for 56). England 374 (D. R. Jardine 127, Robins 55, Ames 47, Walters 46, Martindale 5 for 73).

AT The Oval. August 12 *to* 15. England won by an innings and 17 runs. England 312 (A. H. Bakewell 107, C. J. Barnett 52, M. S. Nichols 49, Martindale 5 for 93). West Indies 100 (C. S. Marriott 5 for 37) and 195 (Roach 56, Marriott 6 for 59).

England in West Indies 1934-35

AT Kensington. January 8 *to* 10. England won by four wickets. West Indies 102 (G. A. Headley 44, K. Farnes 4 for 40) and 51 for six declared (C. I. J. Smith 5 for 15). England 81 for seven declared (W. R. Hammond 43) and 75 for six (E. A. Martindale 5 for 22).

AT Queen's Park. January 24 *to* 28. West Indies won by 217 runs. West Indies 302 (J. E. D. Sealy 92, L. N. Constantine 90, Smith 4 for 100) and 280 for six declared (Headley 93). England 258 (E. R. T. Holmes 85 not out, J. Iddon 73, E. H. Hendren 41) and 107.

AT Bourda. February 14 *to* 18. Match drawn. England 226 (G. A. E. Paine 49, Hammond 47, L. G. Hylton 4 for 27) and 160 for six declared (R. E. S. Wyatt 71). West Indies 184 (Headley 53, K. L. Wishart 52, W. E. Hollies 7 for 50) and 104 for five.

AT Sabina. March 14 *to* 18. West Indies won by an innings and 161 runs. West Indies 535 for seven declared (Headley 270 not out, Sealy 91, R. S. Grant 77, Paine 5 for 168). England 271 (L. E. G. Ames 126, Iddon 54, Hendren 40) and 103 (Martindale 4 for 28).

West Indies in England 1939

AT Lord's. June 24 *to* 27. England won by eight wickets. West Indies 277 (G. A. Headley 106, J. B. Stollmeyer 59, W. H. Copson 5 for 85) and 225 (Headley 107, Copson 4 for 67). England 404 for five declared (L. Hutton 196, D. C. S. Compton 120) and 100 for two. *AT Old Trafford. July* 22 *to* 25. Match drawn. England 164 for seven declared (J. Hardstaff 76) and 128 for six declared (L. N. Constantine 4 for 42). West Indies 133 (Headley 51, Grant 47, Bowes 6 for 33) and 43 for four.

AT The Oval. August 19 *to* 22. Match drawn. England 352
(Hardstaff 94, N. Oldfield 80, Hutton 73, W. R. Hammond 43,
Constantine 5 for 75) and 366 for three (Hutton 165 not out,
Hammond 138). West Indies 498 (K. H. Weekes 137, V. H.
Stollmeyer 96, L. N. Constantine 79, G. A. Headley 65, J. B.
Stollmeyer 59, R. T. D. Perks 5 for 156).

England in West Indies 1947–48

AT Kensington. January 21 *to* 26. Match drawn. West Indies 296
(G. E. Gomez 86, J. B. Stollmeyer 78, J. C. Laker 7 for 103) and
351 for nine declared (R. J. Christiani 99, E. A. V. Williams 72,
W. Ferguson 56 not out, R. Howorth 6 for 124). England 253
(J. Hardstaff 98, J. D. B. Robertson 80, P. E. Jones 4 for 54) and
86 for four (Robertson 51 not out).

AT Queen's Park. February 11 *to* 16. Match drawn. England 362
(S. C. Griffith 140, Laker 55, Ferguson 5 for 137) and 275
(Robertson 133, Ferguson 6 for 92). West Indies 497 (A. G.
Ganteaume 112, G. M. Carew 107, F. M. Worrell 97, Gomez 62)
and 72 for three.

AT Bourda. March 3 *to* 6. West Indies won by seven wickets.
West Indies 297 for eight declared (Worrell 131 not out, R. J.
Christiani 51, K. Cranston 4 for 78) and 78 for three. England 111
(J. D. C. Goddard 5 for 31) and 263 (Hardstaff 63, Ferguson 5 for
116).

AT Sabina. March 27 *to April* 1. West Indies won by 10 wickets.
England 227 (Robertson 64, L. Hutton 56, H. H. Johnson 5 for 41)
and 336 (W. Place 107, Hardstaff 64, Hutton 60, Johnson 5 for 55).
West Indies 490 (E. D. Weekes 141, Ferguson 75, K. R.
Rickards 67, C. L. Walcott 45) and 76 for no wicket (Goddard 46
not out).

West Indies in England 1950

AT Old Trafford. June 8 *to* 12. England won by 202 runs. England
312 (T. G. Evans 104, T. E. Bailey 82 not out, A. L. Valentine
8 for 104) and 288 (W. J. Edrich 71, L. Hutton 45, J. C. Laker 40).
West Indies 215 (E. D. Weekes 52, J. B. Stollmeyer 43, R. Berry
5 for 63) and 183 (Stollmeyer 78, W. E. Hollies 5 for 63, Berry 4
for 53).

AT Lord's. June 24 *to* 29. West Indies won by 326 runs. West
Indies 326 (A. F. Rae 106, Weekes 63, F. M. Worrell 52, R. O.
Jenkins 5 for 116) and 425 for six declared (C. L. Walcott 168
not out, G. E. Gomez 70, Weekes 63, Worrell 45, Jenkins 4 for 174).
England 151 (S. Ramadhin 5 for 66, Valentine 4 for 48) and 274
(C. Washbrook 114, W. G. A. Parkhouse 48, Ramadhin 6 for 86).

AT Trent Bridge. July 20 *to* 25. West Indies won by 10 wickets.
England 223 (D. Shackleton 42, N. W. D. Yardley 41) and 436
(C. Washbrook 102, R. T. Simpson 94, Parkhouse 69, J. G. Dewes

67, Evans 63, Ramadhin 5 for 135). West Indies 558 (Worrell 261, Weekes 129, Rae 68, Stollmeyer 46, A. V. Bedser 5 for 127) and 103 for no wicket (Stollmeyer 52 not out, Rae 46 not out).

AT The Oval. August 12 to 16. West Indies won by an innings and 56 runs. West Indies 503 (Worrell 138, Rae 109, Gomez 74, J. D. C. Goddard 58 not out, D. V. P. Wright 5 for 141). England 344 (Hutton 202 not out, D. C. S. Compton 44, Goddard 4 for 25, Valentine 4 for 121) and 103 (Valentine 6 for 39).

England in West Indies 1953–54

AT Sabina. January 15 to 21. West Indies won by 140 runs. West Indies 417 (J. K. Holt 94, C. L. Walcott 65, J. B. Stollmeyer 60, E. D. Weekes 55, C. A. McWatt 54, G. E. Gomez 47 not out, J. B. Statham 4 for 90) and 209 for six declared (Weekes 90 not out). England 170 (S. Ramadhin 4 for 65) and 316 (W. Watson 116, P. B. H. May 69, L. Hutton 56, E. S. M. Kentish 5 for 49).

AT Kensington. February 6 to 12. West Indies won by 181 runs. West Indies 383 (Walcott 220, B. H. Pairaudeau 71, D. S. Atkinson 53, J. C. Laker 4 for 81) and 292 for two declared (Holt 166, F. M. Worrell 76 not out). England 181 (Hutton 72, Ramadhin 4 for 50) and 313 (D. C. S. Compton 93, Hutton 77, T. W. Graveney 64 not out, May 62).

AT Bourda. February 24 to March 2. England won by nine wickets. England 435 (Hutton 169, Compton 64, T. E. Bailey 49, Ramadhin 6 for 113) and 75 for one. West Indies 251 (Weekes 94, McWatt 54, Holt 48 not out, Statham 4 for 64) and 256 (Holt 64, Stollmeyer 44).

AT Queen's Park. March 17 to 23. Match drawn. West Indies 681 for eight declared (Weekes 206, Worrell 167, Walcott 124, Atkinson 74, Stollmeyer 41, Holt 40) and 212 for four declared (Worrell 56, Atkinson 53 not out, Walcott 51 not out, W. Ferguson 44). England 537 (May 135, Compton 133, Graveney 92, Bailey 46, Hutton 44) and 98 for three.

AT Sabina. March 30 to April 3. England won by nine wickets. West Indies 139 (Walcott 50, Bailey 7 for 34) and 346 (Walcott 116, Stollmeyer 64, Atkinson 40, Laker 4 for 71). England 414 (Hutton 205, J. H. Wardle 66, G. S. Sobers 4 for 75) and 72 for one.

West Indies in England 1957

AT Edgbaston. May 30 to June 4. Match drawn. England 186 (P. E. Richardson 47, S. Ramadhin 7 for 49) and 583 for four declared (P. B. H. May 285 not out, M. C. Cowdrey 154, D. B.

Close 42). West Indies 474 (O. G. Smith 161, C. L. Walcott 90, F. M. Worrell 81, G. S. Sobers 53, R. B. Kanhai 42, J. C. Laker 4 for 119) and 72 for seven.

AT Lord's. June 20 to 22. England won by an innings and 36 runs. West Indies 127 (T. E. Bailey 7 for 44) and 261 (E. D. Weekes 90, Sobers 66, Bailey 4 for 54). England 424 (Cowdrey 152, T. G. Evans 82, Richardson 76, R. Gilchrist 4 for 115).

AT Trent Bridge. July 4 to 9. Match drawn. England 619 for six declared (T. W. Graveney 258, Richardson 126, May 104, Cowdrey 55) and 64 for one. West Indies 372 (Worrell 191 not out, Sobers 47, Kanhai 42, F. S. Trueman 5 for 63) and 367 (Smith 168, J. D. C. Goddard 61, D. S. Atkinson 46, J. B. Statham 5 for 118, Trueman 4 for 80).

AT Headingley. July 25 to 27. England won by an innings and five runs. West Indies 142 (Kanhai 47, P. J. Loader 6 for 36) and 132. England 279 (May 69, Cowdrey 68, D. S. Sheppard 68, Worrell 7 for 70).

AT The Oval. August 22 to 24. England won by an innings and 237 runs. England 412 (Graveney 164, Richardson 107, Sheppard 40, Evans 40, Ramadhin 4 for 107). West Indies 89 (G. A. R. Lock 5 for 28) and 86 (Sobers 42, Lock 6 for 20).

England in West Indies 1959-60

AT Kensington. January 6 to 12. Match drawn. England 482 (E. R. Dexter 136 not out, K. F. Barrington 128, G. Pullar 65, R. Swetman 45) and 71 for no wicket (Pullar 46 not out). West Indies 563 for eight declared (G. S. Sobers 226, F. M. Worrell 197 not out, C. C. Hunte 42, R. B. Kanhai 40, F. S. Trueman 4 for 93).

AT Queen's Park. January 28 to February 3. England won by 256 runs. England 382 (Barrington 121, M. J. K. Smith 108, Dexter 77) and 230 for nine declared (Barrington 49, R. Illingworth 41 not out). West Indies 112 (Trueman 5 for 35) and 244 (Kanhai 110, Hunte 47).

AT Sabina. February 17 to 23. Match drawn. England 277 (M. C. Cowdrey 114, W. W. Hall 7 for 69) and 305 (Cowdrey 97, Pullar 66, P. B. H. May 45, C. Watson 4 for 62). West Indies 353 (Sobers 147, E. D. A. McMorris 73, S. M. Nurse 70) and 175 for six (Kanhai 57, Hunte 40, Trueman 4 for 54).

AT Bourda. March 9 to 15. Match drawn. England 295 (Cowdrey 65, D. A. Allen 55, Hall 6 for 90) and 334 for eight (Dexter 110, R. Subba Row 100, Pullar 47, Worrell 4 for 49). West Indies 402 for eight declared (Sobers 145, Kanhai 55).

AT Port-of-Spain. March 25 to 31. Match drawn. England 393 (Cowdrey 119, Dexter 76, Barrington 69, J. M. Parks 43, S.

Ramadhin 4 for 73) and 350 for seven declared (Parks 101 not out,
Smith 96, Pullar 54, Dexter 47). West Indies 338 for eight declared
(Sobers 92, Hunte 72 not out, C. L. Walcott 53) and 209 for five
(Worrell 61, Sobers 49 not out).

West Indies in England 1963

AT Old Trafford. June 6 to 10. West Indies won by 10 wickets.
West Indies 501 for six declared (C. C. Hunte 182, R. B. Kanhai 90,
F. M. Worrell 74 not out, G. S. Sobers 64) and one for no wicket.
England 205 (E. R. Dexter 73, L. R. Gibbs 5 for 59) and 296
(M. J. Stewart 87, Gibbs 6 for 98).

AT Lord's. June 20 to 25. Match drawn. West Indies 301 (Kanhai
73, J. S. Solomon 56, Hunte 44, Sobers 42, F. S. Trueman 6 for 100)
and 229 (B. F. Butcher 133, Trueman 5 for 52, D. Shackleton 4 for
72). England 297 (K. F. Barrington 80, Dexter 70, F. J. Titmus
52 not out, C. C. Griffith 5 for 91) and 228 for nine (D. B. Close
70, Barrington 60, W. W. Hall 4 for 93).

AT Edgbaston. July 4 to 9. England won by 217 runs. England 216
(Close 55, Sobers 5 for 60) and 278 for nine declared (P. J. Sharpe
85 not out, Dexter 57, G. A. R. Lock 56, Gibbs 4 for 49). West
Indies 186 (M. C. Carew 40, Trueman 5 for 75, Dexter 4 for 38) and
91 (Trueman 7 for 44).

AT Headingley. July 25 to 29. West Indies won by 221 runs. West
Indies 397 (Sobers 102, Kanhai 92, Solomon 62, Trueman 4 for
117) and 229 (Butcher 78, Sobers 52, Kanhai 44, Titmus 4 for 44).
England 174 (Lock 53, Griffith 6 for 36) and 231 (J. M. Parks 57,
Close 56, J. B. Bolus 43, Gibbs 4 for 76).

AT The Oval. August 22 to 26. West Indies won by eight wickets.
England 275 (Sharpe 63, Close 46, Griffith 6 for 71) and 223
(Sharpe 83, Hall 4 for 39). West Indies 246 (Hunte 80, Butcher 53)
and 255 for two (Hunte 108 not out, Kanhai 77).

West Indies in England 1966

AT Old Trafford. June 2 to 4. West Indies won by an innings and
40 runs. West Indies 484 (G. S. Sobers 161, C. C. Hunte 135,
S. M. Nurse 49, B. F. Butcher 44, F. J. Titmus 5 for 83). England
167 (J. M. Parks 43, L. R. Gibbs 5 for 37) and 277 (C. Milburn 94,
M. C. Cowdrey 69, Gibbs 5 for 69).

AT Lord's. June 16 to 21. Match drawn. West Indies 269 (Nurse
64, Butcher 49, Sobers 46, K. Higgs 6 for 91) and 369 for five
declared (Sobers 163 not out, D. A. J. Holford 105 not out, R. B.
Kanhai 40). England 355 (T. W. Graveney 96, Parks 91,
G. Boycott 60, W. W. Hall 4 for 106) and 197 for four (Milburn
126 not out).

AT Trent Bridge. June 30 *to July* 5. West Indies won by 139 runs. West Indies 235 (Nurse 93, P. D. Lashley 49, J. A. Snow 4 for 82, Higgs 4 for 71) and 482 for five declared (Butcher 209 not out, Sobers 94, Kanhai 63, Nurse 53). England 325 (Graveney 109, Cowdrey 96, B. L. D'Oliveira 76, Sobers 4 for 90, Hall 4 for 105) and 253 (Boycott 71, D'Oliveira 54, C. C. Griffith 4 for 34).

AT Headingley. August 4 *to* 8. West Indies won by an innings and 55 runs. West Indies 500 for nine declared (Sobers 174, Nurse 137, Hunte 48, Kanhai 45, Higgs 4 for 94). England 240 (D'Oliveira 88, Higgs 49, Sobers 5 for 41) and 205 (R. W. Barber 55, Milburn 42, Gibbs 6 for 39).

AT The Oval. August 18 *to* 22. England won by an innings and 34 runs. West Indies 268 (Kanhai 104, Sobers 81) and 225 (Nurse 70, Butcher 60). England 527 (Graveney 165, J. T. Murray 112, Higgs 63, Snow 59 not out).

England in West Indies 1967–68

AT Queen's Park. January 19 *to* 24. Match drawn. England 568 (K. F. Barrington 143, T. W. Graveney 118, M. C. Cowdrey 72, G. Boycott 68, J. M. Parks 42, C. C. Griffith 5 for 69). West Indies 363 (C. H. Lloyd 118, R. B. Kanhai 85, S. M. Nurse 41) and 243 for eight (B. F. Butcher 52, G. S. Camacho 43, Nurse 42).

AT Sabina. February 8 *to* 13. Match drawn. England 376 (Cowdrey 101, J. H. Edrich 96, Barrington 63, W. W. Hall 4 for 63) and 68 for eight. West Indies 143 (J. A. Snow 7 for 49) and 391 for nine declared (G. S. Sobers 113 not out, Nurse 73).

AT Kensington. February 29 *to March* 5. Match drawn. West Indies 349 (Butcher 86, Sobers 68, Camacho 57, Snow 5 for 86) and 284 for six (Lloyd 113 not out, Butcher 60). England 449 (Edrich 146, Boycott 90, Graveney 55, B. L. D'Oliveira 51).

AT Queen's Park. March 14 *to* 19. England won by seven wickets. West Indies 526 for seven declared (Kanhai 153, Nurse 136, Camacho 87, Sobers 48, Lloyd 43) and 92 for two declared (M. C. Carew 40 not out). England 404 (Cowdrey 148, A. P. E. Knott 69 not out, Boycott 62, Barrington 48, Butcher 5 for 34) and 215 for three (Boycott 80 not out, Cowdrey 71).

AT Bourda. March 28 *to April* 3. Match drawn. West Indies 414 (Sobers 152, Kanhai 150, Snow 4 for 82) and 264 (Sobers 95 not out, Nurse 49, Snow 6 for 60). England 371 (Boycott 116, G. A. R. Lock 89, Cowdrey 59) and 206 for nine (Cowdrey 82, Knott 73 not out, Gibbs 6 for 60).

West Indies in England 1969

AT Old Trafford. June 12 *to* 17. England won by 10 wickets.

England 413 (G. Boycott 128, T. W. Graveney 75, J. H. Edrich 58, B. L. D'Oliveira 57, J. N. Shepherd 5 for 104) and 12 for no wicket. West Indies 147 (D. J. Brown 4 for 39, J. A. Snow 4 for 54) and 275 (R. C. Fredericks 64, B. F. Butcher 48, G. S. Sobers 48, M. C. Carew 44).

AT Lord's. June 26 *to July* 1. Match drawn. West Indies 380 (C. A. Davis 103, G. S. Camacho 67, Fredericks 63, Snow 5 for 114) and 295 for nine declared (C. H. Lloyd 70, Fredericks 60, Sobers 50 not out, Camacho 45). England 344 (R. Illingworth 113, J. H. Hampshire 107, A. P. E. Knott 53) and 295 for seven (Boycott 106, P. J. Sharpe 86).

AT Headingley. July 10 *to* 15. England won by 30 runs. England 223 (Edrich 79, D'Oliveira 48, Knott 44, V. A. Holder 4 for 48) and 240 (Sobers 5 for 42). West Indies 161 (B. R. Knight 4 for 63) and 272 (Butcher 91, Camacho 71, D. L. Underwood 4 for 55).

West Indies in England 1973

AT The Oval. July 26 *to* 31. West Indies won by 158 runs. West Indies 415 (C. H. Lloyd 132, A. I. Kallicharran 80, K. D. Boyce 72, G. G. Arnold 5 for 113) and 255 (Kallicharran 80, G. S. Sobers 51, R. G. A. Headley 42). England 257 (G. Boycott 97, Boyce 5 for 70) and 255 (F. C. Hayes 106 not out, R. Illingworth 40, Boyce 6 for 77).

AT Edgbaston. August 9 *to* 14. Match drawn. West Indies 327 (R. C. Fredericks 150, B. D. Julien 54) and 302 (Lloyd 94, Sobers 74, R. B. Kanhai 54, Arnold 4 for 43). England 305 (Boycott 56, D. L. Amiss 56, K. W. R. Fletcher 52) and 182 for two (Amiss 86 not out, Fletcher 44 not out, B. W. Luckhurst 42).

AT Lord's. August 23 *to* 27. West Indies won by an innings and 226 runs. West Indies 652 for eight declared (Kanhai 157, Sobers 150 not out, Julien 121, Lloyd 63, Fredericks 51, R. G. D. Willis 4 for 118). England 233 (Fletcher 68, A. W. Greig 44, Boyce 4 for 50, Holder 4 for 56) and 193 (Fletcher 86 not out, Boyce 4 for 49).

England in West Indies 1973–74

AT Queen's Park. February 2 *to* 7. West Indies won by seven wickets. England 131 (K. D. Boyce 4 for 42) and 392 (D. L. Amiss 174, G. Boycott 93, M. H. Denness 44, L. R. Gibbs 6 for 108). West Indies 392 (A. I. Kallicharran 158, B. D. Julien 86 not out, P.I. Pocock 5 for 110) and 132 for three (R. C. Fredericks 65 not out).

AT Sabina. February 16 *to* 21. Match drawn. England 353 (Boycott 68, Denness 67, A. W. Greig 45) and 432 for nine (Amiss 262 not out). West Indies 583 for nine declared (L. G. Rowe 120, Fredericks 94, Kallicharran 93, Julien 66, G. S. Sobers 57, C. H. Lloyd 49).

AT Kensington. March 6 *to* 11. Match drawn. England 395 (Greig

148, A. P. E. Knott 87, Julien 5 for 57) and 277 for seven (K. W. R. Fletcher 129 not out, Knott 67). West Indies 596 for eight declared (Rowe 302, Kallicharran 119, D. L. Murray 53 not out, Greig 6 for 164).

AT Bourda. March 22 to 27. Match drawn. England 448 (Greig 121, Amiss 118, Knott 61, Denness 42, Fletcher 41). West Indies 198 for four (Fredericks 98, R. B. Kanhai 44).

AT Queen's Park. March 30 to April 5. England won by 26 runs. England 267 (Boycott 99, Amiss 44) and 263 (Boycott 112, Fletcher 45, Knott 44). West Indies 305 (Rowe 123, Fredericks 67, Lloyd 52, Greig 8 for 86) and 199 (Greig 5 for 70).

West Indies in England 1976

AT Trent Bridge. June 3 to 8. Match drawn. West Indies 494 (I. V. A. Richards 232, A. I. Kallicharran 97, R. C. Fredericks 42, D. L. Underwood 4 for 82) and 176 for five declared (Richards 63, J. A. Snow 4 for 53). England 332 (D. S. Steele 106, R. A. Woolmer 82, W. W. Daniel 4 for 53) and 156 for two (J. H. Edrich 76 not out).

AT Lord's. June 17 to 22. Match drawn. England 250 (D. B. Close 60, J. M. Brearley 40, A. M. E. Roberts 5 for 60) and 254 (Steele 64, Close 46, Roberts 5 for 63). West Indies 182 (C. G. Greenidge 84, C. H. Lloyd 50, Underwood 5 for 39, Snow 4 for 68) and 241 for six (Fredericks 138).

AT Old Trafford. July 8 to 13. West Indies won by 425 runs. West Indies 211 (Greenidge 134, M. W. W. Selvey 4 for 41) and 411 for five declared (Richards 135, Greenidge 101, Fredericks 50, Lloyd 43). England 71 (M. A. Holding 5 for 17) and 126 (Roberts 6 for 37).

AT Headingley. July 22 to 27. West Indies won by 55 runs. West Indies 450 (Greenidge 115, Fredericks 109, Richards 66, L. G. Rowe 50, Snow 4 for 77) and 196 (C. L. King 58, Willis 5 for 42). England 387 (A. W. Greig 116, A. P. E. Knott 116) and 204 (Greig 76 not out, P. Willey 45).

AT The Oval. August 12 to 17. West Indies won by 231 runs. West Indies 687 for eight declared (Richards 291, Lloyd 84, Fredericks 71, Rowe 70, King 63) and 182 for no wicket declared (Fredericks 86 not out, Greenidge 85 not out). England 435 (D. L. Amiss 203, Knott 50, Steele 44, Holding 8 for 92) and 203 (Knott 57, Steele 42, Holding 6 for 57.

PARTNERSHIP RECORDS

England:

1st	212	C. Washbrook and R. T. Simpson	Nottingham	1950
2nd	266	P. E. Richardson and T. W. Graveney	Nottingham	1957
3rd	264	L. Hutton and W. R. Hammond	The Oval	1939

4th	411	P. B. H. May and M. C. Cowdrey	Edgbaston	1957
5th	130*	C. Milburn and T. W. Graveney	Lord's	1966
6th	163	A. W. Greig and A. P. E. Knott	Bridgetown	1974
7th	197	M. J. K. Smith and J. M. Parks	Port-of-Spain	1960
8th	217	T. W. Graveney and J. T. Murray	The Oval	1966
9th	109	G. A. R. Lock and P. I. Pocock	Georgetown	1968
10th	128	K. Higgs and J. A. Snow	The Oval	1966

West Indies:

1st	206	R. C. Fredericks and L. G. Rowe	Kingston	1974
2nd	249	L. G. Rowe and A. I. Kallicharran	Bridgetown	1974
3rd	338	E. D. Weekes and F. M. Worrell	Port-of-Spain	1954
4th	399	G. S. Sobers and F. M. Worrell	Bridgetown	1960
5th	265	S. M. Nurse and G. S. Sobers	Leeds	1966
6th	274*	G. S. Sobers and D. A. J. Holford	Lord's	1966
7th	155*	G. S. Sobers and B. D. Julien†	Lord's	1973
8th	99	C. A. McWatt and J. K. Holt	Georgetown	1954
9th	63*	G. S. Sobers and W. W. Hall	Port-of-Spain	1968
10th	55	F. M. Worrell and S. Ramadhin	Nottingham	1957

†Seventh-wicket record partnership was ended when Sobers retired ill at 155; 231 runs were added overall for the wicket with K. D. Boyce joining Julien to replace Sobers.

West Indies
v.
Australia

OVERALL RECORD	Played	Won by W. Indies	Won by Australia	Drawn	Tied
In West Indies	15	2	6	7	0
In Australia	26	5	18	2	1
TOTALS	41	7	24	9	1

HIGHEST TOTALS

Australia in West Indies:
758 for 8 declared   Kingston   1955
West Indies in West Indies:
573   Bridgetown   1965
Australia in Australia:
619   Sydney   1968–69
West Indies in Australia:
616   Adelaide   1968–69

LOWEST TOTALS

Australia in West Indies:
144   Georgetown   1965
West Indies in West Indies:
109   Port-of-Spain   1973
Australia in Australia:
82   Adelaide   1951–52
West Indies in Australia:
78   Sydney   1951–52

MOST RUNS IN A SERIES

Australia in Australia:	702	G. S. Chappell	1975–76*
Australia in West Indies:	650	R. N. Harvey	1955
West Indies in Australia:	503	R. B. Kanhai	1960–61
West Indies in West Indies:	827	C. L. Walcott	1955

*Six Tests in series.

MOST WICKETS IN A SERIES

Australia in Australia:	33	C. V. Grimmett	1930–31
	33	A. K. Davidson	1960–61
Australia in West Indies:	26	M. H. N. Walker	1973
West Indies in Australia:	24	A. L. Valentine	1951–52
	24	L. R. Gibbs	1968–69
West Indies in West Indies:	26	L. R. Gibbs	1973

Euphoria for a fast bowler: Michael Holding, the Jamaican 'discovery' of 1976, has bowled Alan Knott in the final Test at The Oval, where he performed one of history's most amazing feats—14 wickets on a perfect pitch, 12 of them bowled or leg-before.

Gordon Greenidge, of Barbados and Hampshire, was the hero of the 1976 Manchester Test, scoring a century in each innings. Here he drives with characteristic freedom against Mike Selvey.

both Patrick Eagar

Learie Constantine was an electrifying performer on the cricket field, one of those ra
players whose reputation will last forever, founded not upon statistics but dashing ba
manship, bursts of hostile fast bowling, and fielding that was out of this world. This le
handed catch at gully cost Stan McCabe his wicket in the Test match at Brisbane in 19:
when West Indies suffered the third of four successive heavy defeats in a series that,
the whole, they would rather forget.

est Indies' fortunes were not greatly improved on their second tour of Australia, in 1951–
, 21 years after the first. Jeff Stollmeyer, opening the batting at Sydney in the second
st, is struck on the head by a bouncer from Ray Lindwall.

e crowd at Kensington Oval, Bridgetown, pay tribute to one of the most extraordinary
nds in Test cricket history: Denis Atkinson (left) and Clairemonte de Peiza put on 347
r West Indies' seventh wicket against Australia in 1955—still a world record.

Barbados Advocate

Cricket can be a dangerous game. Jackie Hendriks, the West Indies wicketkeeper, is str
on the head while batting at Bridgetown in the 1965 Test. Australia's captain, Bob Simps
signals for assistance, while Graham McKenzie, the bowler, Garry Sobers, and Brian Bo
rush to Hendriks' aid. Australian wicketkeeper Wally Grout is in the foreground.

Barbados Daily N

Express bowler Wes Hall forces Australian batsman Norm O'Neill to duck a fiery boun
at Brisbane in the first Test of the thrilling 1960–61 series.

Sydney Morning Her

West Indies v. Australia

HAVING long established contact with English cricket, the West Indies broke new ground in 1930 with their first tour to Australia. To West Indians of that era, with no jet travel, no television, no running radio commentary, Australia was as distant as the moon. The common bond of cricket, however, bridged the gap and initiated the exchange between the teams which has become so frequent of late.

It is said that the great Australian batsman C. G. Macartney was mainly responsible for the series materialising. He had seen the West Indies in England in 1928 and was anxious that they should come to Australia. The West Indian players were equally keen, particularly after their heartening performances against England in the Caribbean in 1929-30, and the nucleus of the 16 chosen for the series set out on their adventure in October confident of doing well. Like almost all those West Indian teams which have gone to Australia since, their optimism proved misplaced. This particular one was really no match for what was a very powerful opposition and their one slice of comfort was victory in the fifth and final Test which at least restored their pride after four heavy and successive losses.

Like so many pioneers, the West Indies expected one thing and, instead, were confronted with something totally different when they arrived at their destination. In this case, they had been led to believe that Australian pitches would be quick, bouncy and true and, as a result, banked heavily on fast bowling. Herman Griffith, Learie Constantine and George Francis had proven themselves as three bowlers of the highest class, each possessing real speed with the experience to make it worthwhile. Edwin St Hill, a Trinidadian, was added to boost this form of attack. This left the selection somewhat unbalanced and there was a definite deficiency in spin. Yet it was a gamble. After all, if the conditions did suit fast bowling, as they were reputed to, what use would an excess of spinners be?

Alas, the pitches, virtually throughout, proved to be slow and lifeless and the West Indies were thrown into confusion. They were forced to press Martin, primarily a batsman, into service as a slow left-armer and in both the Tests and in the first-class matches he bowled more than anyone else. Scott, the only specialist spinner, took 40 first-class wickets with his leg-breaks and googlies and bowled well in the first two Tests.

Still, the West Indian fast bowlers were not without their moments of glory and when, at the tailend of the tour, the groundstaff at Sydney provided them with a pitch more to their liking (reportedly on the instructions of M. A. Noble, the former Australian captain) they showed their true worth by routing New South Wales for 190. Griffith, who bowled consistently throughout, had the satisfaction of removing the great Bradman twice cheaply, bowling him for a duck in the final innings of the series.

When all was said and done, however, Australia won for no other reason than they were the better team, well balanced, particularly strong in batting and spin bowling, with a long experience of playing together. This the West Indies lacked, for inter-island cricket was not yet well established and several members only met for the first time on the ship taking them to Australia. Indeed, the captain, Jackie Grant, joined them from England, where he was at Cambridge University. He had never captained anything before and had been out of direct touch with West Indies cricket, but his advance as captain, batsman and close fielder in the series was one of the features of the tour.

Bradman, Ponsford, Kippax, McCabe, Woodfull and Fairfax all took toll of the West Indian bowling at some stage and their spinners, the diminutive Grimmett with his leg-breaks and googlies, and the aged Ironmonger with his accurate left-arm deliveries, constantly tantalised their batsmen. Only the masterful Headley, only just past the age of maturity, and Grant did their reputations any good although Martin made a praiseworthy century in the final Test. The talent was evident for all to see in players like Roach, Bartlett and the teenaged Sealy but it had been nurtured principally on weekend club matches, which was not the best preparation for difficult Test cricket in a strange land.

There could hardly have been a more cheerless start for the West Indians, who suffered three successive defeats by State teams before the first Test at Adelaide. Only Headley's genius against Victoria at Melbourne saved face for them, an innings of 131 out of a total of 212 evincing the sort of reviews reserved for the Very Greats. Headley had announced himself to the discerning public with two polished displays against New South Wales in the opening match. The first yielded only 25 but Learie Constantine rated it as some of the best batting of the tour and his century at Melbourne was confirmation that he had quickly settled down on what was his first tour outside the West Indies.

However, he and his team-mates were contending with sharp cricketing brains and a plan was soon devised to contain their most dangerous adversary. Noting Headley had scored mostly on the off side, the Australians decided to bowl at his legs and, for a time, the scheme worked. For eight consecutive innings, he could not get past 20, until he improvised a method to counter the tactics. He opened his stance and the result was immediate with centuries in the third and fifth Tests and more than 1000 runs on the tour. In the end, Grimmett was describing Headley as the best on-side player he had ever bowled to, whereas at the beginning he had been hailed as a magnificent off-side player.

Yet Headley's first Test innings of the series ended first ball—caught close-in on the on side off Grimmett—but the other batsmen applied themselves so well that a total of 296 was raised. Roach opened with an accomplished half-century, Grant contributed a dogged, undefeated 53, and the innings of the day was 84 by Bartlett, the dapper little right-hander whose strokeplay matched his impeccable dress. Grimmett's 7 for 87 was an ominous portent for the rest of the series.

The West Indies fast bowlers dismissed Ponsford, Jackson and Bradman for 64 but then a missed chance off Kippax spoiled the effort. That mistake and the easy-paced pitch allowed Australia to recover, Kippax (146) and McCabe (90) adding 182 for the fourth wicket, a partnership which took the sting from the West Indian tail. Even though Scott wrapped up the innings by taking four wickets without conceding a run on the third day, the lead was still 80, very useful in any circumstances. It put the pressure on the West Indies and they did not bat well enough to save themselves.

Grimmett and the off-spinner Hurwood bowled 72 overs between them and took four wickets each, Grant doing his utmost to summon enough runs to set his opponents a challenge to worry them. He batted admirably for 71 not out, bringing his total in the match to 124 without being dismissed. However, only his vice-captain, Birkett, resisted the spin for any time and Ponsford and Jackson knocked off the 172 for victory without being bothered or separated.

All things considered, the West Indian performance was not a bad one but, for some reason, their cricket deteriorated in the next month. It is true they easily beat Tasmania and Queensland and only went under to South Australia by one wicket but in the second, third and fourth Tests their totals were 107 and 90, 193 and 148, and 99 and 107. Puny efforts but all the more so against a team with the likes of Bradman, Ponsford, Kippax and McCabe. Australia's two-to-one victories could be the only consequence.

The gods frowned on the West Indies for the second Test at Sydney. They lost the toss, stuck manfully to their task under perfect batting conditions on the first day and then were forced to bat on a treacherous, rain-affected pitch. In addition, Bartlett broke a finger catching Kippax early in the match and took no further part, a cruel blow in every sense.

Australia's position was virtually secure at the end of the opening day, when Ponsford and Woodfull were together at 323 for four, having added 183. Rain washed out the second day and it was clear that the pitch would not be the same again, leaving the West Indies with the forlorn hope that the adverse weather would continue. It did not and, on the third day, 20 wickets fell for 220 runs. Ponsford, whose 183 took five and three-quarter hours, was eighth out at 361 and only eight were added after he left.

There could have been little elation in the West Indian dressing-room over the quick demise of the Australian innings for they knew it was a disastrous augury for them. They were out just after tea for 107 and it took Australia only 30 overs to rout them for 90 a second time. It had been an unfair and unequal contest and the weather was the villain.

The third Test was no less unequal but this time the West Indies had nothing to blame but their inept batting and faulty catching. Again Australia batted first but Francis struck immediately, dismissing Jackson for a duck. A few minutes later, Bradman touched Constantine to first slip and was dropped. He was then 4 and went on to make 223 in devastating fashion, the highest individual Test score by an Australian in Australia at the time. He and Ponsford, with his second consecutive century, added 229 for the second wicket, and he and Kippax 193 for the third. The board showed a daunting 423 for three at the end of the first day, not a position to encourage a peaceful night's rest for the fielding team. Although Bradman was out without addition on the second morning, and Australia slipped to 558 all out, the West Indian batsmen appeared resigned to defeat.

All, that is, except Headley, who was clearly determined to put his succession of low scores behind him. His changed stance negated the effect of the packed leg side the Australians had used effectively against him earlier on and, regaining lost confidence, he became the first West Indian century-maker against Australia just before the innings closed at 193. He was again top scorer in the follow-on but he could not repeat his first-innings endeavour and there was another collapse and another huge Australian victory, Grimmett finishing with 9 for 144 in the match.

If the West Indian batting was an insult to their true ability at Brisbane, it was even more so at Melbourne for the fourth Test, where Ironmonger, 7 for 23, and Grimmett, 2 for 46, ran through them as if they were no more than a school team. They had the advantage of batting first for the first time since the opening Test yet lost within two days.

Headley's 33 was exactly a third of the first innings total, a dismal performance overall, and one which Australia passed effortlessly. Woodfull and Bradman put on 212 for the second wicket and, on a pitch breaking up prematurely, Woodfull declared 229 ahead. This time, the West Indian batsmen could survive only 25.4 overs from Fairfax, Ironmonger and Grimmett and the home team were 4-0 up.

Sydney was the last stop on the tour and it was at this eleventh hour that Grant's beleaguered men showed their best colours. They had every reason to be despondent for, on top of everything else, the Australian Board informed them the tour was going so badly financially that they would have to take the trams, not taxis, to practice! Yet they not only beat a strong New South Wales team, then Sheffield Shield champions, in their final state match but also won the final Test as well. At least, they could carry home something.

It was no secret that the West Indian players suspected the pitches had been doctored to thwart their fast bowlers throughout the tour and, with the series decided, they taunted the Australian authorities into preparing livelier conditions for them at Sydney. On it, Constantine took 6 for 45 and Griffith 2 for 36 as New South Wales, including Bradman, Kippax and McCabe, were bowled out for 190 in their first innings. Their batsmen, too, enjoyed the change and totalled 339 and 403 and, even though Kippax and McCabe scored second-innings hundreds, the State was beaten fairly and squarely.

The final Test, which followed immediately, was an intriguing game and, even though they were this time favoured by the fickle Sydney weather, the West Indies achieved their victory by dint of application, purposeful batting, excellent bowling and, not least, the foresight of their captain.

They had wasted enough opportunities already in the series and were determined to waste no more. On an ideal batting pitch, they ended the first day 298 for two. Headley batted brilliantly for two and a quarter hours for his second century of the series but the steady support of Martin during a partnership of 152 for the second wicket was equally crucial. Martin, who had done little in previous games, carried his bat through the innings before Grant declared at 350 for six after rain during the night had affected the wicket.

It was a correct reading of the situation, for Australia never recovered from the loss of five wickets for 89 and trailed by 126. Again, the nature of the West Indies second innings was considerably influenced by the elements, with Grant's instructions being to gather runs as quickly as possible. The third day ended with the West Indies 124 for five, 250 in the lead and, whatever the conditions, well-placed. As it happened, rain completely washed out the fourth day, soaking the uncovered wicket, and when the weather broke on the fifth with bright sunshine, it was obvious that batsmen were going to have a tough time of it.

But for how long? How quickly would the pitch improve? These were questions which Grant had to consider before taking the bold gamble of declaring right away, leaving Australia, with its galaxy of batting, a relatively modest challenge.

Again, Grant's assessment was correct and, even though Australia made a real fight of it, they fell 30 runs short. The turning point was probably Bradman's dismissal for 0, bowled by Griffith after surviving a maiden over from the Barbadian fast bowler most uncomfortably, a large feather in the cap for the bowler.

More than that, the victory was a feather in the cap for West Indies cricket and went some way towards lifting the gloom caused by the earlier reversals. The West Indian players returned home to find a strong desire for the Australians to return the visit, for Caribbean crowds longed to see the likes of Bradman, Ponsford, Grimmett and the others. Unfortunately, they never did.

West Indies in Australia 1951–52

West Indian cricket took a giant step forward in England in 1950. Stollmeyer and Rae, Ramadhin and Valentine had not only brought their team an outstanding victory in the series but had become names to conjure with throughout the cricket world. Everyone wanted to see them, not least the Australians, and even before they had completed that tour an invitation had been extended to the West Indies Board by its Australian counterpart.

Not everyone was keen to see the West Indies go. Jimmy Cozier, who covered the 1950 series for the Caribbean press, reported a conversation with Alan Kippax in which the old Australian batsmen advised against it. "In Australia, you'll be murdered. Make them come to you and you'll win for sure," Cozier quoted Kippax as saying. Cozier strongly recommended that the suggestion be accepted but the Board decided otherwise.

This was strange for the West Indians were thirsty for Test cricket. They had seen England beaten 2-0 in 1948 but could only follow the triumphs over India in 1949 and England in 1950 from a distance. Ramadhin and Valentine were as unfamiliar to most West Indians as they were to Australians, their appearances at home limited by the dearth of inter-territorial cricket. Even more incomprehensible was the Board's acceptance of an itinerary which allowed the team only one first-class match as preparation for the first Test.

For all this, the West Indians arrived in early October amidst excited anticipation. For the first time, but certainly not for the last, they were to be engaged against Australia for the unofficial cricket championship of the world. Sadly, the great expectations came to nothing and the result was, as it was 21 years earlier, 4-1 to Australia.

Reasons for the West Indian debacle were myriad. Their leading batsmen, who had so enjoyed themselves at the expense of the bowlers of England and India, were woefully disappointing. Worrell and Stollmeyer registered the only centuries in the Tests, there was no average higher than Gomez's 36, and Weekes (24.50), Rae and Walcott (14.50 each) were shadows of the players they had been in England. All teams can expect a major batsman or two to be off-colour in a particular series but the complete and simultaneous eclipse of so many was more than the West Indies could take.

Why did such indisputably powerful batting fail so? For one thing, misfortune followed the West Indies around. Weekes tore hamstring muscles in both legs so badly in the opening first-class match that he never moved freely for the rest of the series; Walcott broke his nose early on and, later, developed serious back trouble which not only forced him to abandon wicketkeeping altogether but also to miss two Tests. Chiefly, however, the batsmen languished against fast bowling the likes of which they had not encountered before on pitches which were often far from perfect.

Lindwall and Miller, probably at the peak of their celebrated careers, took 21 and 20 wickets respectively, while the tall, rangy Johnston proved the ideal foil bowling left-arm fast-medium over the wicket, taking 23 wickets. Against them the West Indies could total more than 300 but once in 10 innings. In England in 1950, the same batsmen passed 500 twice in six innings and only once fell below 200. England, it should be noted however, had no one faster than Bailey; Australia's attack possessed men capable of awesome hostility and not averse to using the bouncer.

The West Indies were incapable of responding in kind for the emphasis was, not unexpectedly, on the spin of Ramadhin and Valentine which had served them so well in England. Jones and Trim were two ageing fast bowlers and played only one Test each. Gomez and Worrell, with swing instead of speed, used the new ball and the conditions admirably and Valentine, whatever the state of the pitch and the attitude of the batsmen, underlined his quality by claiming 24 wickets. It was Ramadhin on whom Goddard relied to puzzle the batsmen as he had done in England and, for a time, it appeared as if he would. Whereas the Englishmen were prepared to play him from their creases, however, the Australians, typically, were not. Lindwall and Miller—with the bat not the ball—went after him with boisterous tactics in the first and second Tests and, although he often bowled well, he was never quite the same threat when positive methods were used against him. Perhaps if Goddard had put less faith in his spinners and more in his fast and medium-pace bowlers his returns might have been richer.

The captain of any losing side can anticipate his share of criticism and Goddard got his in no small measure. Worrell felt the captain was cut off by those who had given him useful advice in England and, left on his own, was at a loss. All round he was judged harshly for his lack of control during the critical stages of the fourth Test when Australia's last pair, Ring and Johnston, scored 38 runs to win and when there appeared to be three or four skippers on the field. Eventually, Goddard did not appear in the final Test and Stollmeyer took over, the official reason being unfitness. There was a strong body of opinion that there was more to it than that. Whatever the truth, no-one could be in doubt about Goddard's dedication to the job and there was a great deal of sympathy for him in Australia and outside. After all, there was little he could do about the loss of batting form and the numerous dropped catches which blighted his team's efforts. In the end, too, 4-1 was hardly a just margin, for two of the Tests, the first and the fourth, were so close that they could have gone either way.

The Brisbane Test provided a marvellous start to the series, an enthralling contest from first ball to last, Australia scraping home by three wickets. The highest total was 245 and the bowlers always held sway on a pitch which was, in the modern jargon, a slow turner.

Slow or not, the West Indian batsmen soon found themselves hard-pressed against the fast bowling. Rae, his high grip on the bat and exaggerated backswing encouraging a yorker, got one third ball and was far too late on it, and by lunch Stollmeyer and

Worrell had joined him in the dressing-room. Worrell and Weekes appeared to settle quickly but were out in the 30s. Walcott was leg-before first ball and only stout work by the men not expected to contribute much low down allowed the West Indies to pass 200.

Whether they could keep themselves in the match or not depended on whether Ramadhin and Valentine could torment the Australians as they had done the Englishmen and there was tension in the air when Goddard quickly introduced them into his attack. They did not let their captain down—nor, for that matter, the spectators who had heard so much of their mystical powers. Ramadhin, small in stature, busy in method, with his cap pulled tightly on his head and sleeves buttoned to the wrist, could have been an Indian magician and the batsmen found it difficult to detect his tricks. As usual, Valentine was the model of accuracy and variation and, in fact, it was he who picked up the wickets. Australia struggled to 129 for five with their main batsmen gone before Lindwall and Miller, particularly the former, added 59 in just over half an hour, probably the most crucial period of the series. Aided by plenty of dropped catches and plenty of luck, they demonstrated that the bogey of Ramadhin and Valentine could be destroyed with forthright methods.

Even so, Australia's lead was only 10 and they were to bat last on a pitch already generous to spin. Rae and Stollmeyer again failed to make an impact but, at the start of the last over of the second day, the board read 88 for 2. At the end of it, with Worrell and Goddard gone, it was 88 for 4. This soon became 96 for 5 but fine, attacking batting by Weekes and reliable support by Gomez and Marshall carried the total to 245 before Ring, the leg-spinner, claimed the last wicket, and his sixth, of the innings. Australia required 236 and, on such a pitch, a keen scrap was guaranteed.

What a scrap! Australia's batsmen, never entirely at ease yet grimly determined, managed to get there after 85 overs and seven balls with only three wickets standing, an average of less than three per eight-ball over. Morris, Hassett, Harvey, Hole and Lindwall all played their parts but none worked harder than the two youthful West Indian spinners, who each bowled 40 consecutive overs.

Goddard tried almost everything, changing the field, switching ends and even claiming the second new ball and rubbing it in the dirt before handing it to his tried and trusted spinners. An uncommon occurrence, to say the least, and one which stirred immediate debate. Yet nothing could shift Hole, an upright, blond, 21-year-old South Australian and, 45 not out at the end, he saw Australia through to a famous victory.

The West Indies of 1930–31 had happy memories of Sydney but there was no repetition of their successes in the second Test this time. They were outbatted and lost by seven wickets.

Worrell, Walcott, Christiani and Gomez all scored half-centuries after the West Indies had been sent in and 362 seemed a creditable total. It was to be the best of the series but it was inadequate. On a pitch offering not an iota of assistance to spin, Hassett and Miller scored centuries in a fourth-wicket partnership of 235 and the later batsmen so severely flogged a weary attack that the last three wickets contributed 145.

Ramadhin, in contrast to Brisbane, held no terrors, conceding 143 runs without taking a wicket, and Australia's 517 gave them a lead of 155. As has so often been the case, an unaccepted chance could have made all the difference, for Hassett, when 9, was dropped by Walcott behind the wicket—a difficult one—off Jones from an attempted hook which was gloved. If only, the West Indians moaned then—as they had done so many times 21 years earlier and were to on future Australian visits.

If the West Indies were to avert defeat they needed to bat most of the final two days, but they could not. Weekes played brilliantly and Gomez, Goddard and Stollmeyer (despite a muscle injury and a blow on the head from a Lindwall bouncer) doggedly. But no-one stayed long enough and Australia, fittingly with Hassett and Miller at the wicket, won with plenty of time to spare.

Defeats against Western Australia and South Australia followed in the interim before the third Test, which meant the West Indies had lost six of their seven first-class matches on tour and drawn the other, a bleak record indeed and far from stimulating for a team unaccustomed to such results. That they managed to win the third Test at Adelaide, and by the handsome margin of six wickets to boot, represented a spirited revival which kept the rubber alive.

There was a bizarre start, 22 wickets falling for 207 on a rain-affected pitch on the first day. Oddly, Morris, leading Australia instead of the injured Hassett, decided to bat first after winning the toss and it did not take long for everyone to realise that batting would be a torture. The ball behaved strangely and, inside two hours, Australia were all out for 82, Worrell (6 for 38) and Goddard (3 for 36), who had experienced several such pitches in Barbadian club cricket, doing the damage.

The West Indies fared little better after the effects of the roller wore off and were out for 105. Just as Worrell had done, another left-arm medium-pacer, Johnston, took six wickets, and this inconceivable first day ended with Australia sending in their tailenders and losing two of them for 20.

To add another freakish touch, one of those tailenders, Ring, in the exalted position of No. 4, took his role seriously enough to topscore with a vigorous 67, an innings not capitalized on by his more illustrious team-mates. Valentine, as was customary, shared most of the bowling with Ramadhin, and the left-hander took 6 for 102. Australia, all out 255, set the West Ind·es 233 to maintain their interest in the series. By now, the wicket had dried out and its behaviour had improved.

The West Indies started their quest on Christmas Eve, realising there could be no more welcome present than victory on the following day. Marshall and Stollmeyer laid a sound foundation with an opening stand of 72 and, when the innings faltered after lunch with the dismissals of Worrell and Weekes at 141, Gomez and Christiani checked it and carried it through to the target without being separated. The merry-making that night was bacchanalian, deserved and spontaneous. The West Indies were back in the fight.

If they could win the fourth Test, starting on New Year's Eve, the fifth would be a grand finale. It was not to be. They won everywhere except where it mattered, at the end, when they badly panicked as Ring and Johnston, through the generosity of their opponents, performed their little miracle.

The West Indies first innings of 272 was built around a courageous 108 by Worrell, contrived over three and three-quarter hours against the fastest bowlers in the game with a right hand made swollen and painful by three successive blows on it from bouncers. No other batsman scored more than 37 against the hostility of Lindwall, Miller and Johnston, who bowled all but 18 overs in the innings, a tribute to Worrell's tenacity. Australia's reply was one partnership and oneal one, a fourth-wicket association between Harvey and Miller which was responsible for 124 of their 216 runs. Their last five wickets fell for eight runs and the destroyer was not Ram nor Val nor Gomez nor Worrell but Trim, the big, affable fast bowler, who took 4 for 12 in his last six overs with the second new ball and 5 for 34 overall.

The West Indies lead of 56 was not ·nsignificant by any means but much of the advantage was soon lost by Goddard's peculiar decision to shuffle the batting order for the final 25 minutes of the day. He put Guillen, the wicketkeeper, in first with Stollmeyer and went one down himself and, within a few minutes, was regretting the move, Lindwall dismissing both in the very first over.

Even though Stollmeyer and Gomez batted confidently for half-centuries the following day and Worrell, his injured hand strapped and padded like a Korean War veteran's, put together 30, the West Indian innings did not fully recover from its early shocks. Still, Australia were asked to score 260, 24 more than they got to take the first Test, and on a pitch sowing the seeds of suspicion in the minds of the batsmen by the unpredictability of its bounce, the odds slightly favoured the mercurial visitors.

The final day was to be one of the most stirring climaxes Test cricket has known. The balance swung one way and then the next, no team ever quite gaining the upper hand until the ninth Australian wicket fell at 222, leaving Ring, the No. 9, and Johnston, the No. 11. Surely, the West Indies simply had to win from there? Throughout, they had given little away as Ramadhin and Valentine, over after over, bowled for victory. Hassett, with faultless technique and steely resolve, defied them for just over five hours to score his first Test century on his home ground and both Harvey and Lindwall suggested, while partnering him, that Australia would make it with wickets to spare. Despite this optimism, the last pair was left with a well nigh impossible mission.

However, as the two brought victory nearer and nearer, the West Indies lost their grip. Ring's powers of hitting were well known to them from his exploits in the second and third Tests yet he was allowed to swing freely with the field only three-quarter-way, and not right, back. Johnston, on the other hand, found he could pick up his singles comfortably. In Goddard's defence, it must be said that the MCG is an enormous ground and field-setting, in these circumstances, difficult. As they realized a certain win was slipping away from them, the West Indies appeared to be running around, as one of the players later commented, like chickens without heads. The last straw was when Ramadhin, holding the back of his thigh, limped off the field in the dying moments, and Australia won when Johnston hit the winning run into the leg side.

The final Test was of mere academic value and Australia won by 202 runs. Stollmeyer, leading the team in the absence of Goddard, scored a second-innings century but Gomez, who enjoyed such a wonderful series, claimed the personal honours—7 for 55 and 3 for 58, just reward for one West Indian whose standing in the cricket world had been enhanced several times over during the series. Overall, however, the reverse was true.

Australia in West Indies 1955
THE popularity of Australian cricket in the Caribbean has always stood second to none and their first long-overdue tour to the

region, early in 1955, entrenched that standing. They brought with them several of the great names of post-war cricket, the majority of whom had been responsible for West Indies' defeat in Australia in 1951–52. Harvey, Morris, Lindwall, Miller, Johnston, and the new captain, Johnson, had all played their parts in that series and were the subjects of conversation from the shops of Kingston to the docks of Georgetown.

Immediately prior to their West Indian engagement, Australia had undergone a humiliating exercise at home against England, who, spearheaded by the fast bowling of Tyson and Statham, had regained the Ashes by winning three successive Tests after losing the first by an innings. A year earlier, the West Indies had fought a 2-2 result against England. Could they take their revenge for the indignities of 1951–52 against a crestfallen Australian team?

They should have known that such things as "crestfallen Australian teams" are rare. Although there was only a month between the final Test against England at Sydney and the first against the West Indies at Kingston, Australia never showed the slightest apprehension because of their performance against England. One series was gone and quickly forgotten; this was the time for a fresh start against new opponents in different conditions. With this attitude and against bowling devoid of anything remotely approaching the speed and hostility of Tyson, the Australians swept all before them. They batted with prodigious consistency which only Walcott of the West Indians could match and became the first team to win a series in the Caribbean—by the irrefutable margin of 3-0.

It was a batsman's series. An extraordinary 21 centuries were recorded, Walcott more than compensating for his disappointments in Australia by notching five himself. Twice in the same Test he had centuries in each innings and he ended the series with an aggregate of 827 runs. Harvey and Miller scored three each for Australia and, in one of cricket's great partnerships, Denis Atkinson at No. 7 and Clairemonte dePeiza at No. 8 put on 348 for the seventh wicket for the West Indies in a crisis in the fourth Test. Australia passed 500 in the first Test, 600 in the second and fourth and amassed 758 for 8 in the fifth—still their highest ever. Not before or since has the public of the West Indies witnessed such a glut of scoring in a single rubber.

A shortage of fast bowlers, ideal batting conditions and the loss of form of Ramadhin and Valentine, the two experienced spinners, put pressure on the West Indies. But the reasons for the home team's defeat could also be found off the field, an eternal complaint of West Indian cricket, particularly when playing at home.

Great contention surrounded the appointment of the all-rounder Atkinson as captain when Stollmeyer, through injury, missed the first and then the fourth and fifth Tests. Atkinson, a white Barbadian, an insurance salesman and comparatively inexperienced at Test level, had been chosen as vice-captain for the series months before and when he found himself pitch-forked into the leadership, he also found himself the butt of a campaign to remove him. Organizations in Jamaica, particularly, but in one or two other territories as well, accused the Board of discrimination, called for Atkinson to be replaced by Worrell and went to great lengths to press their campaign. Public meetings were held, resolutions passed, cables despatched.

This was a time of political and social transition in the Caribbean and the furore was part and parcel of that transition. Yet it did nothing for the unity of the West Indies cricket team nor, it might be added, the West Indies as a whole. As for Atkinson himself, he chose the best, and perhaps only, way to answer his detractors with his grand personal feat in his native Kensington Oval in the fourth Test—when besides his double-century and his epic stand with dePeiza he also took five Australian second-innings wickets.

It was in that Test that the backlash of the crusade against Atkinson was felt in a far more unsavoury way than Atkinson's own response. At the time, the former Test fast bowler Hylton was facing execution in Jamaica for the murder of his wife, a sordid matter; yet when Holt, a Jamaican, dropped more than his fair share of catches in the game, a few spectators, with a warped and ghoulish sense of humour, carried placards proclaiming: "Hang Holt, save Hylton".

Nor did the selectors do much to aid the West Indian cause. No fewer than 19 players were picked, three wicketkeepers were used in the first three Tests, the 21-year-old Jamaican Collie Smith, who started his career with a century in the first Test, was unceremoniously left out of the third after "bagging a pair" in the interim, both Ramadhin and Valentine were dropped for the third Test only for the former to be summoned back for the game at the eleventh hour on the evidence of the nature of the pitch in the territorial match. And so on and so on. In no Test were there fewer than three changes to the team. The Australians, on the other hand, only altered the composition of their team if injury warranted it and seven of their men played all five Tests.

The Australian batsmen established their pattern for the series on the very first day which they finished at 266 for 2, a first-rate beginning which culminated at 515 for 9 declared at the end of the second day. McDonald and Morris laid the foundation but Harvey and Miller erected the rest of this immense structure with a third-wicket stand of 224, leaving the others to add the finishing touches. Harvey scored 133 and Miller 147 before Walcott, now being utilized as a slow-medium off-cutter, got both. Nine West Indian bowlers were used in the innings, of whom Ramadhin and Valentine delivered 100 overs between them. It was a clear sign of things to come.

The West Indies batsmen could not make a match of it against an attack with fast bowling, as expected, predominant. Lindwall took six wickets, Miller five and Archer four, but despite the thrashing their team received, the Jamaican crowd had cause for satisfied cheering at the impressive debut of O'Neil Gordon Smith, universally and affectionately known as Collie. An orphan, raised in the heart of Kingston, he had come to public attention while playing Senior Cup cricket in Jamaica for Boy's Town, a club for boys from the capital's poor areas.

The Australians noted his potential when he scored 169 against their bowling in the island match (adding 277 for the sixth wicket with the wicketkeeper Binns). In the Test, he shared a century partnership with Walcott in the first innings, while going in at number three in the second he became one of the elite who have scored a century in their first Test. He did little else in the series but, before his accidental death in a car crash in England in 1959, he had proven beyond any question that his century against the Australians was no flash in the pan.

If the size of Australia's total here was to become the norm for the remainder of the series, so too was the scoring of Walcott, whose 108 and 39 was the only West Indian batting of quality— apart from Smith's and that of Holt, the opener, who scored a polished 60 in his second innings.

The Queen's Park Oval, Port-of-Spain, venue for the second Test, had not produced an outright decision in years as batsmen thrived on its placid, matting wicket. This time, it was an unknown quantity since a new turf square had been laid. If anything, it proved more docile than its predecessor and, with rain causing the loss of over three hours on the first day, a mere 23 wickets fell in a drawn match during which 1255 runs were scored.

Walcott and Weekes were the dominant batsmen for the West Indies, the former completing two centuries in the match and the latter being only 13 short of emulating that feat when stumps were finally drawn. In the first innings, their third-wicket partnership of 242, still a record, was filled with all the best in batsmanship. It was not often that the West Indians batted like this together but they appeared to favour the Trinidadian crowds with their vintage performances. A year earlier, Weekes had helped himself to a double, and Walcott and Worrell single, centuries against England. Now the crowds were treated to another feast. Those who were there can also claim to have seen the only six Weekes ever hit in his 48 Tests and 4455 Test runs—off Bill Johnston in the first innings. It is one of the most unlikely statistics in the game.

The Australians were not to be outdone in this extravaganza and each of their first three batsmen carried a three-figure score back with him to the pavilion—McDonald 110, Morris 111 and Harvey 133. Archer scored 84 and Johnson 66 so that Australia's lead was 218, but on such a pitch, the West Indies had no difficulty playing out time. In the midst of all these runs, Lindwall's 6 for 95 in the West Indies innings and Collie Smith's "pair" were untypical, and contrasting, figures.

The third Test at Georgetown, which Australia won by eight wickets, was the notable exception to the rule of heavy scoring which the series followed. The previous year the West Indian batting twice failed at the same Bourda ground against England, and the match had been lost. It was the batting which again caused defeat by flunking its obligations on the first day when the pitch, which later crumbled, was at its best.

By lunch, the advantage of winning the toss had been wasted with the total 86 for 5 and, although Weekes stroked the ball confidently for 81, he got no aid and an all-out 182 was a ticket to defeat. Benaud's leg-spin demolished the West Indian tail (4 for 15) and when it was the Australians' turn to bat it was the all-rounder's assertive batting which curbed the spin of Sobers, Ramadhin, Atkinson and Norman Marshall on a turning pitch. McDonald and Morris added 71, and Benaud made 68. Yet Australia were hard-pressed to eke out a lead of 75.

Whatever hopes the West Indies had of recovering evaporated with the loss of three second-innings wickets at 25. For a time, Walcott and Worrell lifted the depression which had settled over the ground by adding 125, but Dame Fortune was simply playing a cunning trick on the home team. When 73, Walcott, playing Lindwall into the leg side, stepped back onto his stumps; 12 runs later, Worrell, cutting Benaud, went too far back and hit the off stump with his bat, two unusual dismissals which just about settled the result of the game. Johnson, aided and abetted by a strong cross breeze, a turning pitch and an alert wicketkeeper, scattered the tail, the last seven wickets falling for 57—the Australian captain taking 7 for 44 with his off-spin, Langley stumping three in addition to two earlier catches. Australia made light work of the 133 needed and went into an impregnable series lead.

The fourth Test at Barbados reverted to the high scoring of the first two—at least for the first two innings. Australia, bettering their highest score every match, surpassed the 600 of Port-of-Spain with 668 and batted into the third day, a painful experience for any fielding side. Eight West Indian bowlers sent down 236 overs between them and none was more impressive than Dewdney, the Jamaican fast bowler, who took four wickets in his first Test. It might have been more but Holt, at slip, missed early chances off McDonald and Lindwall, suffering particularly for the latter as the fast bowler proceeded to clout the ball all over the ground for 118. Miller flawlessly compiled 137 and Archer, the third of the pace trio, 98.

When Langley dived to catch Smith off Miller late on the third day for the sixth West Indian wicket at 146, another overwhelming loss was in store for the home team. Barbadians have abiding faith in their cricketers but even to them it was pure fantasy to suggest Atkinson and dePeiza, resuming on the fourth day, would achieve anything heroic. Atkinson's batting form had been poor and, in any case, what with the controversy over the captaincy, and the situation of the game and series, he had enough to worry about. dePeiza, a customs clerk from the same Empire Club as Worrell and Weekes, had never before come close to a first-class century. Yet on and on they went, Atkinson the senior partner taking charge, dePeiza keeping his end going mainly with a long forward defensive prod which prompted some wit to dub him "The Leaning Tower dePeiza".

They were not separated until the first over of the fifth day, when their stand was worth 348, four more than the previous seventh-wicket record set in 1902. A quick collection around the ground raised over $1000, and Atkinson and dePeiza were the toast of their small island for weeks to come. Even so, Australia led by 158 and could have enforced the follow-on under the rules of the time. They didn't, quite content with a draw which seemed inevitable. But the match was not entirely dead, first the West Indies and then Australia pressing to convert favourable positions into victory. Neither did, and a draw it was, Atkinson and dePeiza appropriately playing out the final half hour with six wickets down and the Australian fast bowlers trying desperately to seize an impossible win.

The series ended as it began, at Sabina Park, with Australia easy victors, Walcott scoring heavily for the West Indies (yet again, centuries in each innings) and Australia amassing a huge total—758 for 8 to be exact—and this after the first two wickets had fallen for seven runs. Harvey led the way with a double-century, while McDonald, Miller, Archer and Benaud got single centuries, and five of the six West Indian bowlers used conceded over 100 runs. The odd man out was Sobers, who had one for 99! Depressing enough statistics for any West Indian but the extent of Australia's dominance was emphasised when Benaud came to the wicket at 597 for six to hit two sixes and 15 fours in his 121, passing his century in 78 minutes. It was, in short, a massacre.

Walcott restored some West Indian pride with his exploits and Sobers, with an elegant 64 during which he and Walcott put on 179, continued his development as a batsman. As to the outcome of the rubber, however, there was not the slightest doubt about the vast superiority of Australia. The West Indies had endured the worst beating they had ever received at the hands of a visiting team and it was some years before they shook off the effects of it.

West Indies in Australia 1960–61

"Nobody loves a loser," American sports coaches are fond of reminding their teams.

To use another American expression, it ain't necessarily so, a point vividly illustrated on the streets of Melbourne on 17 February, 1961 when thousands of Australians gathered to cheer a West Indian cricket team which had just been beaten in a Test series. In an era in which increasing emphasis was being placed on avoiding the reputed ignominy of defeat at all costs, the West Indies team which toured Australia that season provided a refreshing change. Collectively, they proved that, even at the highest level of international sport, it was not so much whether they won or lost but how they played the game that mattered.

It was, quite simply, the most thrilling series ever played. It would have been remembered for all time if only for its first match, which produced the wonderful and unprecedented climax of the only tied result in Test cricket. It was, surely, the greatest Test ever played, a match of constantly fluctuating fortunes which produced 1474 runs over its five days and ended on the last-but-one ball.

It couldn't last, everyone logically said. All that followed *had* to be an anti-climax. Amazingly, the two teams, evenly matched and positive in intent, managed to maintain the momentum to the very last ball of the series. Australia won the second Test, the West Indies the third. It took a defiant last-wicket partnership, enduring one and a quarter agonizing hours, to deny the

West Indies victory in the fourth, and Australia won the fifth by two wickets amidst great excitement.

For West Indians, it will always be remembered as Worrell's tour, for the new West Indian captain's influence on proceedings was most pronounced. He had been named to the post some years after the vigorous public campaign in the West Indies advancing his claims had been mounted, and those who had played with him and knew him well had no doubt that he would have been a success. Yet only a cock-eyed optimist would have predicted such wonders as Worrell was able to achieve.

Worrell was a shrewd and intelligent man and cricketer, able to read the game as well as he could read people. He had a calm, persuasive way about him which commanded respect. West Indians, generally speaking, are a volatile lot, prone to shout when making a point or when in an argument. Captains and managers of many eras have commented that their charges are often difficult to control but Worrell's manner, unflustered yet firm, helped overcome such problems. Perhaps it was because he never shouted that he held such control.

Besides his personality, there were many other factors going for him. He was the first black man to lead a touring West Indian team, the significance of which escaped neither Worrell himself not the men under him. That the period corresponded with the development of political independence in the area, through the West Indies Federation, was a coincidence which played its part in unifying the cricket team.

There was, also, the generation gap between himself and his players. It was a disparity in years which was to Worrell's advantage for it generated an affection and respect which a younger man may have found impossible to maintain. Worrell, as a player, had established a considerable reputation and, despite his age (he was 36 at the time), he proved his worth with bat and ball. He certainly was not a captain alone.

Of course, the series was not the success it was only because of Worrell's leadership. It takes two to tango and the response of Richie Benaud, the Australian captain, to the West Indian attitude to the game was emphatically positive. And it was all well and good for Worrell and Benaud to agree, tacitly, on a policy of attack but neither could have implemented it without resources. Fortunately, both possessed them.

In Kanhai and Sobers, the West Indies had two young batsmen who, after a few years' apprenticeship, developed into great players on this tour. Hunte and Smith were unconventional opening batsmen, unconventional, that is, because they attacked the new ball as soon as the innings was under way. Alexander, the wicketkeeper whom Worrell had succeeded as captain, Worrell himself and Solomon were stalwarts low in the order. Hall's speed, generated from a long, fearsome run, was awesome but he lacked support. Like Kanhai and Sobers with the bat, the off-spinner Gibbs emerged as a bowler of rare class.

For Australia, Simpson and O'Neill were often brilliant. McDonald and the gum-chewing left-handed Mackay used less attractive but equally effective methods. The two outstanding Australians, however, were the captain, with his leg-spin bowling and ability to hit hard, and Davidson, who took 33 wickets with his left-arm fast-medium swing bowling and averaged 30 with his free-wheeling batting.

Finally, the value of the rubber was enhanced because nothing much was expected of it. It was a surprise packet and a most agreeable one.

The portents early on, in fact, were not encouraging. In contrast to 1951 there were several matches leading up to the first Test but the West Indies had been so inconsistent in them that critics gave them little chance in the series. Western Australia had beaten them by 94 runs and New South Wales had beaten them by an innings, yet they had trounced Victoria by the same margin and held their own against a strong Combined XI.

If they were encouraged by winning the toss in the first Test at Brisbane on a pitch most observers guessed would yield to spin in its latter stages, the West Indies were quickly in trouble at 65 for three, all to Davidson, within 70 minutes. This was the occasion Sobers chose to transform the match, and possibly the series, with an innings which those who saw it classify in the very highest category. Johnnie Moyes concluded that "it ranks with the most outstanding seen in Australia since the halcyon days of Bradman and McCabe"; Worrell, who watched all of it from the other end while he himself scored 65 in a partnership of 174, called it "dazzling" and he was not inclined to hyperbole; Sir Donald Bradman personally came to the dressing-room to hail Sobers after it was over.

Until then, Sobers' form had been patchy and the Australian press had made much of the fact that Benaud had bowled him for a duck against New South Wales. Sobers couldn't pick the googly, they said. Whether he did or not that day, he launched a fierce attack against the Australian captain (and all other bowlers besides), reaching his century in 125 minutes and finally being caught off a full-toss from Meckiff for 132 after batting 174 minutes, hitting 21 fours. It was a perfect exhibition of counter-attack and served as an example for his team-mates for the rest of the tour—indeed, for the rest of the decade.

With Worrell almost unobtrusively, yet importantly, lending support, the fourth-wicket partnership shifted the advantage away from Australia and half-centuries of varying methods from Solomon, Alexander and Hall low in the order pushed the total to 453, the highest by the West Indies in a Test in Australia.

It did not daunt Australia. McDonald and Simpson provided a sound foundation with a first-wicket partnership of 84 but the backbone of the innings of 505 was supplied by O'Neill, who took advantage of two chances in the 40s and played a capital knock of 181, batting nearly six and a quarter hours all told and guaranteeing there was no embarrassing deficit. Favell, Mackay and Davidson all shared valuable stands with him and, in fact, Australia enjoyed a lead of 52.

In most any other Test, such scores would mean only one result —a draw. But this was already shaping into an extraordinary match and, with two entire days remaining, an outright decision was not out of the question by any means.

An engrossing struggle now ensued, the West Indian second innings faltering, then recovering and, finally, faltering again. Steady batting by Worrell, Kanhai, Hunte and Solomon put 200 on the board with only four wickets down but there was an erosion of the last half of the order, six wickets falling for 74, leaving Australia 233 to win. Davidson took 6 for 87 for match figures of 11 for 222, yet even then his enormous role in the match was not at an end.

Australia were left all but 50 minutes of the final day to reach their goal, surely enough time. If Benaud and his team considered the task a straightforward one, Hall quickly shattered their confidence. "Pace like fire" was, in later years, to become a catch-phrase and the title of Hall's autobiography, and the big fast bowler was aflame in his early spell, which accounted for Simpson, Harvey, O'Neill and Favell. Worrell also bowled McDonald in this period and Australia, five down for 57, suddenly found themselves in choppy waters.

Mackay and Davidson, two left-handers, steadied the ship for an hour or so before Ramadhin, a little more rotund than he had been on his previous tour of Australia nine years earlier, produced one to bowl Mackay, making Australia 92 for 6 with not much left. At this point it was the West Indies' match. At tea, Australia, 109 for 6, required 124 in the final two hours with Davidson and Benaud together.

They might have been inclined to hold out for a draw but,

sensibly, they played the way they knew best, brazenly playing their shots and scampering any run that appeared available. The tactics paid off so well that the pair added 134, carrying Australia a mere seven runs short of the victory which, certainly, was now theirs. Davidson, who batted so intelligently in trying circum- stances for 80, perished through no fault of his own, run out by Solomon's direct throw from square leg after Benaud had urged him into yet another sharp single. Perhaps a little weary, Davidson found it too sharp. Solomon's accuracy, as it turned out, was a preview of what was to follow.

As Hall started the very last over of the match, six were needed, and for the few thousand who were there to witness it, for the players and for the hundreds of thousands of others following the proceedings on their radios, it was to be an unforgettable experi- ence. The recorded radio commentary, the action photographs and the film which record it for posterity will always remain among the treasures of cricket history.

A leg-bye came off the first ball. Benaud, hooking at a bouncer bowled against the captain's instructions, was caught behind off the second, and the fourth yielded a stolen bye. Off the fifth, amidst furious excitement, Hall dropped Grout at square leg off a skyer off his own bowling, and another single was taken. The sixth was hit firmly by the No. 10, Meckiff, down to backward square leg, one taken, then a second and a third attempted with Hunte swiftly gathering the ball and throwing to wicketkeeper Alexander. The ball landed on top of the stumps, a superb throw by Hunte at such a moment, and Grout's desperate dive to make his ground was in vain.

So two balls remained, with Kline, the last man, on his way in. Worrell, standing with no apparent emotion at mid-off, sauntered across and whispered to Hall: "Whatever you do, don't bowl a no-ball, Wes, or they won't let you back into Barbados." Whether the remark registered with the panting, sweating fast bowler is unclear but Hall's foot was well behind the crease when he delivered the seventh ball. Kline, as pre-arranged with his partner, scampered off as soon as he made contact, but Meckiff, by his own later admission, was fractionally hesitant. Solomon, at square leg, was not and, for the second time within a few minutes, he picked up and shattered the stumps for the most famous run-out decision in history.

Pandemonium immediately broke loose. Several West Indians on the field believed victory was theirs. In Barbados, at just past 4 am, the anchor-man in the radio studio announced to bleary- eyed listeners that the West Indies had won by one run. It took some time for the realisation to sink in—it had ended in a tie, a unique result for a unique match.

In the fortnight to the start of the second Test, the West Indies were badly beaten by New South Wales through the brittleness of their batting and when their batting failed again at Melbourne Australia won comfortably by seven wickets, although the toss did present them with an undoubted advantage of batting first.

The West Indies had the better of the early exchanges, limiting Australia near the end of the first day to an unsatisfactory 251 for eight. However, the 100-degree heat took its toll, particularly of Hall, and Mackay and Martin, a left-arm wrist-spinner batting at No. 10 in his first Test, lifted the Australian innings with a partnership of 97.

Australia, al out 348, routed the West Indies for 181, the scorecard being a curious-looking one. Nurse at number three with 70 and Kanhai at number four with 84 were the only batsmen in double figures and their partnership was responsible for 123 of the runs. Yet again, Davidson was the menace with 6 for 53. They fared little better in the follow-on, Hunte's 110 and Alexander's defiant 72 being the only worries to Australia.

It was, in most respects, a rather ordinary match but there was one incident to titillate those who thrive on the bizarre. In the West Indies second innings, Solomon's cap dropped from his head as he pulled a ball from Benaud and landed on the stumps, dislodging the bails. There was no alternative but for umpire Colin Hoy to uphold Benaud's appeal for hit-wicket, a rare dismissal indeed and one which the crowd, ignorant of the laws or perhaps over-sympathetic to the poor batsman, did not appreciate. For some time Benaud was roundly jeered and booed.

If Australia's good fortune in batting first at Melbourne had been a factor in their victory, the West Indies were even more favoured by the capricious flick of the coin in the third Test at Sydney. On a pitch which deteriorated as the match progressed, Australia's batsmen had no answer to the contrasting spin of Valentine, 4 for 67 and 4 for 86, and Gibbs, whose selection over the veteran Ramadhin was a bold one and who captured 8 for 112. They were out for 202 and 241 and lost by 222 runs, a margin which broached no argument. Since, in their two earlier matches against New South Wales, they had been soundly beaten by an innings, it was sweet revenge for Worrell's men.

Sobers set it up with a superlative 168 on the first day, an innings to match, if not quite surpass, his display at Brisbane. In four and a half hours, he played hardly a false shot, 26 of them finding the boundary, 25 fours and a six. With Nurse's 43 the next-best score, the match was virtually all Sobers, though Davidson, with what had become monotonous consistency, picked up another five wickets.

Hall accounted for the first two Australian wickets in quick order but Australia's nemesis was the spin of the wily Valentine and the colt Gibbs. The last five of their wickets fell on the third morning for 30 runs, three of them to the lanky off-spinner in four balls—two in the last three balls of one over, the other off the first of the next. Behind by 137, Australia were left with a great leeway and they never made it up.

The loss of Davidson through a muscle strain early in the West Indian second innings was an almost insurmountable handicap. The left-hander had, once more, caused early West Indian consternation by taking 3 for 33 in eight overs, leaving the board at 22 for 3, but he could not bowl again in the innings. Even so, it was the lesser batting lights of the visiting team which shone brightest.

Alexander, in great form, came to the wicket at 159 for 6; he left it last man out at 326 with 108, the value of which could not be overstated. Smith, the ever-smiling insurance salesman from Barbados, played his best hand of the series for 55 and Worrell batted with the unhurried assurance on which his reputation had been built for 82. On a pitch which batsmen were now regarding with much suspicion because of its unpredictable bounce, Australia's chances of scoring the 464 in nine hours to win were remote in the extreme.

By the end of the fourth day, Australia had played themselves back into the game or, more accurately, Harvey and O'Neill had done so. With boldly aggressive tactics, two of Australia's finest post-war batsmen put on 99 in the final hour and a half's play, and at 182 for 2, the foundation had been laid. The next morning, it crumbled rapidly before Gibbs and Valentine and before lunch the series was level.

Dame Fortune was not kind to the home team for Harvey, whose 85 was his highest of the series, pulled a muscle early on which affected his movements. After he was brilliantly caught at cover by Sobers off Gibbs, the rest of the batting offered no resistance. The Sobers-Gibbs combination also claimed O'Neill and, during the remaining play, Gibbs took 5 for 27 and Valentine 3 for 29.

By now, the evenness of the contest and the nature of the cricket had caught the imagination of Australia and the drama was far from over. There was excitement galore in both the fourth Test, at Adelaide, and in the fifth and final in that giant stadium, the Melbourne Cricket Ground.

At Adelaide, the West Indies, clearly believing in their ability to beat Australia and brimful of self-confidence, thoroughly outplayed their opponents so that, with the final session of the match to go, victory was virtually theirs. Australia's last pair were at the wicket and, if one partner, Mackay, was known to be capable of such defiance as was needed to save the game, the other, Kline, had no pretentions to batsmanship. Still, in three previous innings in the series, Kline had not once been dismissed —nor was he to be this time as he and his fellow left-hander grimly hung on until the end.

Quite apart from a conclusion which tested the nervous system of participants and spectators alike there were many good things about the cricket all the way through this Test. Kanhai, with centuries in each West Indian innings, touched the heights of genius of which he was so frequently capable, while captain Worrell and vice-captain Alexander also batted splendidly, the former for 71 and 53, the latter, continuing to emphasise his immense value low in the order, for 63 and 87, undefeated each time. Hunte's 79, and his second-wicket stand of 163 with Kanhai in the second innings, was an innings to match any for its wide range of stroke-play. However, the 113 scored by Worrell and Alexander together was the most important partnership for it carried the match completely out of Australia's grasp.

For all this, undoubtedly the individual highlight was Gibbs' hat-trick, the first against Australia this century, in which he dismissed Mackay, leg-before, Grout, caught low down at leg slip, and Misson, bowled, with successive deliveries. What else would this exceptional contest produce? It was not very long after that piece of history that Mackay and Kline were creating theirs. When Mackay was 17, and with over an hour remaining, the West Indians believed Sobers to have caught him close in on the on side off Worrell. But the batsman and the umpire were of a different opinion and the fielders who had started for the pavilion had to despondently return to their places. In the remaining play, the new ball, constant changes of bowling, the presence of ten fielders clustered like vultures around the bat, and the great tension could not sway the batsmen from their task, and they held out.

The teams therefore moved to Melbourne, on February 10, for the decider—and, for once, there was a return to the stern attrition for which Test cricket had become infamous, with the scoring rate throughout never rising above four per eight-ball over. For all the attacking spirit of the earlier matches, the result of the rubber hinged on this match and neither team, naturally, was willing to sacrifice it completely in the cause of entertainment. Still, the cricket was never dull—only comparatively so in view of what had gone before.

The West Indies, put in to bat, did not fully utilize a good batting pitch and were all out for 292, Sobers managing 64 without being at his best, and Lashley and Solomon bolstering the middle and lower order with 40s. As Simpson and McDonald replied with a resolute first-wicket partnership of 146 on the Saturday, cricket's largest crowd—90,800—which filled the concrete stadium must have been satisfied the home team was building an invincible position.

However, the West Indies, fielding quite spectacularly and bowling tightly, never lost grip of the situation and the Australian total was limited to 356. Sobers, as fit and athletic as anyone who ran on this ground four years earlier in the Olympics, took 5 for 120 bowling 44 overs at fast-medium pace. Gibbs, exhibiting all the subtleties of the off-spinner's craft, backed him with 4 for 74.

Trailing by 64, the West Indian openers soon had 54 within an hour, but the start was deceptive. No batsman remained long enough to fashion the type of innings his team wanted, although the dependable vice-captain, now worthy of the sobriquet Alexander the Great, for the umpteenth time batted superbly for 73. Davidson, an equally crucial figure in the series, paid no attention to a muscle injury which reduced him to a pronounced limp, and claimed 5 for 84.

Australia started the final innings of the series needing 258 to win, a challenge which warranted a close finish, but throughout they always appeared likely winners.

Simpson launched an assault on Hall at the start of the innings late on the fourth day in which he took 18 off the first over, including four boundaries, and left the big fast bowler's analysis after three overs at 0 for 31. Inevitably, he became more subdued when play resumed the following morning but his innings of 92, ended immediately after lunch when he played-on to Gibbs, was a match-winning one. Fourth out at 176, he returned to the stands to watch what the others would make of his effort.

He saw three more wickets fall by 248 and, at 254, one of the several strange incidents which had marked the series occurred. For some reason, not immediately apparent to umpires Egar and Hoy, Grout's off bail was dislodged after he cut at a ball from Valentine. The batsmen took two as Alexander and Valentine pointed to the fallen bail and appealed. After consulting his square-leg colleague, Egar ruled "not out" and, even though Grout deliberately skyed a catch to cover the same over, the matter

somewhat sullied the end of a great Test series. Australia won by
two wickets and, as a consequence, became first holders of the
Frank Worrell Trophy, presented by the Australian Board of
Control for International Cricket for perpetual competition
between the two teams—a great and heartfelt tribute to the
West Indies captain who, during the four and a half months he
spent in Australia, had won the warmth and affection of the public
at large for him and his team.

It was to be the beginning of a mighty era in West Indian
cricket.

Australia in West Indies 1965

The West Indian public had become accustomed to gritting its
teeth and bearing the bitter disappointment of defeat against
Australia when Bobby Simpson and his team arrived in Jamaica
in February, 1965 for the fifth series between the teams. Until
then, Australia had proved invincible and their only previous tour
to the Caribbean had resulted in a crushing and humiliating rout
for the home team.

This time, however, there was real optimism and West Indians
sensed that this was the occasion for sweet revenge. They had
followed the development of a young, strong and well-balanced
team under the astute guidance of Worrell and were confident
that it was fully capable of reversing the depressing trend against
Australia.

Worrell himself announced his retirement after the 1963 tour
of England but, by then, he had moulded the side into a tightly-
knit unit. To no-one's surprise, the brilliantly versatile Sobers was
chosen to succeed him. Hunte had been vice-captain and there
was a case for his being given the post but, somehow, Sobers,
with his flair and feel for the game, seemed the natural choice.

Significantly, Worrell's influence was not lost with his retirement. He was chosen as manager for the West Indies team and
the value of his presence in the background could not be underestimated.

The series followed a curious pattern. After three Tests, the
West Indies were 2-0 up and their supporters were, even then,
celebrating their first success against Australia with the claim that
it made Sobers' team "world champions". It was, of course, a
purely unofficial title but, having won 5-0 over India in 1962 and
3-1 over England in 1963, not a far-fetched one.

By the time the tour moved to Barbados, Australian stocks
were shockingly low. Phil Tresidder, the respected correspondent
of the Sydney *Daily Telegraph*, wrote after the third Test at

Georgetown: "There was a lack of backbone, an absence of traditional fight. It became all too easy for the West Indies." This, about an Australian team!

Cause of this uncharacteristic frailty was, partly, the all-round strength and efficiency of the Australians' opponents, who possessed two of the fastest and most hostile bowlers the game has known in Hall and Griffith, in addition to a quite magnificent off-spinner, Gibbs, the all-round genius of Sobers, and a batting order rich in talent.

Yet this was far from the full story. The Australian spirit, the will to fight, even to concentrate on the challenge which faced them, was undermined by their own overwhelming obsession with the bowling action of Griffith.

It was an issue which soured the series and which was first raised publicly by Benaud, the former Australian captain, so admired throughout the West Indies following his role in the memorable 1960–61 series. Benaud was covering the tour for several newspapers, including some in the Caribbean, and he caused an immediate sensation on the fourth day of the first Test when he wrote that he considered Griffith a thrower. Photographs he himself had taken were used as evidence.

It was not a new charge; there had been previous doubts about the legality of the big Barbadian's basic action in the West Indies and in England, where he enjoyed such success during the 1963 tour. Yet the West Indies Board had gone to great lengths to determine for themselves whether the delivery was fair or not. They had not chosen him for the Tests against India in 1962, when he was clearly worth a place on merit, and had screened films of him before deciding to pick him for the series in England.

There he passed the scrutiny of the English umpires and those critics in the press box. Certainly Benaud himself, who watched that series, raised no voice against Griffith then. West Indians, therefore, were at liberty to question his motives for doing so at a time when Australia, not England, was on the receiving end.

It was no secret that Benaud's views were shared by most, if not all, the Australian players, not least by the captain himself. To his credit, however, Simpson's only comment was: "We abide by the umpires' decisions." Unfortunately, they allowed the matter to dominate everything else. They shot hundreds of feet of film of Griffith in action and spent hours in their hotels viewing it and convincing themselves that he was, indeed, "chucking". It was a pointless and self-destructive attitude.

It is pertinent that two of those who appeared to concern themselves least with the affair, the left-handed batsman Cowper and the opening bowler Hawke, did best, and that, as the tour neared its end and the subject eventually became a bore, Australia's performances improved. With double-centuries from Lawry and Simpson in an opening partnership of 382, Australia reached 650 for 6 declared in the fourth Test, while there was the satisfying consolation of a victory in three days by 10 wickets in the final Test. By then, however, it was too late and West Indies had confirmed themselves as the strongest team in Test cricket.

The die had been cast in the first Test at Kingston. There the West Indies won a low-scoring match by 179 runs and Jamaicans, who had been subjected to two massive defeats at Sabina at the hands of Johnson's team 10 years earlier, were exultant.

There had been nothing to suggest the Australian collapses in this Test. They started their tour with innings victories over the Jamaican Colts and Jamaica, Simpson, Cowper and O'Neill taking centuries in a total of 547 for 5 declared in the latter match. The first day of the Test, in fact, ended with Australia promisingly placed.

On a fast pitch, so glossy that it reflected the image of the players from its surface, the West Indies were dismissed for 239 and they only reached that many because of the robust hitting of the all-rounder White. Playing his first Test, he arrived at the crease when Butcher, Sobers and Solomon had all fallen with the total at 149; he was still there, 57 not out, an hour and a half later when the innings closed. By the end of the day, Simpson and Lawry had 32 on the board, a confident beginning.

Fortunes began to swing with the very first ball of the second day, from Hall, which Simpson edged to slip. Seven runs later, Hall struck again, having Lawry leg-before, and Australia never recovered. They were undone by demanding fast bowling, Hall reviving memories of his great performance against England five years earlier and Griffith lending him telling support not reflected in the statistics.

With a narrow lead, the West Indies began their second innings uncertainly before the reliable Hunte and Butcher, a batsman new to Australians, steadied the innings with a partnership of 116. When it faltered again at 247 for 6, Solomon disregarded the psychological barrier of three successive ducks in his previous Test innings and batted with real authority to give his team the initiative.

Mayne's Test debut for Australia was an impressive one. Bowling fast and straight, he added four wickets to those he had taken in the first innings to claim eight in the match, but it was Philpott's leg-spin which tested the West Indies most—scarcely a bad ball in 47 overs and Kanhai, Butcher and Sobers among his four victims.

The West Indies totalled 373 and left Australia 396 to win, a daunting task. Their batsmen never suggested they would even come close. By the end of the fourth day, Lawry and Simpson were gone and the West Indies achieved their first home victory over Australia just before 4 pm the following afternoon. Each of the six bowlers used by Sobers claimed a wicket but it was the fast bowling, Hall's especially, which proved decisive. Hall's match figures were 9 for 105 from 43 overs; Griffith's 4 for 95 from 33 overs. Yet again, a great fast-bowling partnership had emphasised its value.

The second Test, at the Queen's Park Oval, yielded a glut of runs on a pitch which drew condemnation from both frustrated captains. It was so dreadfully slow that neither batsmen nor bowlers could be seen to best advantage and Sobers afterwards advised that it should be dug up, a suggestion made, but not heeded, several times in subsequent years.

Simpson caused a predictable stir by opting to field first after winning the toss, a decision generally interpreted as a compliment to Hall and Griffith. Perhaps the Australian captain was apprehensive about the effect the West Indian fast bowlers would have had in unsettled weather, but the West Indian batsmen had no qualms. Hunte and yet another new partner, the Trinidadian Bryan Davis, started with a partnership of 116 which set the pattern for the match.

After they had departed, Hunte brilliantly caught by Simpson at slip 11 short of his century, a crowd of 27,000 was treated to the best batting of the innings by Butcher and Sobers in a stand of 160. It might have been much more had not both been run out by throws of pin-point accuracy from Booth at fine leg, Butcher for 117 and Sobers for 69.

The West Indian tail made little difference to the overall total and Australia before lunch on the third day were facing 429. After Griffith quickly had Lawry caught at slip, he yorked Simpson and then forced O'Neill to retire hurt (for the second time in the series) after striking him on the forearm with a bouncer. The home crowd prepared for a debacle similar to that of Sabina.

At this point, Cowper and Booth stood firm, the former batting with little panache but plenty of determination to register his first Test century. Booth, with the benefit of chances at 14 and 67, stayed with him until midway through the fourth day before the partnership, worth 225, was broken. By then, the match was clearly going to be a draw. Australia, in fact, were not dismissed until well into the fifth day with a lead of 87 and Sobers decided to use the rest of the time for batting practice for his players, the majority of whom had no opportunity for competitive cricket outside the Tests.

The third Test, at Georgetown's Bourda Oval, began with the kind of ludicrous discord which might have amounted to light-hearted reading in the world's press but which only served to highlight the trifling insularity which remained in the West Indies. The local umpires' association took such strong objection to the decision by the West Indies Board to appoint Cortez Jordan, of Barbados, as one of the umpires for the Test that it directed one of its members, Cecil Kippins, who was the other appointee, not to stand. It meant flying in a replacement, Bertie Jacelon, from Trinidad, but when flight difficulties delayed his arrival, the Board, with the consent of the Australians, were forced to turn to Gerry Gomez, the former West Indies all-rounder, current Board member and selector, to do the job.

Gomez was a qualified umpire and active in the formation of the West Indies Umpires' Association but he had never carried a first-class match before. In the event, he did an excellent job, his influence being evident before a ball was bowled as he ordered the remarking of the creases, which had been incorrectly laid. In his active playing days, Gomez had done a lot of yeoman work on the field for the West Indies but he could hardly have been more exhausted than as he must have been now. He not only umpired but also helped select the side, attended Board meetings and summarised each day's cricket for radio!

If Gomez remained strictly impartial in his judgments on the field, it would have been unnatural for him not to have been overjoyed with the result of the match—a win by 212 runs for the West Indies.

Sobers won the toss and, at the end of the opening day, Kanhai and Butcher had seen to it that the start was a good one, 201 for two. That was enough, for the pitch became progressively respon-sive to spin, a characteristic complicated by its inclination to play at varying heights.

Batsmen of both teams viewed it and the opposing bowlers with increasing suspicion and 38 wickets fell for 657 runs. The fact that there were two rest days, Good Friday and Easter Sunday, meant there was that much longer for the pitch to last; it was clear by Thursday that there was no way it would.

Kanhai, out of touch previously, approached his best form in his first innings (89) before Hawke conjured up a ball to bowl him which the wicketkeeper, Grout, described as one of the best he had seen. It swung into the batsman, pitched middle and leg, and cut away to clip the top of the off stump. Thereafter, no batsman reached 50 in the match and, even though the West Indies' 355 was appreciably lower than seemed likely at the start of the second day, it was beginning to appear in true perspective by the end of it when Australia were 92 for 4 in reply.

Australia's batting was an unceasing and unavailing struggle and they fell 176 in arrears, Gibbs' 3 for 51 foreshadowing the events which were to follow. Hawke, who had taken 6 for 72 in the first innings, had 4 for 43 and Philpott 4 for 49, with the West Indies finding run-scoring equally as difficult in their second innings. But they still set Australia 357 to win. At another time, in another place, it would have been possible; in this match it was only a question of time before the West Indies won.

Yet Australia's start was such as to cause some West Indian anxiety. When tea was taken on the fourth day, with Lawry and Cowper together, the score read 80 for one, a comforting beginning. It was then that a shrewd piece of strategy dramatically altered the position. Sobers switched ends with Gibbs after the interval after the off-spinner had complained of bowling into a stiff breeze. The move worked like magic. In the final session, Gibbs bowled Lawry, had Cowper stumped, and removed O'Neill, Booth and Philpott, two caught by Sobers in his famous short-leg position. Lawry was Gibbs' 100th Test wicket and by the close of play the West Indies only needed to remove McKenzie to formalise their victory. Gibbs did so with the second ball he delivered on the final morning.

That Gibbs (9 for 80 in the match), Kanhai and Butcher—all Guyanese—should have contributed so much to the West Indian triumph made it doubly satisfying for the people of Guyana, who had not seen Test cricket for five years following the cancellation of India's visit there in 1962 because of political upheavals. It was, however, very much a team effort under the captaincy of Sobers, who made several inspired decisions in the game besides scoring 45 and 42, taking four wickets in each of his bowling styles and holding four catches.

There was just cause for despondency in the Australian camp but, at last, they now demonstrated true grit. In between the third and fourth Tests they faced a powerful Barbados team including Sobers, Hall, Griffith, Hunte, Nurse and White and they responded, with the aid of an ideal batting pitch, positively. Simpson, O'Neill and Thomas each scored centuries in a drawn game in which Hall and Griffith managed only a wicket apiece.

he sensational finish at Brisbane, 1960. Joe Solomon throws from square leg and hits the
umps with Ian Meckiff short of the crease, and the Test ends in a frantic tie. Others in
e picture are (from the left): Wes Hall (bowler), Garry Sobers, Frank Worrell (bowler's
d), Rohan Kanhai (leaping), Meckiff, Lindsay Kline.   *Melbourne Age*

nother pulsating moment in the 1960–61 series: Frank Misson is bowled by Lance Gibbs,
ho thus achieves the first Test hat-trick in Australia for 57 years.   *Associated Press*

Lawrence Rowe's career is seriously interrupted by an ankle injury during the third West Indies–Australia Test of 1972–73, at Port-of-Spain. Clive Lloyd and Maurice Foster carry him off, followed by an anxious Lance Gibbs. *Patrick Eagar*

The Frank Worrell Trophy goes to Australia again, presented to captain Ian Chappell by Worrell's widow, Lady Velda, at Queen's Park Oval in 1973. *Trinidad Express*

A capacity crowd need be no problem for agile fans such as these temporary tree-dwellers at Sabina Park, Kingston during Jamaica's first Test match Sunday, West Indies v. Australia, 1973.

Jamaica Gleaner

One of the few bright spots for West Indies in their 1975–76 encounter with Australia w.
Roy Fredericks' fast and furious innings of 169 at Perth. Ian Chappell and Rod Marsh follo
a vicious pull to the boundary off Mallett.

Patrick Eag

Guyana off-spinner Lance Gibbs has just crowned a long and honourable career with h
308th Test wicket, passing Trueman's world record. His team-mates congratulate hi
after his dismissal of Australia's Ian Redpath in the sixth Test, at Melbourne, in 1976.

John Jones

It was just the tonic Australia needed and its effect was seen in the record-breaking opening partnership between Simpson and Lawry in the Test. Until then, the best they had managed for the first wicket in Tests was 39 and Simpson's highest Test score was 30, while Lawry's was 22. They proceeded to bat as if intent on erasing all the unhappy memories of the early part of the tour, capitalizing on the conditions prepared for them to the fullest, and batting, with hardly a blemish, well into the second day before Simpson played on to Hall just 31 short of the first-wicket Test wicket record held by the Indians, Mankad and Roy.

Simpson's double-century was soon followed by Lawry's, and that, at least, was unique. No other pair of openers had ever recorded double-centuries in a Test before. Nor was the feast of runs over, for Cowper also completed an attractive century off the exasperated bowlers.

In all this run-gathering, Simpson had to be aware of the position in the series. His team, after all, was 2-0 down and with only two to play. He had to win here to have a chance of levelling. Midway through the third day, he reckoned he had enough runs and declared at 650 for 6, his bowlers then taking two early wickets, in addition to the temporary retirement of Hunte (hit in the face while hooking at McKenzie). The West Indies had a long way to go to make it safe.

But by the end of the fourth day, it was—just. Kanhai and the local players Nurse and Hunte saw to that before a packed Saturday afternoon crowd. In eight previous Tests, spread over four series, Nurse had not made a century; by the close, he was 183 out of 424 for 3, having shared a 200-run partnership with Kanhai. Next day, he became the third batsman in the match to score a double-century. Before it was over, he was celebrating yet another "double"—his wife had given birth to twin girls, a happy coincidence for a happy cricketer.

The West Indies comfortably avoided the follow-on, Simpson declaring his second innings at 175 for 4, challenging the West Indies to get 253 in 267 minutes. It was a feasible proposition but, logically, the West Indies would only chase them if they were first certain they could not lose. Hunte and Davis provided the solid start needed by adding 145 but, although there was great excitement in the dying minutes, the West Indies could not quite maintain the momentum needed and fell 11 short with four wickets remaining, Hendriks following proceedings from his hospital bed where he was still being kept five days after being struck on the side of the head by a ball from McKenzie while batting. It was ironic that it was an Australian bowler who should have caused two injuries to batsmen in this match while the most the West Indians could achieve was a warning from umpire Kippins (reinstated after the Georgetown incident) to Griffith for the over-use of bouncers!

It was ironic, too, that within a week of clinching a deserving and signal triumph over Australia in a series, the West Indies were being beaten by 10 wickets inside three days. Perhaps Sobers' team allowed itself to unwind too soon after the high tension of the first four Tests; perhaps the Australians had, finally, found their true form. Whatever the reasons, the West Indies were well and truly beaten, mainly because of inept batting on a Queen's Park Oval pitch entirely different in character to that used for the second Test.

In the circumstances, there were two outstanding innings played for the home team. Kanhai scored 121 out of a first-innings total of 224, according to Richie Benaud "a great innings by a great player"; Hunte soldiered on during a second-innings debacle, batting through for 60 undefeated in an all-out 131. Hawke brought his tally of wickets in the series to 24 by claiming six wickets in the match while there were other outstanding fast-bowling performances by McKenzie (5 for 33 in the West Indies' second innings) and Griffith (6 for 46 in Australia's first).

It was a disappointing match, and an anti-climax to a series which had generated great international interest and controversy. It was impossible, however, to spoil the occasion for West Indians. The Tests had provided them with some of their finest moments and the overall outcome was the source of considerable euphoria.

West Indies in Australia 1968–69

By the time the West Indies returned to Australia in October, 1968 for their fourth tour the cracks were beginning to show in the structure of the formidable team which had dominated the game for much of the decade. They had first become visible during the short series in India in 1966–67 and were accentuated during the MCC tour of the Caribbean early in 1968.

Whether the selectors noticed the decline or not, they decided that this was not the time for change. All the familiar names were included in the 17 announced in April, nine of them over 30, and the average age of the group just over 29. Almost inevitably, it proved a handicap against opponents who were not only younger and fitter but who were at the start, not the end, of their careers. The West Indians of that year had already created their reputations; the youthful Australians were anxious to make theirs.

These were the main but by no means the only reasons for the three massive victories Australia recorded in the five Tests. Yet most of the West Indian problems stemmed from the age differential which can count so heavily in sport at international level— problems of fitness, reflexes, and attitude.

As captain, Sobers failed to provide the guidance and inspiration which was so necessary, particularly with the few new, young members of the side. It was, perhaps, understandable. He had always adopted the attitude that his players were all experienced cricketers—"big men" as he would refer to them—capable of taking care of themselves. They surely did not need his advice about what time to get to bed, how hard and often to practise, where to go and not to go.

When Sobers, therefore, spent much of his spare time on the golfcourse playing the game he had come to love with a passion or when he left his team in Brisbane, just prior to the first Test, to travel to Melbourne to meet the girl who eventually became his wife, it was nothing unusual. He had done no different in 1966 in England or in 1967 in India, where he had even announced his engagement to an Indian actress. On those occasions, however, the West Indies were winning and winning well, and such issues were secondary. Now they were losing, and they were contributing factors.

After the West Indies had lost successive matches to a Combined XI at Perth and to South Australia at Adelaide early in the tour, the manager, Berkeley Gaskin, who had served in that capacity on two previous tours of India and England, admonished his players and told the press: "The party is over." It was a comment which rankled with the team, the majority of whom were not prepared to attribute their performances on the field to their attitudes off it, and for whom such discipline, publicly aired, was foreign and unnecessary.

As it turned out, the West Indies found it difficult to measure up to the high standards expected of them and the tour was to prove a sad finale to one of the finest eras West Indian cricket has known. The batting was frequently inconsistent, despite a second-innings total of 616 in the fourth Test and the fact that Sobers, Kanhai, Nurse, Butcher and Carew of the old brigade, and Lloyd of the new, occasionally demonstrated their class. With Hall and Griffith only shadows of the menacing pair they were in 1965 and seldom fit together, the balance of the attack was seriously affected and, before long, Gibbs found himself having to fill the role of stock bowler, a cruel injustice. It was, however, the fielding which was the weakest department. Sobers estimated 34 catches were dropped by his fielders in the five Tests, many of them at crucial stages. It was not a pleasant sight for West Indian eyes to watch as Sobers, in the end, was searching for positions to hide men in the field.

Australia, on the other hand, were quick to capitalise on their opponents' shortcomings. Their captain, Lawry, had a score to settle after his experiences on the 1965 tour of the Caribbean and he knew he had the resources to regain the Worrell Trophy. It is significant that Lawry was one of only three survivors of the 1965 Australian team to play in the series (the fast bowler McKenzie, who took 30 wickets, and the wicket-keeper, Jarman, were the others) while there were no fewer than eight West Indians who had been on the victorious side on that occasion.

Lawry himself, his captaincy and his batting reflecting a fierce determination to avenge the indignities of three years earlier, Ian Chappell and Walters dominated the batting, which passed 500 an innings in each of the final four Tests.

Lawry recorded a double-century at Melbourne and single centuries at Brisbane and Sydney in dogged fashion and, requiring only a draw to clinch the series, refused to enforce the follow-on despite a first-innings lead of 340 in the final Test. Chappell took five centuries off the tourists in various matches, two in Tests, and was nicknamed "Cathedral" by frustrated West Indian supporters listening through the night on their radios to the ball-by-ball commentaries. Walters, who missed the first Test through injury, scored with Bradmanesque consistency in the others—699 runs in six innings with centuries in the third and fourth Tests and the then-unequalled feat of a double and a single century in the same Test, the fifth. Had all the catches offered by this trio been held, the record books would read very differently but, in their contrasting ways, they gave no quarter and made the West Indies suffer for their mistakes.

The Australian bowling revolved around McKenzie, Connolly and Gleeson. McKenzie, big and strong with a model side-on action, had been surprisingly overshadowed by Hawke in the Caribbean in 1965. Now he demonstrated his true worth, accounting for most of his 30 victims with late swing, and every so often bowling with real speed and hostility. He had 14 batsmen caught either by the 'keeper or in the slips. Connolly was the ideal foil. Also a six-footer with broad shoulders, he was no more than quickish medium but his control, variations of pace and capacity for hard work made his contribution to his team's effort the equal of any other bowler. Gleeson, an amiable, unathletic individual, was the trick artist—a spinner who gripped the ball abnormally and who flicked it on its way with the middle finger. He turned it each way, if only a little, and he troubled batsmen who found his methods baffling. Iverson and Ramadhin had had the same effect with their unorthodox spin in previous eras. It was only in the fourth Test, when they decided to get after him, that the West Indies extinguished Gleeson's threat—much as the Australians had done to Ramadhin 17 years earlier—but, by then, he had served his purpose and Australia had established an actual and psychological advantage which they never wasted.

They had established that lead after losing the first Test at Brisbane by 125 runs. The West Indies owed that victory mainly to the winning of the toss, which put Australia under the pressure of batting last on a pitch which became progressively responsive to spin. Gibbs, Sobers (bowling orthodox spin) and Holford used it to best advantage and Australia failed to reach 300 in either innings.

It was not bowling alone, however, that was responsible for the only West Indian win of the series. Carew, the loose-limbed Trinidadian who had been a surprise choice for the tour and, for that matter, this Test as well, played two crucial hands, Kanhai batted with real authority in the first innings and Lloyd conclusively shifted the balance of an evenly-contested match with a brilliant second-innings 129.

Each innings, with the exception of Australia's second, revolved around one sizable partnership. In the first it was a second-wicket association between Carew and Kanhai that yielded 165 before the rest collapsed to an all-out 296; in Australia's reply, Lawry and Chappell gave warning of events to follow by each scoring centuries in a second-wicket stand of 217; when West Indies were 178 for 6 and only 190 ahead in their second innings, Lloyd and Carew (batting at number seven because of injury) brought life back to the sagging cause with a stand of 120.

The West Indian performance at Brisbane was every bit as convincing as the many which had earned them the unofficial "world champions" designation. They dropped no catch and took several good ones, they counter-attacked brilliantly through Lloyd (who hit 18 fours and a six, and 100 of whose runs were scored in the final session of play) and Sobers' magic worked. When Lawry and Chappell were entrenched on the second day, he tossed the ball to Lloyd, who removed both in the space of a couple of overs, appropriately the captain himself catching both. Sobers' second-innings figures of 6 for 73 were his best in Test cricket.

Yes, Sobers, criticised heavily for his golf and his trip to

Melbourne before the match, had cause for satisfaction.

It was to be short-lived. By the time the series moved to
Melbourne on Boxing Day, the West Indies had been embarras-
singly outplayed by South Australia for the second time and the
euphoria created by the Brisbane victory had quickly evaporated.
To add to their woes, the weather on the opening day was
diabolical, cold, grey and damp, and Sobers lost the toss. In
such conditions, only the newcomer Fredericks of the West Indian
batsmen seemed inclined to concentrate on the job after Lawry
had sent them in. Kanhai, in fact, came in as low as number
seven, reluctant to risk further aggravating a heavy cold.

McKenzie was the destroyer, dismissing every batsman,
except Nurse and Butcher, for 71. All out for 200, the West Indies
claimed an early wicket through Edwards, playing his first Test,
but a missed chance to gully by Chappell off the same bowler
when 10 proved a critical error. It was the first in a spate of
dropped catches which effectively set the seal on the match.

Lawry and Chappell proceeded to dominate an attack which
possessed only two bowlers of Test experience (Holford having
been dropped against Sobers' wishes), adding 298 in 310 minutes.
Lawry was badly missed by Sobers at 117, off his own bowling,
and off Edwards at 132 and, after Chappell had gone (16 fours),
Walters came to re-establish himself in the team, putting on a
further 123 with his captain. He, too, escaped through a fielding
error early in his innings, Davis at slip spilling a straightforward
slip catch off Sobers. At that stage, Walters was battling, none
too impressively, to overcome poor form. It was, in every respect,
a crucial opportunity wasted.

Australia eventually accumulated a lead of 310 and the West
Indies never appeared likely to save the match, despite a fifth-
wicket partnership of 134 between Nurse and Sobers filled with
delightful strokeplay. Australia won in the last over of the
fourth day by an innings and 30 runs and the series was level.

The pattern of the third Test at Sydney, which followed
immediately, was much the same. The West Indies batted incon-
sistently despite an excellent pitch which, to the contrary,
Australia's batsmen fully appreciated. Walters and Redpath
flogged an inept attack, and left it tired and frustrated. Freeman
at number eight and the last pair, Gleeson and Connolly, rubbed
salt in the wounds and Australia's lead was a formidable 283.

The West Indies, despite the great odds against them, batted
with more purpose in their second innings than they had done in
their first. Fredericks and Kanhai had a century stand for the
second wicket and Butcher batted just over four hours for a

deserved 101. But only he and Kanhai managed to pass 50, and it required much more than that to prevent Australia winning yet again.

Sobers and his team by now could only have been in a state of shock. In the space of a fortnight, they had squandered the advantage gained by the Brisbane victory and Australia had suddenly and decisively established an immense superiority. There were 15 days between the end of the Sydney Test and the start of the fourth at the Adelaide Oval and, during them, the West Indies could relax with two upcountry games and two on the pleasant island State of Tasmania.

If the break had any beneficial effect, it was not immediately evident on the return to Adelaide. It is true that Sobers batted on the opening day of the fourth Test as a man inspired, unleashing shots in every direction in a wonderful display, yet his team could only total an unsatisfactory 276. The captain's insistence on batting at number six despite widespread advice that he should go higher once again was shown to be folly. He came to the wicket with Australia already in command with the total 107 for four and left at 261 for eight; in other words, he had scored 110 of the 154 made during his 132 minutes' batting (two sixes, 14 fours).

Almost inevitably, Australia's batsmen consolidated the advantage their bowlers had secured. Lawry, Stackpole, Chappell and Redpath laid the foundations of another huge total, Walters followed to score his second successive hundred and Sheahan and McKenzie brought the number of half-century-makers in the innings to six. Australia's lead was, yet again, substantial—257.

The similarity between this and the preceding two Tests was, until this stage, uncanny and even the staunchest West Indian supporter must have been resigned to another ignominious defeat at the start of the West Indian second innings. It was cause for immense satisfaction, therefore, when the batting finally came good at this vital moment. At last, this ageing, much-maligned team showed that its spirit was not entirely broken yet. And how it fought.

Every man Jack, with the exception of Gibbs, scored over 20. Butcher led the way with yet another competent hundred, full of grit and determination. Carew registered his highest score of the series, Kanhai got 80—as did Holford—at last shaking off the insecurity of an eternity of batting failures. Sobers made 52 and if Nurse's contribution was only 40 it was the type of innings always to be remembered. The total when McKenzie bowled Gibbs in the first over of the final day was 616, the West Indies' best in Australia, leaving Australia 360 in five and three-quarter hours—a steep task but, on the evidence thus far, by no means impossible.

It was an equation which led to a marvellous climax, reviving memories for those listening and watching of the series eight years earlier. Australia's batsmen, brimful of confidence, set off after the target with a succession of bold, positive strokes. Stackpole led the way with 50 in an hour and a half and Lawry, Chappell and Walters, the trio which had perpetually harassed West Indian bowlers throughout the season, each scored so freely that Australia entered the final hour, in which at least 15 eight-ball overs had to be bowled, needing 62 with seven wickets standing.

Uncharacteristically, Australia panicked. There were three run-outs and, suddenly, at 333 for nine with 3.2 overs remaining, the West Indies were on the verge of squaring the rubber. This, however, was as far as they got. Sheahan and Connolly, the last pair, survived, Sobers claiming the new ball and wasting it by swinging it down the leg side, too far, too often.

During the early part of the Australian innings, there was an incident which caused heated reaction at the time and much argument subsequently. Redpath, backing up at the non-striker's end as Australia sought quick runs, was run out by the bowler, Griffith, during the delivery stride. Although Sobers apologised to the Australians during the tea interval and although a large block of opinion was against Griffith, there were several who supported the action on the grounds that the Australians were running sharp singles, that one batsman (Chappell) had previously been warned (by Holford) and that Redpath was a full yard out of his ground when Griffith removed the bails. It is worth mentioning that Redpath was caught in the same embarrassing predicament in the final Test, this time by Hall, but the bowler did not remove the bails.

The subject, naturally, caused divided opinion in the press box —and produced a delightful piece of repartee from Bill "Tiger" O'Reilly, the former Australian spinner. O'Reilly was supporting Griffith when someone pointed out that he had never resorted to such tactics in all his years of bowling, although he must often have had the opportunity. "Ah", replied O'Reilly, "when I was bowling they weren't so anxious to get to the other end."

The West Indies entered the fifth Test with the opportunity of sharing the rubber—and thereby retaining the Worrell Trophy. But they had to win the match and, for all the drama of Adelaide, for some months they had not looked capable of doing so.

Still, they started prosperously after Sobers had decided to field first, only to be betrayed by the faulty catching which had stalked them throughout the tour. Hall, fully aware it was his final appearance in a Test in Australia, summoned all his resources at the start of the Australian innings for a spell of beautiful outswing bowling, while Sobers, left-arm over the wicket, brought the ball back the other way. It was a testing combination and, inside an hour and a half, they had removed Stackpole, Chappell and Redpath for 51. By then, however, two of Hall's two best deliveries had brought the big-hearted fast bowler only the pain of seeing chances dropped in the slips off Chappell. Later, Lawry, at 44, and Walters, at 76, also escaped through the generosity of the fielders, the former off Griffith, the latter off Hall.

Thereafter, the match was one long tale of woe for the West Indies which only ended when their last wicket fell early on the final day to give Australia victory by 382 runs. The partnership between Lawry (151) and Walters (242 with 24 fours) added 336 and the total reached 619, by which time the match was as good as over. The West Indies clearly had little heart for proceedings after that, especially after Lawry's mean streak in batting a second time despite his mammoth first-innings lead after the West Indies had fallen for 279. It was a decision which presented Walters with the opportunity of yet another hundred and left the West Indies 735 to win!

Sobers and Nurse prevented it being more humiliating than it was with two sparkling centuries, starting with the innings in a shambles at 102 for five. But no-one else stayed around very long—not even the spectators, of whom there were barely 300 to watch Lawry, beaming contentedly, receive the Worrell Trophy on behalf of his team and, unquestionably, on behalf of those who had lost it in the Caribbean three years earlier.

West Indian feelings on the defeat were summed up by Don Norville, of the Barbados *Advocate-News*, whose pointed comment was: "The time has come for some tree-shaking to let the old fruit drop." Within a month, the selectors did shake the tree and several of the old fruit did drop, bringing a great era in West Indian cricket unmistakably to its end.

Australia in West Indies 1973

The moods of the two teams were sharply contrasting when Australia started their third tour of the Caribbean in February, 1973.

West Indian cricket was in a state of melancholy, bred principally by a protracted period of depressing results. Of the previous 26 Tests they had played, the West Indies had won a mere two and the defeat at the hands of India in 1971 and the inability to achieve one positive result against New Zealand in 1972, both at home before an ultra-critical public, were traumatic experiences.

Australia, on the other hand, had been buoyed by the performances of an essentially young team under the captaincy of Ian Chappell in England the previous summer and at home against Pakistan in their own season. The Australians arrived in the Caribbean fresh from winning all three Tests against the Pakistanis, a stimulating tonic.

These differences were reflected in the cricket the teams played, in the way they responded to the crises which they encountered and, finally, in Australia's victories in the third and fourth Tests which ensured the retention of the Worrell Trophy.

Against England and Pakistan, Australia's bowling had been carried by the speed of Lillee, the newest in a long line of outstanding Australian fast bowlers, the swing of Massie, who had astounded everyone by taking 16 wickets in his debut Test at Lord's the previous June, and the off-spin of Mallett, one of the most successful of his type to have played for Australia. As it turned out, Lillee broke down with a back injury very early on and played only the first Test (in which he took no wicket for 132), Massie entirely lost form and played no Test cricket at all and Mallett was unavailable to tour for personal reasons. So Australia were forced to build an entirely new attack, a handicap which they overcame with typical efficiency.

Walker, a native Tasmanian and adopted Victorian, nicknamed "Tanglefoot" by team-mates because of his unorthodox, wrong-footed delivery, had only played his first Test in January, yet he constantly troubled batsmen with his deep inswing, excellent control and amazing stamina. Immensely strong and fit he bowled 100 more overs in the Tests than any of his team-mates and took 26 wickets at 20 apiece. Hammond, a boyish, freckled-faced South Australian, had toured England without playing a Test and was, it seemed, chosen as a back-up fast bowler to do the work in the territorial matches. When his opportunity came, he seized it by bowling fast and straight and with great spirit. Jenner and O'Keeffe, leg-spinners of differing styles, played their parts, particularly at the Queen's Park Oval, while Walters and Greg Chappell occasionally contributed telling spells.

At all times the bowling was supported by wonderful ground fielding, never more importantly than in the pre-lunch period of the third Test when the West Indies appeared heading for a notable victory, and Chappell exuded an aggressive confidence which permeated right through his team.

In contrast, the West Indies were bedevilled by adversity,

much of it off the field and much of it of their own making. It left their new captain, the experienced Kanhai, with a huge task, even more difficult than it would normally have been.

Much of the controversy, as usual, involved selection.

The most contentious issue surrounded the position of Sobers, whose resignation as captain, after 39 consecutive Tests, was evidence of a certain mental and physical weariness. The choice of his successor in itself was the cause of a certain amount of inter-territorial rivalry but there appeared to be general acceptance once Kanhai's appointment was announced.

Sobers had undergone surgery for the removal of a cartilage in England in the summer and was struggling to get fit when the series started. At his own request, he was not considered for the first Test but, when he was also omitted from the second, he announced that he was ready, willing and able to rejoin the team. The selectors and the West Indies Board, however, were wary. They demanded that the great left-hander be cleared by a specialist first and asked him to play in a two-day exhibition game in St Vincent in betweeen the second and third Tests as a sort of fitness test.

Sobers was indignant. He said he had always kept faith with the Board during his long career and, whenever unfit, had been quick to declare himself so. Now he expected the Board to accept his word. Understandably, the impasse provoked a welter of comment through the area and rivalled the cricket itself for the public's attention. The individual concerned, after all, was not just another player but a phenomenon.

Whether fit or not, Sobers' absence from the team was a major loss and Ian Chappell's comment after the series that his team's triumph would have been much more meaningful had Sobers played was a pertinent one.

But Sobers' was not the only selectorial quarrel. There was a furore in Trinidad when Charlie Davis, so successful in 1971 and 1972 against India and New Zealand, was omitted from the first three Tests through lack of form; while Guyana's Prime Minister Forbes Burnham personally sent for Lloyd, then playing club cricket in Australia, when the West Indies Board decided he would not be one of the chosen few paid to return home from their professional assignments.

The West Indies also found themselves affected by injuries at crucial periods, none more so than that to Rowe, who was put out of the match and the series when he wrenched an ankle on the first day of the third Test, a tense, closely-fought match which Australia eventually won by 44 runs.

The first two Tests, both drawn, suggested that neither side possessed the bowling strength to produce a conclusive result.

Both were affected to some extent by the weather, which caused an important loss of time but, even so, there were six centuries on either side and Australia's 324 in the second Test was the lowest all-out total.

Australia, batting consistently right down the order, declared at 428 for 7 near the end of the second day at Sabina Park but the West Indies responded in kind to level the scores exactly. Stackpole's 142 in Australia's second innings was full of hefty strokes but as it was being compiled it was clear what the result would be.

It was a match of mixed fortunes for Jamaicans before their home crowd, which overflowed the tiny ground so that even the light pylons were packed with spectators, precariously perched on the steel structure. The young fast bowler Dowe was so punished by Stackpole for persistent short bowling that Jamaicans instituted their own commandment. "Dowe shalt not bowl!" they chorused after a while. However, Foster's maiden Test century, attractively made with his accustomed penchant for the leg side, and Rowe's 76 more than compensated for Dowe's disappointment and brought a rapturous response from the adoring public.

The West Indies began the second Test encouragingly, taking the wickets of Stackpole and Redpath in the first three-quarters of an hour and, despite a third-wicket stand of 129 between the Chappell brothers, Australia ended the first day unsatisfactorily placed at 243 for six. Overnight rain then delayed the start of play on both the second and third days, taking over three hours off the overall time and diminishing the prospects of a result.

Greg Chappell's 106 was executed with commanding authority but it was the effervescent wicketkeeper Marsh who lifted Australia from the insecurity of 218 for six to an eventual 324, following his 97 in the first Test with 78. The West Indies also faltered in their reply, Walker testing their main batsmen in a marathon spell lasting two and three-quarter hours on the third day. Fredericks played confidently for 98 but it was only a sixth-wicket stand of 165 between Kanhai (105) and Murray (90, his highest Test score) which sent the home team into the lead. By then, it was well into the fourth day and the match thereafter was reduced to batting practice, Ian Chappell and Walters helping themselves to unbeaten centuries in Australia's second innings.

There was little to separate the teams at this point and their evenness provided crowds at the Queen's Park Oval in Port-of-Spain with a most fascinating match in the third Test, the West

Indies frittering away a wonderful opportunity after lunch on the final day and Australia, never conceding, fighting grimly for their triumph.

With Trinidad experiencing a protracted drought, the outfield was bone hard and bare of grass and, throughout, the pitch favoured spin, with several catches taken close in, frequently off bat and pad. The West Indies decided to use Lloyd as opening bowler and relied heavily on the spin of Gibbs and the two young left-armers Inshan Ali and Willett, a shy, 19-year-old native of Nevis who had made his Test debut at Bridgetown.

Australia's attack was better balanced, although the leg-spin of Jenner and O'Keeffe and the off-spin of Greg Chappell played vital roles.

Australia, batting first, owed their 332 to the innings of the series, a brilliant 112 by Walters, who unleashed a wide range of strokes and completely dominated the bowling. He came to the wicket on resumption after lunch and was 100 by tea, a rare accomplishment by a batsman who had formed a liking for West Indian bowling four years earlier on his home pitches. That the last seven wickets fell for 92 after his dismissal was indicative of the significance of Walters' two and a half hours at the wicket.

The West Indies responded with determination and application but there was no major individual contribution and they fell 52 short, a worrying deficit in such conditions. Australia increased it by 281, despite some challenging bowling by Gibbs (5 for 102) and Willett (3 for 33 from 28 overs). Their captain led the way with a resolute 97 in an innings of nearly four hours but probably the most vital runs were provided by the last two wickets, which put on 50 during a period when the West Indies bowling tactics were suspect.

The West Indies therefore required 334—a Herculean task in any circumstances but doubly so with a major batsman (Rowe) short and on a pitch of slow turn and unpredictable bounce. Yet their batsmen approached the task so diligently that they went into lunch on the final day with the score at 268, with five wickets standing and Kallicharran and Foster seemingly well entrenched. The two left-handers, Fredericks and Kallicharran, built the foundations for the epic struggle with an aggressive second wicket partnership of 102 and it was the latter who was to be the linch-pin of the West Indian effort.

Meeting every delivery with a broad bat and superb technique, he had been batting just over four and three-quarter hours at the first interval on the final day. By then, the crowd had already begun its celebrations but they proved premature. Kalluicharran's efforts had taken a lot out of him and lunch served to break his concentration. Chappell claim the second new ball immediately on resumption—his "one last hope"—and Kallicharran followed Walker's very first ball wide of the off stump, and touched a catch to the 'keeper. The domino theory of one fall, all fall now went into effect and, before a shocked crowd, the West Indies slumped to defeat.

Disappointed they may have been but the Trinidadians kept their unique sense of humour right to the bitter end; as Gibbs strolled out, the last man, they chanted: "Amen, amen!" The Australians, naturally jubilant, owed their win on this final day as much to the exceptional ground fielding as to the bowling. They saved dozens of precious runs with acrobatic, bone-jarring saves, a tribute to their never-say-die spirit.

If the Trinidad crowds had been subjected to a frustrating anti-climax those in Guyana for the fourth Test had even more to complain about of their team. Simple statistics illustrate the extent of the West Indian decline. Batting first for the only time in the series, they ended the opening day 269 for three, gained a narrow first-innings lead and yet were losing by 10 wickets inside half an hour on the final day.

The hero of the first day was unquestionably Lloyd. With Prime Minister Burnham basking in the reflected glory, the loose-limbed left-hander reinstated himself in the team and erased doubts about his real merit as a Test player. Abandoning the contact lenses he had used in Trinidad and reverting to spectacles, he was in irresistible mood, attacking confidently and hitting a six and 24 fours before he was out on the second morning for 178. He added a record 187 for the fourth wicket with Kanhai but no-one else scored more than 30, the last seven wickets collapsing for 89 on the second day.

As they had done in Barbados, Boyce and Holder gained an early breakthrough in Australia's first innings but the West Indies again failed to seize the initiative, Ian Chappell scoring a typically efficient 109, his brother 51, and Walters, exuding confidence, 81. The 200 was passed with only three wickets down but the innings suddenly went into decline against steady bowling, the last six wickets yielding only 112 and the West Indies carrying a lead of 25 into their second innings.

What followed was an inexplicably lame display by a batting team which, until then, had been commendably consistent throughout the series. Fredericks and Kallicharran were quickly gone, the latter to a marvellous catch at long leg by Walker off Hammond, and it was this combination which consolidated

Australia's advantage with inspired bowling. Each took four wickets and, in 52 overs and four balls, the West Indies were dismissed for 109. Their spirit broken, there was little effort to make Australia even fight for the 135 needed for victory.

A pall of gloom descended over West Indies cricket, a predictable culmination of the discord which had afflicted it in so many ways throughout that season, and its manifestation was seen in the final, now meaningless, Test at the Queen's Park Oval. Over 90,000 all told had watched the five gripping days of the third Test; now a tenth of that total turned out to see the final rites to the series. Some days barely 1000 were present. West Indies, it seemed, had had enough of the buffeting which their national sport had suffered both on and off the field.

The atmosphere for the match was unreal and neither team played with much zest, the matching ending in a draw very much in Australia's favour. For the West Indies, it was to be the last of their frustrations. Within a few months, virtually the same team under the same captain, away from the trials and tribulations of the Caribbean, was to score a resounding triumph in England.

West Indies in Australia 1975-76

Arranged as a substitute for a scheduled tour by South Africa, there was the expectation of a rich cricketing feast for the West Indies' fifth visit to Australia. The ingredients were perfect. Each team contained a number of aggressive batsmen of high repute, each possessed bowlers of rare speed and hostility, and the two most successful off-spinners in contemporary international cricket were on opposite sides. Above all, they appeared evenly matched.

The aperitif, served up in England the previous summer in the form of the first World Cup competition, provided a mouth-watering prelude, being the most entertaining and competitive cricket witnessed for years.

The West Indies captain, Clive Lloyd, had enjoyed an immensely successful initiation to the job. His basically young team had triumphed 3-2 in the series in India in 1974-75 and had been the first World Cup champions, beating Australia on the two occasions the countries met, including the final at Lord's.

Lloyd himself wrote before the start of the series: "There is not much between the two teams where talents and skills are involved and you don't need a crystal ball to predict the outcome could hang on a slender thread."

It was a widely-shared opinion. Yet, after a wonderful start, the contest deteriorated into a one-sided anti-climax, Australia comfortably winning the last four of the six Tests for a 5-1 advantage.

Disappointment was no stranger to West Indian teams in Australia. All those before—even, to a certain extent, that of 1960-61—had endured it but not quite so sharply as Lloyd's. It lost the first Test by eight wickets but the margin of defeat did not accurately indicate the closeness of the struggle. It then won the second Test by an innings and 87 with a magnificent performance in which all that is best about West Indian cricket was shown to advantage. From that point onwards, little went right for it and its spirit was irreparably broken by a combination of Australia's fast bowling, injury, lack of form of leading players, faulty catching and questionable umpiring.

They were factors familiar to West Indian teams in Australia and, as had been the case before, the situation degenerated from bad to worse. In the end, the West Indian players, dejected by their own performances, were merely going through the motions, none more so than the captain, who found it impossible to hide his bitter disappointment.

The Australians, never ones to show mercy in such circumstances, had appeared psychologically shaken after their massive defeat at Perth in the second Test. The West Indian fast bowling, spearheaded by Roberts and the 21-year-old Holding, devastated their batting, and the West Indian strokemakers were equally severe on their bowlers. At this stage, the visitors held a distinct advantage.

The West Indies appeared to become complacent after their success, a grave misjudgment. Immediately following their victory, they allowed themselves to slip into an embarrassing tangle against a sub-standard South Australia team purely and simply because of a lethargic attitude to the match. The Australians saw this as a sign of weakness, which they themselves would never allow, regrouped their forces and put the debacle of Perth behind them. The contest was not the same thereafter.

Australia's dominance from that match was built around the consistency of their batting, with their new captain, Greg Chappell, outstanding, and the havoc wreaked by the pace of Thomson and Lillee, but more especially the former, admirably supported by the left-arm swing of the talented and youthful Gilmour. Between them they claimed 76 of the 110 West Indian wickets that fell and subjected the batsmen to the constant threat of physical injury which was never far from their minds. Almost all the major West Indian batsmen were hit about the face and body at one time or another—Kallicharran had his nose broken by Lillee at Perth, Julien's thumb was cracked when he was used as an opener, and Lloyd and Holding forced to retire hurt at Sydney, as was Ali at Brisbane.

The West Indians generally chose to counter-attack against such bowling but the result was that 14 wickets were lost to the hook shot while numerous others went to catches behind the wicket and in the slips area, Marsh claiming a record-equalling 26 catches as wicketkeeper.

Roberts and Holding suggested that they were capable of replying in kind by their display in the second Test but a pulled muscle sustained by the young Jamaican then separated them for the crucial third Test and, subsequently, Roberts' flame dwindled under the strain of overwork. He was unable to play at all in the final Test, by which time Holding, again, and Boyce were also well below the fitness required for five-day cricket.

No less of a handicap to Lloyd was the failure of the recognised opening pair. Greenidge completely lost form and confidence and Fredericks found himself carrying Julien, Kallicharran and, finally, Richards to the middle as partners. Fredericks himself, usually so reliable, had one unforgettable innings of 169 at Perth but achieved little else of note and it was no surprise that there was only one first-wicket partnership in excess of 50.

Not for the first time, the standard of umpiring angered the touring team and its effect, indirectly if not directly, could not be underestimated. Decisions given by one particular umpire, Jack Collins of Melbourne in the third Test, led to a public protest from the West Indies captain and an open demonstration on the field by the senior player, Gibbs. In the Sydney Test, the refusal of an appeal for a catch at the wicket against Ian Chappell first ball off Holding by umpire Reg Ledwidge occasioned a tearful and much-publicised reaction from the bowler. By then, it was no secret that the West Indians believed, along with everything else, that the umpiring was also against them, just another worry to distract their attention away from the cricket itself.

The outcome of the first Test was virtually decided by lunch on the first day when the West Indies contrived to be 125 for six, a remarkable start to the series. Belligerent and uncharacteristic batting by Murray carried the total to 214 but, on an easy-paced pitch, it was clearly insufficient.

A polished century by Greg Chappell and the left-handed Turner's 81 were mainly responsible for Australia's passing 300 with only four wickets down, a seemingly impregnable position which only a late-order collapse could spoil. It was spoiled, principally by the off-spin of Gibbs, who took four of the last six wickets which fell for 49, and Australia's lead was not 300 as had appeared probable, but 152.

With the West Indies 50 for three in their second innings, Australia were set for a quick and handsome victory before the balance was shifted by the left-handed Kallicharran and the right-handed Rowe. Becoming entrenched after unsettled beginnings, they caused Australia real concern in a partnership of 198 which lasted four hours ten minutes.

The West Indies were in the lead by 96 with six wickets left when Rowe was out for 107, in what was his first Test match outside the Caribbean, a dismissal which led to a complete transformation in the match. In quick succession, Lloyd and Richards succumbed through careless cricket, and Kallicharran followed, bowled off his body sweeping, for an accomplished 101. Murray again bolstered the lower order with his second half-century of the match but the challenge offered Australia, to score 219, while not to be scoffed at, was not enough.

Gibbs bowled beautifully on a pitch responding to spin and Australia might have been hard-pressed to get home had Inshan Ali not dropped Ian Chappell off his own bowling when he was 12. The kudos, however, belonged to Greg Chappell, who, in his first match as captain, completed his second century and hit the winning run. His elder brother's influence in an unbroken stand of 159 was also considerable.

Australia's lead in the rubber was short-lived. To say that the West Indies drew level by winning by an innings and 87 runs at Perth simply indicates the statistical dimensions of their superiority; the quality of the cricket which achieved it could not be surpassed for its attacking brilliance.

The first day was ordinary enough, Ian Chappell's 15th Test century providing the backbone of an Australian total of 317 for 7 which ended at 329 on the second morning when Holding took the final three wickets in the same over. A fierce onslaught by the West Indian batsmen and fast bowlers followed which completely rattled the home team and which did not cease until the last ball had been bowled early on the fourth day.

The blitz was started by Fredericks, who played the innings of his life, a devastating demonstration of strokeplay in all directions against all bowling. He hooked his second ball, from Lillee, for six, stroked 27 fours and batted a mere three and a half hours for 169, truly one of the great Test innings. His salvo was advanced by Lloyd, whose 149 lasted a mere 216 minutes and included a six and 22 fours while Kallicharran, despite his nose injury,

Murray and Boyce, in their differing fashions, made their presence felt as the total mounted to 585, leaving Australia an enormous deficit.

Roberts, almost singlehandedly, saw to it that the West Indies would not be denied. Bowling at great pace with sustained accuracy, he removed the first four batsmen by the end of the third day when Australia were 104 for 4 and quickly added another three on the fourth morning to make his analysis 7 for 54. Julien accounted for the three tailenders in the absence of the injured Holding and the West Indies were home by lunch, a great triumph.

So far, all the expectations of the contest had been fulfilled and a crowd of 85,596 assembled at the vast Melbourne Cricket Ground on Boxing Day to witness the start of the third Test. Only the few West Indian supporters among them, including a visiting steel band, could have been disappointed at the events. Chappell decided to bowl first after winning the toss and Thomson and Lillee finally discovered the form with which they had harassed England a year earlier. They took nine wickets between them and the West Indies were bowled out for 224, an early advantage which Australia never relinquished.

To their credit the West Indian bowlers fought gamely to reinstate themselves but nothing went their way. Redpath, who made a dogged 102, was dropped at 62 and Greg Chappell, who scored 52, at 10; Cosier, the second century-maker of the innings in his first Test appearance, survived what the West Indians considered a clear lbw decision when only 5. These frustrating setbacks took their toll of the West Indian effort as the Australian innings progressed and partnerships of 114 between Cosier and his captain and 88 between Cosier and Marsh guaranteed a sizable Australian lead. It mounted, after robust hitting from Lillee and Thomson, to 261 and by the rest day, with the visitors' total 92 for three, it was clear the West Indies had lost.

They duly succumbed and even a century by Lloyd was no more than small consolation. It was a lone battle by the West Indian captain for no other batsman scored more than 36 and Australia were left with the formality of scoring 52 to win.

As by tradition, the fourth Test followed the third immediately and there appeared an important shift in the West Indies favour when Lillee had to withdraw on the morning of the match through illness. In contrast, the West Indies welcomed back Holding.

Over the first two days, the cricket was well balanced, no side earning a clear ascendancy. After being sent in for the second successive time, the West Indies batted with far more restraint than they had previously and, despite injuries to three of their batsmen, managed a respectable, if not formidable, 355. Several batsmen got going but made nothing of their promising begin-nings.

Australia's batsmen found it difficult to assert themselves, losing four wickets for 103 but a fielding error gave them the chance to shake free without a major collapse. Soon after he came in, Greg Chappell snicked Roberts low to fourth slip where Boyce dropped him, a mistake which Lloyd undiplomatically, if not incorrectly, blamed in a newspaper article a day later for the loss of the series.

Chappell made the most of this opportunity and he with the bat and Thomson with the ball were responsible for a rapid West Indian disintegration. An undefeated 38 at the end of the second day, the Australian captain, upright in stance and straight-batted in technique, batted through his team's innings to be 182 when the last wicket fell. Although he was below his best during the period when he offered his chance, his batting could not be faulted later and he guided his team to a lead of 50 on first innings, a sterling performance.

Still, it was only a narrow margin on an essentially good batting pitch and a decisive result appeared unlikely when the West Indies started their second innings. Incredibly, they lost with more than a day to spare, falling to a pathetic 128 all out.

Thomson and their own folly created the situation. The former, generating such speed that he knocked the stumps of Holding and Murray flying back to the 'keeper, took 6 for 50; for their part, Fredericks, Kallicharran and Richards were all out to needless hook shots when the West Indies batted for the final one and a quarter hours of the third day.

West Indian morale was abysmally low. They knew they had disappointed thousands upon thousands of their followers at home; more importantly, they had disappointed themselves and they could not shake off the morose mood which fell over them for the rest of the tour. Australia encountered little sparkle in their opponents for the final two Tests and duly romped home.

There was one shining light in the West Indian gloom. After the fourth Test, it was decided to use Richards as opener and the strongly-built Antiguan suddenly found the answer to compiling the sizable scores which always appeared within his capacity. He had innings of 64, 93, 160, 107 not out and 99 in minor matches and then rounded off his tour with 30 and 101 in the Adelaide Test and 50 and 98 in the sixth Test. It was a phenomenal sequence which became commonplace for him in the 1976 Tests.

However, no-one else on his team seemed to have much heart for the cricket. True, Boyce scored 95 not out and 69 at Adelaide in typically blazing fashion, Lloyd was at his best with 91 not out in his last innings of the series at Melbourne, and Holder bowled superbly in the fourth Test. The most satisfying individual performance, however, was Gibbs'. After 19 years and 78 Tests he secured the wickets he needed to pass Trueman's record of 307, an achievement which, temporarily at least, revived West Indies morale.

It was Gibbs' third and last tour of Australia and, for the third and last time, he was on the losing side. As he commented, no West Indian defeat had so disillusioned him as this one for he knew this particular team had the potential to accomplish what none before it had—victory over Australia in Australia. A few months later, as they steamrollered over England in England, virtually the same side was confirming Gibbs' estimate of its strength.

West Indies in Australia 1930–31

AT Adelaide. December 12 *to* 16. Australia won by 10 wickets. West Indies 296 (E. L. Bartlett 84, C. A. Roach 56, G. C. Grant 53 not out, C. V. Grimmett 7 for 87) and 249 (Grant 71 not out, L. S. Birkett 64, A. Hurwood 4 for 86, Grimmett 4 for 96). Australia 376 (A. F. Kippax 146, S. J. McCabe 90, A. G. Fairfax 41 not out, O. C. Scott 4 for 83) and 172 for no wicket (W. H. Ponsford 92 not out, A. A. Jackson 70 not out).

AT Sydney. January 1 *to* 5. Australia won by an innings and 172 runs. Australia 369 (Ponsford 183, W. M. Woodfull 58, Scott 4 for 66). West Indies 107 (Grimmett 4 for 54) and 90 (Hurwood 4 for 22).

AT Brisbane. January 16 *to* 20. Australia won by an innings and 217 runs. Australia 558 (D. G. Bradman 223, Ponsford 109, Kippax 84, R. K. Oxenham 48, H. C. Griffith 4 for 133). West Indies 193 (G. A. Headley 102 not out, Oxenham 4 for 39, Grimmett 4 for 95) and 148 (Grimmett 5 for 49).

AT Melbourne. February 13 *and* 14. Australia won by an innings and 122 runs. West Indies 99 (H. Ironmonger 7 for 23) and 107 (Fairfax 4 for 31, Ironmonger 4 for 56). Australia 328 for eight declared (Bradman 152, Woodfull 83).

AT Sydney. February 27 *to March* 4. West Indies won by 30 runs. West Indies 350 for six declared (F. R. Martin 123 not out, Headley 105, Grant 62) and 124 for five declared. Australia 224

(Fairfax 54, Bradman 43, G. N. Francis 4 for 48) and 220 (Fairfax 60 not out, McCabe 44, Griffith 4 for 50).

West Indies in Australia 1951–52

AT Brisbane. November 9 *to* 13. Australia won by three wickets. West Indies 216 (J. D. C. Goddard 45, R. R. Lindwall 4 for 62) and 245 (E. D. Weekes 70, G. E. Gomez 55, D. T. Ring 6 for 80). Australia 226 (Lindwall 61, K. R. Miller 46, A. L. Valentine 5 for 99) and 236 for seven (A. R. Morris 48, G. B. Hole 45 not out, R. N. Harvey 42, S. Ramadhin 5 for 90).

AT Sydney. November 30 *to December* 5. Australia won by seven wickets. West Indies 362 (R. J. Christiani 76, F. M. Worrell 64, C. L. Walcott 60, Gomez 54, Lindwall 4 for 66) and 290 (Goddard 57 not out, Weekes 56, Gomez 41). Australia 517 (A. L. Hassett 132, Miller 129, Ring 65, Lindwall 48, Valentine 4 for 111) and 137 for three (K. A. Archer 47, Hassett 46 not out).

AT Adelaide. December 22 *to* 25. West Indies won by six wickets. Australia 82 (Worrell 6 for 38) and 255 (Ring 67, Morris 45, Valentine 6 for 102). West Indies 105 (W. A. Johnston 6 for 62) and 233 for four (J. B. Stollmeyer 47, Gomez 46 not out, Christiani 42 not out).

AT Melbourne. December 31 *to January* 3. Australia won by one wicket. West Indies 272 (Worrell 108, Miller 5 for 60) and 203 (Stollmeyer 54, Gomez 52). Australia 216 (Harvey 83, Miller 47, J. Trim 5 for 34) and 260 for nine (Hassett 102, Valentine 5 for 88).

AT Sydney. January 25 *to* 29. Australia won by 202 runs. Australia 116 (Gomez 7 for 55) and 377 (Miller 69, Hassett 64, C. C. McDonald 62, Hole 62, Worrell 4 for 95). West Indies 78 (Miller 5 for 26) and 213 (Stollmeyer 104, Lindwall 5 for 52).

Australia in West Indies 1955

AT Kingston. March 26 *to* 31. Australia won by nine wickets. Australia 515 for nine declared (K. R. Miller 147, R. N. Harvey 133, A. R. Morris 65, C. C. McDonald 50, R. Benaud 46) and 20 for one. West Indies 259 (C. L. Walcott 108, O. G. Smith 44, R. R. Lindwall 4 for 61) and 275 (Smith 104, J. K. Holt 60).

AT Port-of-Spain. April 11 *to* 16. Match drawn. West Indies 382 (E. D. Weekes 139, Walcott 126, G. S. Sobers 47, Lindwall 6 for 95) and 273 for four (Walcott 110, Weekes 87 not out, J. B. Stollmeyer 42). Australia 600 for nine declared (Harvey 133, Morris 111, McDonald 110, R. G. Archer 84, I. W. Johnson 66).

AT Georgetown. April 26 *to* 29. Australia won by eight wickets. West Indies 182 (Weekes 81, Benaud 4 for 15) and 207 (Walcott 73, F. M. Worrell 56, Johnson 7 for 44). Australia 257 (Benaud 68,

McDonald 61, Morris 44) and 133 for two (Harvey 41 not out).

AT Bridgetown. May 14 *to* 20. Match drawn. Australia 668 (Miller 137, Lindwall 118, Archer 98, Harvey 74, L. E. Favell 72, G. R. A. Langley 53, McDonald 46, T. Dewdney 4 for 125) and 249 (Johnson 57, Favell 53, D. S. Atkinson 5 for 56). West Indies 510 (Atkinson 219, dePeiza 122, Weekes 44, Sobers 43) and 234 for six (Walcott 83, Holt 49).

AT Kingston. June 11 *to* 17. Australia won by an innings and 82 runs. West Indies 357 (Walcott 155, Worrell 61, Weekes 56, Miller 6 for 107) and 319 (Walcott 110, Sobers 64). Australia 758 for eight declared (Harvey 204, Archer 128, McDonald 127, Benaud 121, Miller 109).

West Indies in Australia 1960-61

AT Brisbane. December 9 *to* 14. Match tied. West Indies 453 (G. S. Sobers 132, F. M. Worrell 65, J. S. Solomon 65, F. C. M. Alexander 60, W. W. Hall 50, A. K. Davidson 5 for 135) and 284 (Worrell 65, R. B. Kanhai 54, Solomon 47, Davidson 6 for 87). Australia 505 (N. C. O'Neill 181, R. B. Simpson 92, C. C. McDonald 57, L. E. Favell 45, Davidson 44, Hall 4 for 140) and 232 (Davidson 80, R. Benaud 52, Hall 5 for 63).

AT Melbourne. December 30 *to January* 3. Australia won by seven wickets. Australia 348 (K. D. Mackay 74, J. W. Martin 55, Favell 51, Simpson 49, O'Neill 40, Hall 4 for 51) and 70 for three. West Indies 181 (Kanhai 84, S. M. Nurse 70, Davidson 6 for 53) and 233 (C. C. Hunte 110, Alexander 72).

AT Sydney. January 13 *to* 18. West Indies won by 222 runs. West Indies 339 (Sobers 168, Nurse 43, Davidson 5 for 80, Benaud 4 for 86) and 326 (Alexander 108, Worrell 82, C. W. Smith 55, Benaud 4 for 113). Australia 202 (O'Neill 71, A. L. Valentine 4 for 67) and 241 (R. N. Harvey 85, O'Neill 70, L. R. Gibbs 5 for 66. Valentine 4 for 86).

AT Adelaide. January 27 *to February* 1. Match drawn. West Indies 393 (Kanhai 117, Worrell 71, Alexander 63 not out, Nurse 49, Benaud 5 for 96) and 432 for six declared (Kanhai 115, Alexander 87 not out, Hunte 79, Worrell 53, Smith 46). Australia 366 (Simpson 85, Benaud 77, McDonald 71, P. J. P. Burge 45, Gibbs 5 for 97) and 273 for nine (O'Neill 65, Mackay 62 not out, Burge 49, A. T. W. Grout 42).

AT Melbourne. February 10 *to* 15. Australia won by two wickets. West Indies 292 (Sobers 64, Solomon 45, P. D. Lashley 41, F. M. Misson 4 for 58) and 321 (Alexander 73, Hunte 52, Davidson 5 for 84). Australia 356 (McDonald 91, Simpson 75, Burge 68, Sobers 5 for

120, Gibbs 4 for 74) and 258 for eight (Simpson 92, Burge 53, O'Neill 48).

Australia in West Indies 1965

AT Kingston. March 3 *to* 8. West Indies won by 179 runs. West Indies 239 (A. W. White 57 not out, C. C. Hunte 41, L. C. Mayne 4 for 43) and 373 (Hunte 81, J. S. Solomon 76, B. F. Butcher 71, Mayne 4 for 56, P. I. Philpott 4 for 109). Australia 217 (N. J. N. Hawke 46 not out, N. C. O'Neill 40, W. W. Hall 5 for 60) and 216 (B. C. Booth 56, Hall 4 for 45).

AT Port-of-Spain. March 26 *to April* 1. Match drawn. West Indies 429 (Butcher 117, Hunte 89, G. S. Sobers 69, B. A. Davis 54, O'Neill 4 for 41) and 386 (Davis 58, Hunte 53, R. B. Kanhai 53, Solomon 48, Butcher 47). Australia 516 (R. M. Cowper 143, Booth 117, G. Thomas 61).

AT Georgetown. April 14 *to* 20. West Indies won by 212 runs. West Indies 355 (Kanhai 89, Butcher 49, Sobers 45, S. M. Nurse 42, Hawke 6 for 72) and 180 (Sobers 42, Philpott 4 for 49, Hawke 4 for 43). Australia 179 (Cowper 41) and 144 (L. R. Gibbs 6 for 29).

AT Bridgetown. May 5 *to* 11. Match drawn. Australia 650 for six declared (W. M. Lawry 210, R. B. Simpson 201, Cowper 102, O'Neill 51) and 175 for four declared (O'Neill 74 not out, Lawry 58). West Indies 573 (Nurse 201, Kanhai 129, Hunte 75, Sobers 55, C. C. Griffith 54, G. D. McKenzie 4 for 114) and 242 for five (Hunte 81, Davis 68).

AT Port-of-Spain. May 14 *to* 17. Australia won by 10 wickets. West Indies 224 (Kanhai 121) and 131 (Hunte 60 not out, McKenzie 5 for 33). Australia 294 (Simpson 72, Cowper 69, Griffith 6 for 46) and 63 for no wicket.

West Indies in Australia 1968-69

AT Brisbane. December 6 *to* 10. West Indies won by 125 runs West Indies 296 (R. B. Kanhai 94, M. C. Carew 83, A. N. Connolly 4 for 60) and 353 (C. H. Lloyd 129, Carew 71 not out, G. S. Camacho 40, J. W. Gleeson 5 for 122). Australia 284 (I. M. Chappell 117, W. M. Lawry 105, L. R. Gibbs 5 for 88) and 240 (Chappell 50, G. S. Sobers 6 for 73).

AT Melbourne. December 26 *to* 30. Australia won by an innings and 30 runs. West Indies 200 (R. C. Fredericks 76, B. F. Butcher 42, G. D. McKenzie 8 for 71) and 280 (S. M. Nurse 74, Sobers 67, Fredericks 47, Gleeson 5 for 61). Australia 510 (Lawry 205, Chappell 165, K. D. Walters 76, Sobers 4 for 97, Gibbs 4 for 139). *AT Sydney. January* 3 *to* 8. Australia won by 10 wickets. West Indies 264 (Lloyd 50, Sobers 49, McKenzie 4 for 85) and 324

(Butcher 101, Kanhai 69, Fredericks 43, Gleeson 4 for 91).
Australia 547 (Walters 118, I. R. Redpath 80, E. W. Freeman 76,
K. R. Stackpole 58, A. P. Sheahan 47, Gleeson 42 not out) and
42 for no wicket.

AT Adelaide. January 24 *to* 29. Match drawn. West Indies 276
(Sobers 110, Butcher 52, Freeman 4 for 52) and 616 (Butcher 118,
Carew 90, Kanhai 80, D. A. J. Holford 80, Sobers 52, Lloyd 42,
Nurse 40, Connolly 5 for 122). Australia 533 (Walters 110, Chappell
76, Lawry 62, Stackpole 62, McKenzie 59, Sheahan 51, Redpath
45, Gibbs 4 for 145) and 339 for nine (Chappell 96, Lawry 89, Stackpole 50, Walters 50).

AT Sydney. February 14 *to* 20. Australia won by 382 runs. Australia
619 (Walters 242, Lawry 151, Freeman 56, H. B. Taber 48,
Gleeson 45) and 394 for eight declared (Redpath 132, Walters 103,
McKenzie 40). West Indies 279 (Carew 64, Lloyd 53, Kanhai 44,
Connolly 4 for 61) and 352 (Nurse 137, Sobers 113).

Australia in West Indies 1973

AT Kingston. February 16 *to* 21. Match drawn. Australia 428 for
seven declared (R. W. Marsh 97, K. D. Walters 72, R. Edwards 63,
I. R. Redpath 46, K. R. Stackpole 44, G. S. Chappell 42, L. R.
Gibbs 4 for 85) and 260 for two declared (Stackpole 142, Redpath
60). West Indies 428 (M. L. C. Foster 125, R. B. Kanhai 84, L. G.
Rowe 76, A. I. Kallicharran 50, M. H. N. Walker 6 for 114, J. R.
Hammond 4 for 79) and 67 for three.

AT Bridgetown. March 9 *to* 14. Match drawn. Australia 324 (G. S.
Chappell 106, Marsh 78, I. M. Chappell 72) and 300 for two declared
(I. M. Chappell 106 not out, Walters 102 not out, Stackpole 53).
West Indies 391 (Kanhai 105, R. C. Fredericks 98, D. L. Murray
90, Walker 5 for 97) and 36 for no wicket.

AT Port-of-Spain. March 23 *to* 28. Australia won by 44 runs.
Australia 332 (Walters 112, Redpath 66, G. S. Chappell 56) and 281
(I. M. Chappell 97, Redpath 44, Gibbs 5 for 102). West Indies 280
(Kanhai 56, Kallicharran 53, Murray 40, T. J. Jenner 4 for 98)
and 289 (Kallicharran 91, Fredericks 76, K. J. O'Keeffe 4 for 57).
AT Georgetown. April 6 *to* 11. Australia won by 10 wickets. West
Indies 366 (C. H. Lloyd 178, Kanhai 57, Walters 5 for 66) and 109
(Hammond 4 for 38, Walker 4 for 45). Australia 341 (I. M. Chappell
109, Walters 81, G. S. Chappell 51) and 135 for no wicket (Stackpole
76 not out, Redpath 57 not out).

AT Port-of-Spain. April 21 *to* 26. Match drawn. Australia 419 for
eight declared (Edwards 74, Walters 70, I. M. Chappell 56, Marsh
56, G. S. Chappell 41) and 218 for seven declared (Gibbs 4 for 66).

West Indies 319 (Fredericks 73, Lloyd 59, Walker 5 for 75, Jenner 5 for 90) and 135 for five.

West Indies in Australia 1975-76

AT Brisbane. November 28 *to December* 2. Australia won by eight wickets. West Indies 214 (D. L. Murray 66, R. C. Fredericks 46, G. J. Gilmour 4 for 42) and 370 (L. G. Rowe 107, A. I. Kallicharran 101, Murray 55). Australia 366 (G. S. Chappell 123, A. Turner 81, R. W. Marsh 48, I. M. Chappell 41, L. R. Gibbs 5 for 102) and 219 for two (G. S. Chappell 109 not out, I. M. Chappell 74 not out).

AT Perth. December 12 *to* 16. West Indies won by an innings and 87 runs. Australia 329 (I. M. Chappell 156, Gilmour 45, M. A. Holding 4 for 88) and 169 (G. S. Chappell 43, A. M. E. Roberts 7 for 54). West Indies 585 (Fredericks 169, C. H. Lloyd 149, Murray 63, Kallicharran 57, K. D. Boyce 49 not out).

AT Melbourne. December 26 *to* 30. Australia won by eight wickets. West Indies 224 (Fredericks 59, I. V. A. Richards 41, J. R. Thomson 5 for 62, D. K. Lillee 4 for 56) and 312 (Lloyd 102). Australia 485 (G. J. Cosier 109, I. R. Redpath 102, Marsh 56, G. S. Chappell 52, Thomson 44, Roberts 4 for 126) and 55 for two.

AT Sydney. January 3 *to* 7. Australia won by seven wickets. West Indies 355 (Rowe 67, Lloyd 51, Fredericks 48, B. D. Julien 46 not out, Richards 44, M. H. N. Walker 4 for 70) and 128 (Murray 50, Thomson 6 for 50). Australia 405 (G. S. Chappell 182 not out, Turner 53) and 82 for three.

AT Adelaide. January 23 *to* 28. Australia won by 190 runs. Australia 418 (Redpath 103, Gilmour 95, G. N. Yallop 47, I. M. Chappell 42, V. A. Holder 5 for 108) and 345 for seven declared (Turner 136, Redpath 65, G. S. Chappell 48 not out, Yallop 43). West Indies 274 (Boyce 95 not out, Kallicharran 76, Thomson 4 for 68) and 299 (Richards 101, Boyce 69, Kallicharran 67).

AT Melbourne. January 31 *to February* 5. Australia won by 165 runs. Australia 351 (Redpath 101, G. S. Chappell 68, Yallop 57) and 300 for three declared (R. B. McCosker 109 not out, Redpath 70, G. S. Chappell 54 not out). West Indies 160 (Richards 50, Gilmour 5 for 34, Lillee 5 for 63) and 326 (Richards 98, Lloyd 91 not out, Kallicharran 44, Thomson 4 for 80).

Overall Record
RECORD PARTNERSHIPS FOR EACH WICKET
Australia

1st	382	W. M. Lawry and R. B. Simpson	Bridgetown	1965
2nd	298	W. M. Lawry and I. M. Chappell	Melbourne	1968-69
3rd	295	C. C. McDonald and R. N. Harvey	Kingston	1955
4th	336	W. M. Lawry and K. D. Walters	Sydney	1968-69
5th	220	K. R. Miller and R. G. Archer	Kingston	1955
6th	206	K. R. Miller and R. G. Archer	Bridgetown	1955

7th	134	A. K. Davidson and R. Benaud	Brisbane	1960–61
8th	137	R. Benaud and I. W. Johnson	Kingston	1955
9th	97	K. D. Mackay and J. W. Martin	Melbourne	1960–61
10th	73	J. W. Gleeson and A. N. Connolly	Sydney	1968–69

West Indies

1st	145	C. C. Hunte and B. A. Davis	Bridgetown	1965
2nd	165	M. C. Carew and R. B. Kanhai	Brisbane	1968–69
3rd	242	C. L. Walcott and E. D. Weekes	Port-of-Spain	1955
4th	198	L. G. Rowe and A. I. Kallicharran	Brisbane	1975–76
5th	210	R. B. Kanhai and M. L. C. Foster	Kingston	1973
6th	165	R. B. Kanhai and D. L. Murray	Bridgetown	1973
7th	347	D. S. Atkinson and C. dePeiza	Bridgetown	1955
8th	74	F. C. M. Alexander and L. R. Gibbs	Sydney	1960–61
9th	122	D. A. J. Holford and J. L. Hendriks	Adelaide	1968–69
10th	37	K. D. Boyce and L. R. Gibbs	Perth	1975–76

West Indies v. New Zealand

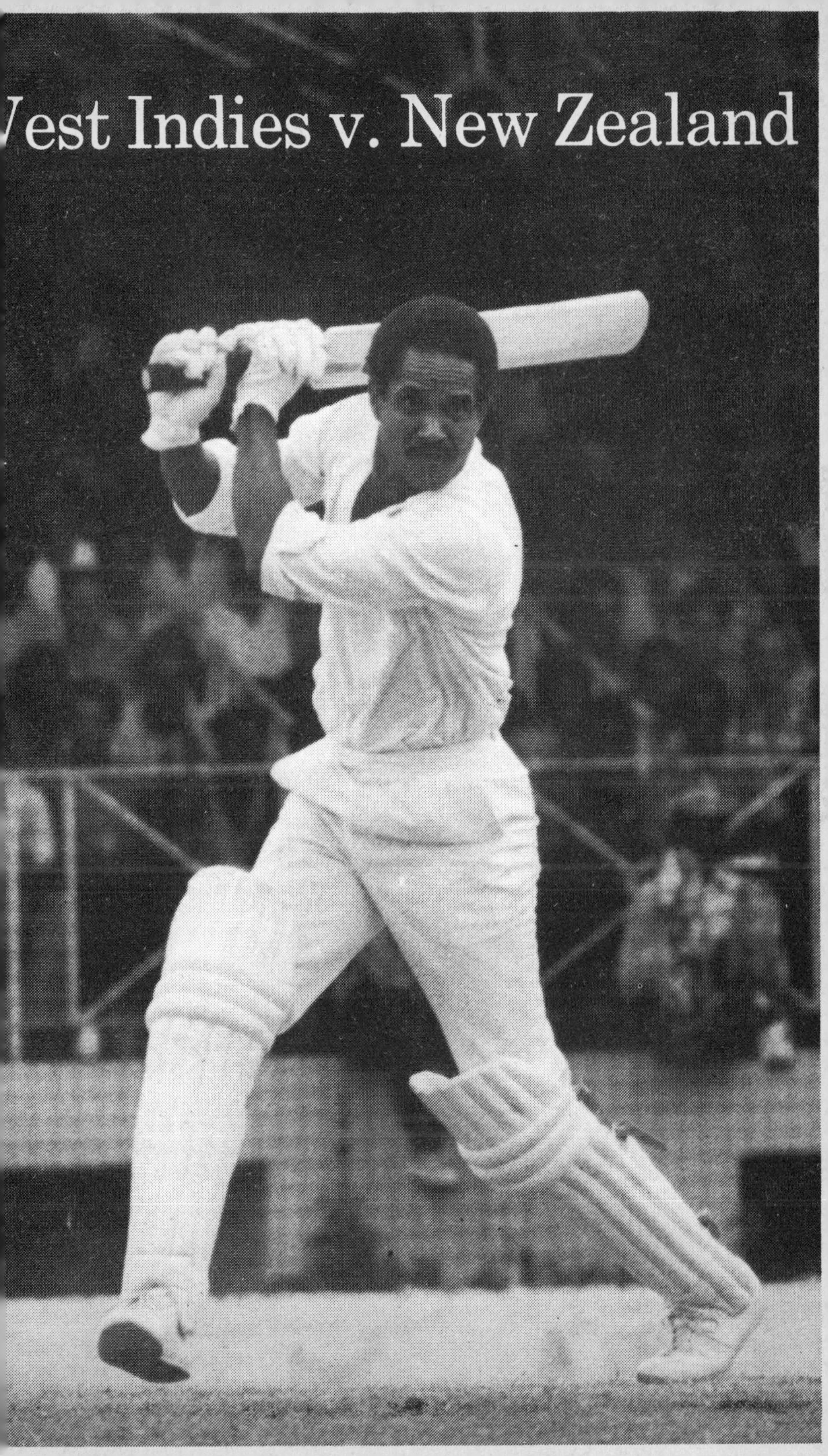

OVERALL RECORD

	Played	Won by W. Indies	Won by NZ	Drawn
In West Indies	5	0	0	5
In New Zealand	9	5	2	2
TOTALS	14	5	2	7

HIGHEST TOTALS
West Indies in New Zealand
　　546 for 6 declared　　　Auckland　　　1952
New Zealand in New Zealand
　　367 for 6　　　　　　　Christchurch　　1969
West Indies in West Indies
　　564 for 8　　　　　　　Bridgetown　　　1972
New Zealand in West Indies
　　543 for 3 declared　　　Georgetown　　　1972

LOWEST TOTALS
West Indies in New Zealand
　　77　　　　　　　　　　Auckland　　　　1956
New Zealand in New Zealand
　　74　　　　　　　　　　Dunedin　　　　　1956
West Indies in West Indies
　　133　　　　　　　　　　Bridgetown　　　1972
New Zealand in West Indies
　　162　　　　　　　　　　Port-of-Spain　　1972

MOST RUNS IN A SERIES
West Indies in New Zealand	558	S. M. Nurse	1969
New Zealand in New Zealand	239	B. F. Hastings	1969
West Indies in West Indies	487	R. C. Fredericks	1972
New Zealand in West Indies	672	G. M. Turner	1972

MOST WICKETS IN A SERIES
West Indies in New Zealand	20	S. Ramadhin	1956
New Zealand in New Zealand	17	R. C. Motz	1969
West Indies in West Indies	12	V. A. Holder	1972
New Zealand in West Indies	27	B. R. Taylor	1972

West Indies v. New Zealand

NEW ZEALAND has been treated as something of a poor relation by its fellow-Test-playing countries and the West Indies have been no exception. Only one series between the teams, New Zealand's first and only one to date in the Caribbean, has been contested over five Tests and two have been tacked on, almost as after-thoughts, to lengthy and wearisome tours of Australia. Yet the West Indians have always been immensely popular in New Zealand and any condescending view that the New Zealanders would not be attractive in the West Indies was given the lie in 1972 when the West Indies Board realised a profit from that sole series.

West Indian cricketers, in fact, played in New Zealand back in 1930 while in transit by boat through Wellington on their way to Australia. Poor weather, however, allowed little play in the one game arranged and West Indian hopes of shaking off the sea legs after a month's journey were frustrated.

West Indies in New Zealand 1952
It was not until 21 years later that the West Indies came to stay a little longer—this time to play two Tests after their Australian jaunt of 1951–52. These were the first Tests between the teams and, although the West Indies won the first by five wickets, the match was far closer than the result suggested. In the second, however, only rain prevented them from victory by a large margin.

The historic inaugural Test was played at Christchurch's Lancaster Park, a match in which the West Indian heroes of their 1950 successes in England filled the major roles. Worrell scored 71 and 62 not out and Walcott 65 in the first innings, when their fourth-wicket stand of 129 was made at a crucial time; Ramadhin and Valentine bowled twice as many overs as anyone else and took 14 of the wickets between them, Ramadhin nine.

Scott and the left-handed Sutcliffe were the best of the home team's batsmen but even they were ill at ease against the spin of Ramadhin and totals of 236 and 189 put too much onus on the bowlers. Even so, the West Indies were forced to fight hard until the very last ball. Tom Burtt's left-arm spin and the accurate medium-pace swing and cut of Hayes caused such a first-innings middle-order collapse after the Worrell-Walcott partnership that four wickets fell in the 180s before the wicketkeeper, Simpson

Guillen, hit out for 54, his highest score in first-class cricket. Whether that particular piece of providence prompted him or not is unclear but Guillen later settled in New Zealand and won his Test cap for the country of his adoption as well, the only West Indian to have done so. That his opponents were the West Indies (during the 1956 series) was what, as a native Trinidadian, he would refer to as lagniappe—a bonus, the icing on the cake.

The West Indian requirement of 139 appeared straightforward enough but, at 99 for five with only Worrell of their main batsmen left, the result hung in the balance. Worrell and the ever-reliable Gomez, with due care and attention, saw them home.

Auckland's Test was a nightmare for Sutcliffe, the New Zealand captain. He won the toss, sent the West Indies in and then, along with his 10 team-mates, was kept in the field for nearly two days while the opponents helped themselves to 546 for six declared. Stollmeyer scored 152 and, with Rae, added 197 for the first wicket; Worrell and Walcott also took centuries and Weekes 51. Rae was unfortunate to be bowled for 99 but, were it not for a generous act of sportsmanship by Moir, the leg-spinner, he would have been run out 90 short of that. In the simple motion of turning to regain his crease after backing up, Rae slipped and fell and lay helpless, short of his ground, when the ball was returned to Moir. The bowler, to mixed feelings, decided against taking advantage of a man when he is down and Rae continued.

With such a total staring ominously down on them from the scoreboard, the New Zealand batsmen, with the sole exception of Scott, who completed an excellent 84, again faded against the spin of Ramadhin and Valentine, with two wickets from Stollmeyer's leg-spin thrown in for good measure. They followed on nearly 400 behind and would almost certainly have been defeated on the final day but for the rain which allowed not a single ball.

West Indies in New Zealand 1956

New Zealand, not unnaturally, laid out the red carpet for the West Indians in 1956 for they were the first team to undertake a separate full-scale tour since England had done so in the 1930s.

The New Zealanders themselves arrived back home just in time for the series after completing the most ambitious overseas venture they had ever undertaken, a 3½-months jaunt through the Indian sub-continent during which they played three Tests against Pakistan and five against India. If their cricket, at times, did show signs of staleness it was not surprising.

For their part, the West Indies brought a largely experimental side, captained by Denis Atkinson. There were several young

West Indies v. New Zealand Tests have had their moments: Lawrence Rowe, who scored 214 and 100 not out in his first Test appearance, is seen, lips pursed in his perpetual whistle, during the double-century. Wicketkeeper is the late Ken Wadsworth.

The dropped catch which probably cost New Zealand victory in the third Test in 1971–72: Sobers, 87, edges Bruce Taylor to slip, where Terry Jarvis, hands apparently ideally positioned, is about to miss the catch.

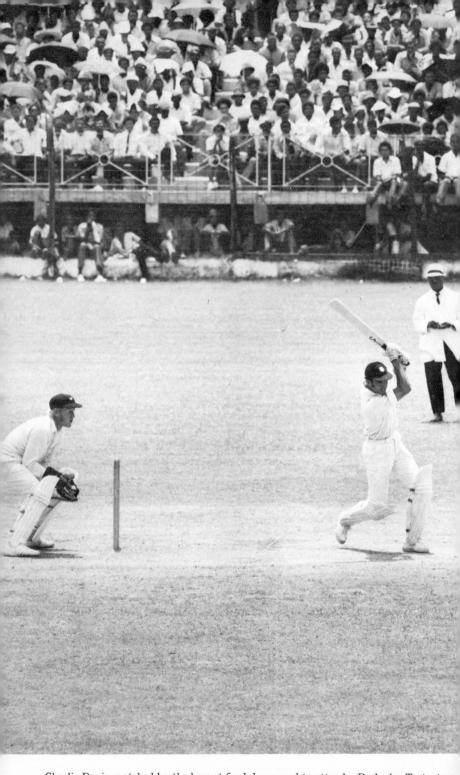

Charlie Davis, watched by the largest final-day crowd to attend a Barbados Test, steps ' to drive during his vital innings of **183** in the third Test against New Zealand, 1971–7.

Willie Alle

ne of New Zealander Bruce Taylor's seven wickets in the West Indies first innings of the
ird Test, 1971–72: the groping David Holford caught behind for three.   *Willie Alleyne*

he saddest incident in a generally sad tour by India in 1962 was the blow their captain,
ari Contractor, suffered while batting against Charlie Griffith in the Barbados match.
owel held to his right temple, Contractor is being helped off the field. A series of operations
ved his life.   *Barbados Daily News*

One of Lance Gibbs' eight wickets in India's second innings of the Bridgetown Test, 1962: Chandu Borde pulls a catch to silly mid-on, where Frank Worrell goes down on his haunches to clutch it

players on their first overseas tours who, it was felt, would benefit from the exposure—the all-rounders Sobers and Smith among them. These were interspersed with a few well-established stalwarts and it was on them that the major responsibility rested for winning the four-Test series 3–1.

Weekes, the only W chosen, made the trip a rousing personal triumph. He treated all bowling almost as he pleased, reeling off six first-class centuries, five of them in succession. In each of the first three Tests he passed three figures in the only innings he batted. He was the main element in the formula for success. The others were Ramadhin and Valentine, whose spin was never properly countered, and Atkinson and Goddard, both of whom fulfilled important roles on and off the field. Goddard had been the captain four years earlier; now he returned as player-manager.

None of the young players lived up to expectations and, from this point of view, the tour was a disappointment for the West Indies.

For New Zealand, the series will always be remembered as the one which brought them their first victory in Test cricket after 26 long years in the wilderness. In the final Test, at Eden Park, they outplayed the West Indies to win, deservedly and conclusively, by 190 runs.

Above all else, the tour was a great success in public relations. At the end of it, L. B. Schauner, president of the New Zealand Cricket Council, wrote to the West Indies Board, stating: "If international cricket were always played as your team played on this tour then no-one could possibly have any fears or doubts about its future and what a boon it would be to international goodwill if international sport could copy the example of your team on this tour".

The West Indies won the first Test at Dunedin by an innings and 71 runs, seizing the initiative on the first day and never slackening it. Ramadhin and Valentine destroyed batsmen shackled by their own self-doubts and a total of 74 took 62.2 painful overs to compile. Ramadhin claimed 6 for 23 from 21.2 overs, Valentine 2 for 28 from 24 and it could have been England, 1950, all over again.

Weekes' first century of the series, a typically ruthless 123, and his third-wicket partnership of 162 in an hour and 40 minutes with Smith emphasised the paucity of New Zealand's total and, even though the home team batted far more steadily second time, arrears of 279 were far too demanding. John Beck, a 20-year-old left-hander in his first full season, played purposefully for the top score of 66 but spin, this time Ramadhin's and Smith's, was again responsible for their dismissal for 208.

The second Test at Lancaster Park followed a similar course. A century by Weekes followed by incisive bowling by the spinners saw the West Indies home by an innings and 64 runs, again inside three days. This time, however, it was not Weekes alone. He had come and gone at the sixth wicket with only 169 scored and it was left to the captain and the manager to rally the cause with a stand of 143 for the seventh wicket.

Atkinson, taking the attack to the bowlers, was finally out for 85, Goddard was undefeated at the end with a more mundane 83, and Ramadhin, who had scored 44 in the first Test, pleased himself with another useful score of 33. He was immediately back at it when New Zealand replied, his 5 for 46 causing another collapse to 158 all out. So New Zealand followed on yet again and, even though Atkinson only called on Ramadhin for nine overs this time, Valentine and Smith were equally troublesome and another large win was the result.

By now, Weekes' mastery of the New Zealanders was entrenched and they suffered yet again on the opening day of the third Test as he powered his way to 156, sharing century stands with Atkinson and the wicketkeeper, Binns, at better than run-a-minute. New Zealand, however, had themselves to blame this time for Weekes was dropped when three. A total of 404 would hardly have been possible had that chance, at slip off Cave, stuck but, judged on earlier performances, it was clearly beyond the capacity of the New Zealanders. They succeeded in scoring just enough to avoid another two-to-one loss.

Beck again played resolutely for 55 in the first innings, when he had useful support from Taylor and the immigrant, Guillen, and Taylor was to the fore in the second with a splendid 77, characterised by several fine shots. But these efforts were far from enough.

New Zealand, therefore, had lost the series by the time it arrived in Auckland for the final match but their most glorious moment in Test cricket was soon to follow. There was no hint of it in the early exchanges. Their batsmen, as usual, struggled and four were down for 87 before their captain, Reid, who had achieved very little with the bat until then, introduced a spirit of adventure into their cricket. His assertive 84 and a partnership of 104 with Beck were responsible for his team's best total of the series, 255. Utilising a pitch freshened by overnight rain, Tom Dewdney took four of the last five wickets to finish with 5 for 21 but the assistance he gained was also an advantage for Mac-Gibbon and Cave, New Zealand's admirable new ball pair. They did not waste it, routing the West Indies for 145 in which 64 by the Trinidadian opener Hammond Furlonge and a steady 28 by an 18-year-old by the name of Alfie Roberts from St Vincent stood out. It was Roberts' first Test innings—and the first time a player from the "small islands" had played in a Test.

For the first time in the series, New Zealand were on top and they remained so. Atkinson bowled his heart out to take 7 for 53 from 40 overs in their second innings but his team was left four hours to get 268 when Reid declared with nine wickets down. In no time, they were 22 for six against the swerve and cut of Cave and Beard and it was clear history was in the making. Offices hurriedly closed and spectators streamed into the ground for the occasion. Weekes and Binns delayed it for a while but, with well over an hour to spare, Cave claimed the last wicket for the New Zealanders' first win in Test cricket, a momentous event. For the West Indies, their total of 77 was their lowest in Tests, lowered seven years later by one run by Pakistan.

West Indies in New Zealand 1969

The West Indies arrived in Dunedin in February, 1969, tired and disillusioned after a most disheartening series in Australia. They appeared to have little heart for the month or so they were to spend in New Zealand and their lack of spirit was clear from their cricket. In addition, they found New Zealand cricket far less reticent than they had been led to expect.

It was, in many ways, a sad tour for the West Indies for it signalled the end of several great careers. Nurse went out in grand style with 558 runs from five innings, his finale being an innings of 258 in the third Test, the last he played. Hall and Griffith, the great fast-bowling association, left the scene with somewhat less flourish, unceremoniously dropped from the team to tour England the following summer. Kanhai, nursing an injured knee, took no part in the tour and also missed that to England. Sobers, on his second visit to New Zealand, achieved nothing with either bat or ball, a major disappointment for the public.

For all that, the cricket produced its great moments and none more so than the first Test. Both sides were positive from the outset and a bold declaration by Dowling, the New Zealand captain, brought a challenging response from the West Indies, who won by five wickets in a stirring finish.

Sobers' decision to field first after winning the toss appeared all but vindicated when only Congdon (with 85) of the earlier New Zealand batsmen displayed any confidence. The total stood at 152 for six when Bruce Taylor, a swaggering, ambidextious all-rounder, strode to the crease. When he left it 110 minutes later, it was 323 all out, Taylor 124 with five sixes and 14 fours. His fifty took half an hour, his century 86 minutes, the fifth-fastest in Test history. It was a thrilling exhibition of power-hitting.

The left-handed Carew brought his form across the Tasman Sea with him and passed his maiden Test century; Nurse was in fine touch for 95. The pair added 172 for the second wicket but then there was such poor batting that New Zealand carried a lead of 47 into their second innings.

Buoyed by their early successes, New Zealand's batting was more full of self-confidence than it had been for some time in the second innings. Dowling and Turner started with a century opening stand and Pollard passed an undefeated half-century. With eight wickets down, Dowling made his widely-acclaimed decision first thing on the final morning—and the West Indies took him up on it. Nurse led the way for them in great fashion with three hours 35 minutes of pure perfection which brought him 168 runs and, by the time he departed, the job needed only the finishing touches which were supplied by Butcher's un-defeated 78.

Dowling's declaration brought no criticism in New Zealand and, if anything, his refreshing spirit appeared to infuse the side with new life for the second Test for it scored a justifiable victory by six wickets.

The quick bowlers generally dominated a match played on a fast, green pitch. Dick Motz, who later that year became the first New Zealand bowler to 100 Test wickets, kept the West Indian first innings down to 297, a total highly dependent on gritty batting by the tailend. He took 6 for 69. Richard Edwards, schooled by the Atkinson brothers in Barbados, was equally effective at similar medium-pace for the West Indies with 5 for 84 and, after New Zealand had passed 150 with only two wickets down, there was little in the first innings.

New Zealand clinched the match on the third day when Motz, Cunis, another medium-pacer, and Yuile, left-arm slow, bowled the West Indies out for 148. Griffith and Edwards reacted to the news that they had been dropped from the team to England with the fastest bowling of the tour and caused the home team a few anxious moments but it was only a temporary phenomenon. New Zealand had levelled the series early on the fourth and final day.

New Zealand had earned new respect for itself in international cricket by now and this was enhanced by the character shown in saving the third and final Test, when Nurse and Carew, the form batsmen, subjected their bowlers to a searching examination. The former stroked the ball with a fine sense of timing and made no error in compiling his highest Test score and the highest individual innings on the ground in eight hours with a six and 35 fours. Carew was more painstaking over 91, which took just over five hours. They added 231 together; the third wicket did not fall until 326 and yet the final total was only 417.

For the only time in the series, New Zealand's batting let them down when they replied and, undone principally by the spin of Gibbs and Holford on a turning pitch, they fell short by 200. When they followed on with more than a day remaining, the West Indies appeared likely to clinch the match and the series but an opening partnership of 115 by Dowling and Turner, followed by a maiden Test century by Hastings (117 not out), made the match safe for the home team by as early as midway through the final day.

The result was, unquestionably, the fairest one for there was little to separate the teams. What was obvious was the fact that the West Indies were in for hard times and that New Zealand, conversely, were entering a period when they could hold their own against any opponents.

New Zealand in West Indies 1972

New Zealand's first tour of the Caribbean produced an unenviable record. It was the first by an international team to end without a result in any of the first-class matches. It is true that, even with the inevitable frustration of drawn matches, there were several days when the cricket was tense and interesting. On the whole, however, the tempo was unbearably slow. Not a single day in the series yielded more than 300 runs.

In addition, the series was unfortunate to have been stricken by perhaps the worst Test match ever witnessed in the West Indies, the fourth at Georgetown. It was a pointless, boring contest over its five days, consumed by a glut of runs. In most cases the New Zealanders were the guilty party in the matter of slow play yet, in many ways, their overall performance was an outstanding one.

They arrived with only 15 players, the smallest touring party ever brought to the West Indies for a five-Tests programme. Before the start of the second Test, the fast bowler Collinge was forced to return home for personal reasons and a replacement had to be sought. Even then the captain, Dowling, was carrying on a vain struggle to recover from a back injury and he took no further part in proceedings after the second Test, also returning home. Reduced to 14 players, the New Zealanders were later without the services of the 41-year-old leg-spinner Alabaster for long periods because of injury.

Allied to these misfortunes, they had to endure a poor start to the tour as they tried to adjust to conditions far removed from what they had been led to expect. When by mid-afternoon on the first day of the second Test they were 99 for six their stocks could hardly have been lower. However, they kept their spirit, recovered in that innings through a spate of dropped catches and never looked back. Paradoxically, it was a dropped catch, on the final day of the third Test, which cost them their best opportunity of winning.

There were three outstanding individuals—the batsmen Turner, who totalled 1214 runs on the tour and emulated Patsy Hendren's 1930 record of four double-centuries in a West Indian season, and Congdon, who succeeded Dowling to the captaincy and led by personal example: and the fast-medium bowler Taylor, who took 27 wickets in the four Tests he played. These were the best performances yet it was still very much a team effort, with the fielding achieving remarkable standards.

Having been beaten by India the previous season, the failure to conclude a single result against New Zealand stirred renewed public dissatisfaction in the West Indies. Two new batsmen in the mould of the great West Indians emerged, the Jamaican Rowe and the Guyanese Kallicharran, but these were small comforts. Sobers, labouring under the handicap of an unsettled team, had clearly become disinterested in the captaincy and, indeed, the game as a whole and it was to be his last series at the helm of the team he took over from Worrell 39 Tests earlier.

Each Test was a recitation of history-making individual feats. From a purely cricket point of view, the third, which the West Indies fought desperately to save, and the fifth, when the roles were reversed, were the best.

The first at Sabina was completely dominated by Rowe and Turner. Rowe, a slim, ice-cool Jamaican, became a national hero by scoring 214 in the first innings and 100 not out in the second of his very first Test, something never before accomplished. Through it all, as he wheeled off an array of effortless strokes, he hardly perspired and his lips were permanently pursed in a whistle. Turner's epic 223 not out was undoubtedly more valuable to his team for it was built from the ruins of 108 for five, replying to 508 for four declared (Fredericks' 163 assisting in a second-wicket stand of 269 with Rowe). Turner and the wicketkeeper, Wadsworth, dismissed the follow-on threat with a partnership of 220 and the determined opener saw all 10 wickets fall during his 563 minutes' batting.

On the final day, there were times when Holford's leg-spin looked capable of seizing victory for the West Indies but Burgess' attractive 101 scotched that.

The second Test, at the Queen's Park Oval, would almost certainly have brought a different result had not the West Indies caught so lamentably on the first day. Congdon, let off three times before he was 30, led the recovery from 99 for six to 348 with 166 not out and, as the pitch became slower and slower, the possibility of a result receded. It was as good as drawn as early as the fourth morning.

There was no such resignation in Barbados. There, on a pitch better for bowling than batting on the opening morning, Sobers erred in going in first after winning the toss. As Taylor used his height to cut and bounce the ball alarmingly, the West Indies retired to lunch in shambles at 44 for five. Thanks to an undefeated 44 from the wicketkeeper, Findlay, they managed to reach 133, Taylor's bag being 7 for 74. Thereafter, they were always engaged in a fierce uphill fight for the pitch had eased and was on its best behaviour while centuries from Congdon and Hastings, in a partnership of 175 for the fourth wicket, carried New Zealand to 422, a lead of 289, with just over two days remaining.

The early part of their second innings did not inspire any confidence among their supporters. When the fifth wicket fell first ball after lunch on the fourth day at 171 and Sobers entered belatedly at No. 7, all was as good as over. Except, of course, that Sobers was there. Davis, as steady a partner as he could wish for, was there too. When the pair carried the score to 297 without being separated at the end of the fourth day, the public sensed something dramatic was in the offing. The ground was packed to capacity for the final day, a Tuesday, and the spectators were not disappointed. Sobers, their idol, scored 142, Davis 183 run out after 10 hours of strict self-denial and the match was drawn. Two spilled chances proved New Zealand's undoing. Davis, when 18, was dropped at slip by Turner off the left-arm spinner Howarth; when 87, Sobers offered a catch to slip off Taylor which Jarvis spilled.

The Bourda Test was another draw—but of a completely different kind. Kallicharran emulated Rowe's earlier feat of scoring a century on his Test debut on his home ground but this was overshadowed by the first-wicket partnership between Turner and Jarvis which lasted seven hours and 186 overs and which realised 387, the second-highest for the wicket in all Test cricket, the highest against the West Indies and, by a long way, the highest for New Zealand. Perhaps the earlier loss of three hours to rain and 20 minutes to a crowd disturbance convinced the New Zealanders that there was nothing to play for but records. Nevertheless, there was no excuse for the crawl to which Turner (who went on to make 259) and Jarvis (182) subjected the spectators.

On a pitch which recognised the rights of the bowlers, the final Test was a keen contest. The West Indies tried desperately to break the deadlock and they came close, but the defiant New Zealanders kept them out, Taylor and Wadsworth batting out the final hour and three-quarters together to ensure that their team did not suffer the frustration of a last-minute defeat.

Kallicharran's second consecutive century was the best in a West Indian total of 368 in which Sobers batted at No. 8. Inshan Ali, the little Trinidadian left-arm chinaman and googly bowler, then presented his captain with the option of enforcing the follow-on by taking 5 for 59 as New Zealand fell for 162, their lowest total of the series. Sobers, however, chose to bat again, press for quick runs and then give his bowlers most of the final two days of the six-day match to clinch victory. As it turned out, rain badly thwarted his plans, restricting play to an hour and a quarter on the fifth day.

Even at that, New Zealand only just managed to hold out. It was fitting that Taylor and Wadsworth should have been the two who remained steadfast at the finish for no cricketers epitomised the great spirit of their team throughout the series better than these two.

West Indies in New Zealand 1951-52

AT Christchurch. February 8 *to* 12. West Indies won by five wickets. New Zealand 236 (V. J. Scott 45, B. Sutcliffe 45, S. Ramadhin 5 for 86) and 189 (Ramadhin 4 for 39). West Indies 287 (F. M. Worrell 71, C. L. Walcott 65, S. C. Guillen 54, T. B. Burtt 5 for 69) and 142 for five (Worrell 62 not out).

AT Auckland. February 15 *to* 19. Match drawn. West Indies 546 for six declared (J. B. Stollmeyer 152, Walcott 115, Worrell 100). New Zealand 160 (Scott 84) and 17 for one.

West Indies in New Zealand 1955–56

AT Dunedin. February 3 *to* 6. West Indies won by an innings and 71 runs. New Zealand 74 (S. Ramadhin 6 for 23) and 208 (J. E. F. Beck 66, B. Sutcliffe 48). West Indies 353 (E. D. Weekes 123, O. G. Smith 64, J. D. C. Goddard 48 not out, Ramadhin 44, R. W. Blair 4 for 90).

AT Christchurch. February 18 *to* 21. West Indies won by an innings and 64 runs. West Indies 386 (Weekes 103, D. S. Atkinson 85, Goddard 83). New Zealand 158 (Ramadhin 5 for 46) and 164 (J. R. Reid 40, A. L. Valentine 5 for 32, Smith 4 for 75).

AT Wellington. March 3 *to* 7. West Indies won by nine wickets. West Indies 404 (Weekes 156, B. H. Pairaudeau 68, Atkinson 60) and 13 for one. New Zealand 208 (Beck 55, D. D. Taylor 43) and 208 (Taylor 77, S. N. McGregor 41, Atkinson 5 for 66).

AT Auckland. March 9 *to* 13. New Zealand won by 190 runs. New Zealand 255 (Reid 84, L. S. M. Miller 47, T. Dewdney 5 for 21) and 157 for nine declared (S. C. Guillen 41, Atkinson 7 for 53). West Indies 145 (H. A. Furlonge 64, H. B. Cave 4 for 22, A. R. MacGibbon 4 for 44) and 77 (Cave 4 for 21).

West Indies in New Zealand 1968–69

AT Auckland. February 27 *to March* 3. West Indies won by five wickets. New Zealand 323 (B. R. Taylor 124, B. E. Congdon 85) and 297 for eight declared (G. T. Dowling 71, V. Pollard 51 not out, G. M. Turner 40). West Indies 276 (M. C. Carew 109, S. M. Nurse 95) and 348 for five (Nurse 168, B. F. Butcher 78 not out).
AT Wellington. March 7 *to* 11. New Zealand won by six wickets. West Indies 297 (J. L. Hendriks 54 not out. Butcher 50, C. H. Lloyd 44, R. C. Motz 6 for 69) and 148 (Butcher 59). New Zealand 282 (Turner 74, Congdon 52, R. M. Edwards 5 for 84) and 166 for four (B. F. Hastings 62 not out).

AT Christchurch. March 13 *to* 17. Match drawn. West Indies 417 (Nurse 258, Carew 91, Motz 5 for 113). New Zealand 217 (Taylor 43 not out, Congdon 42, D. A. J. Holford 4 for 66) and 367 for six (Hastings 117 not out, Dowling 76, Pollard 44, Congdon 43).

New Zealand in West Indies 1972

AT Sabina Park. February 16 *to* 21. Match drawn. West Indies 508 for four declared (L. G. Rowe 214, R. C. Fredericks 163, M. C. Carew 43) and 218 for three declared (Rowe 100 not out, C. A. Davis 41). New Zealand 386 (G. M. Turner 223 not out, K. J. Wadsworth 78) and 236 for six (M. G. Burgess 101, D. A. J. Holford 4 for 55).

AT Queen's Park. March 9 *to* 14. Match drawn. New Zealand 348
(B. E. Congdon 166 not out, R. S. Cunis 51, B. R. Taylor 46, V. A.
Holder 4 for 60) and 288 for three declared (Turner 95, Congdon
82, Burgess 62 not out). West Indies 341 (Davis 90, Fredericks 69,
Taylor 4 for 41) and 121 for five.

AT Kensington. March 23 *to* 28. Match drawn. West Indies 133
T. M. Frindlay 44 not out, Taylor 7 for 74) and 564 for eight
(Davis 183, G. S. Sobers 142, Rowe 51, Holford 50, Carew 45).
New Zealand 422 (Congdon 126, B. F. Hastings 105, Sobers 4 for
64).

AT Bourda. April 6 *to* 11. Match drawn. West Indies 365 for seven
declared. (A. I. Kallicharran 100 not out, G. A. Greenidge 50, C. H.
Lloyd 43, Fredericks 41) and 86 for no wicket (Fredericks 42 not
out). New Zealand 543 for three declared (Turner 259, T. W. Jarvis
182, Congdon 61 not out).

AT Queen's Park. April 20 *to* 26. Match drawn. West Indies 368
(Kallicharran 101, Fredericks 60, Holford 46 ret hurt, Davis 40)
and 194 (Holder 42, Taylor 5 for 41). New Zealand 162 (Jarvis
40, Inshan Ali 5 for 59) and 253 for seven (Congdon 58, Turner
50, Taylor 42 not out, Wadsworth 40 not out, Holder 4 for 41).

PARTNERSHIP RECORDS
West Indies:

1st	197	J. B. Stollmeyer and A. F. Rae	Auckland	1952
2nd	269	R. C. Fredericks and L. G. Rowe	Kingston	1972
3rd	174	S. M. Nurse and B. F. Butcher	Auckland	1969
4th	162	E. D. Weekes and O. G. Smith	Dunedin	1956
5th	189	F. M. Worrell and C. L. Walcott	Auckland	1952
6th	254	C. A. Davis and G. S. Sobers	Bridgetown	1972
7th	143	D. S. Atkinson and J. D. C. Goddard	Christchurch	1956
8th	65	J. D. C. Goddard and S. Ramadhin	Dunedin	1956
9th	46	J. L. Hendriks and R. M. Edwards	Wellington	1969
		Inshan Ali and V. A. Holder	Port-of-Spain	1972
10th	31	T. M. Findlay and G. C. Shillingford	Bridgetown	1972

New Zealand:

1st	387	G. M. Turner and T. W. Jarvis	Georgetown	1972
2nd	119	G. M. Turner and B. E. Congdon	Port-of-Spain	1972
3rd	75	G. T. Dowling and B. E. Congdon	Christchurch	1969
4th	175	B. E. Congdon and B. F. Hastings	Bridgetown	1972

5th	110	B. F. Hastings and V. Pollard	Christchurch	1969
6th	220	G. M. Turner and K. J. Wadsworth	Kingston	1972
7th	90	J. E. F. Beck and A. M. Moir	Dunedin	1956
8th	136	B. E. Congdon and R. S. Cunis	Port-of-Spain	1972
9th	50	F. L. H. Mooney and D. D. Beard	Christchurch	1952
10th	41	B. E. Congdon and J. C. Alabaster	Port-of-Spain	1972

West Indies v. India

OVERALL RECORD

	Tests	Won by W. Indies	Won by India	Drawn
In West Indies	19	8	2	9
In India	18	9	2	7
TOTALS	37	17	4	16

HIGHEST TOTALS

West Indies in India :
> 644 for 8 declared   New Delhi   1958–59

India in India :
> 454   New Delhi   1948–49

West Indies in West Indies :
> 631 for 8 declared   Kingston   1962

India in West Indies :
> 444   Kingston   1953

LOWEST TOTALS

West Indies in India :
> 154   Madras   1974–75

India in India :
> 118   Bangalore   1974–75

West Indies in West Indies :
> 214   Port-of-Spain   1971

India in West Indies :
> 97†   Kingston   1976
> (†Batted with five men absent hurt.)
> 98   Port-of-Spain   1962

MOST RUNS IN A SERIES

West Indies in West Indies :	716	E. D. Weekes	1953
India in West Indies :	774	S. M. Gavaskar	1971
West Indies in India :	779	E. D. Weekes	1948–49
India in India :	560	R. S. Modi	1948–49

MOST WICKETS IN A SERIES

West Indies in West Indies :	28	A. L. Valentine	1953
India in West Indies :	27	S. P. Gupte	1953
West Indies in India :	32	A. M. E. Roberts	1974–75
India in India :	22	S. P. Gupte	1958–59

West Indies v. India

INDIA was the first country visited by the West Indies after World War II, a long and rigorous assignment which was the start of a frequent exchange. Since then, only England have played more Tests against the West Indies than India and, even so, the Indians have toured the Caribbean just as often.

The reasons are not hard to find and involve more than simply cricket. At the turn of the century, hundreds of thousands of Indians were brought to the West Indies as indentured labour to the sugar plantations, mainly in Trinidad and Guyana, where their descendants now comprise half the total populations. To a large extent, they have maintained their cultural and religious heritage and still have strong ties with their ancestral home. None of the four Indian teams which have played in the Caribbean has possessed any extraordinary strength yet each has been massively supported in Trinidad and Guyana. The gates are correspondingly good and the arrangement profitable.

Ethnic divisions between those of East Indian and those of African descent in Trinidad and Guyana have been sharp and a Test match between India (or, to a lesser extent, Pakistan) and the West Indies at the Queen's Park Oval or Bourda accentuates them. In many ways, the attitude of the East Indian in Port-of-Spain or Georgetown corresponds with that of the West Indian in London or Birmingham; both tend to consider themselves immigrants, one of somewhat longer vintage than the other, and both identify with the team representing the country of their origin rather than the country of their adoption.

West Indian cricket has always been held in high esteem in India, a fact immediately obvious to anyone who has been to that vast country. The tradition was first established by the pioneers of the 1948–49 tour.

West Indies in India 1948–49

Pioneers they were in every sense for not only were they the first West Indian team to India but modes of travel and accommodation were, more often than not, unbelievably harsh. Long distances were covered by train, mostly in great heat with few amenities. Some journeys took over 30 hours and one, from Delhi to Poona, fully two days. The fact that it was not long after the traumatic partition of the country aggravated the situation for a tour which started in early october and did not end until early March. Nevertheless the trip was an unqualified success. The team was, generally speaking, youthful and eager to prove that its successes against the MCC a few months earlier had been no flash in the pan. For the great majority, it was the first experience outside the West Indies and they knew that reputations could be established by performances.

There was, almost inevitably, some controversy over the selection of the team. Worrell, playing his first season as professional with Radcliffe, was overlooked when he refused the Board's terms (all travel and accommodation paid for plus "a sum not exceeding £3 15s per week to cover out-of-pocket expenses") and even though India had asked that he be included. The tall Jamaican fast bowler Hines Johnson, who had wrecked England in the final Test in March, also announced he was unavailable. Jimmy Cameron, a Jamaican off-spinner then studying at university in Canada, and Allan Rae, a Jamaican left-handed batsman doing law in London at the time, were chosen among the initial 15. When the Indian Board agreed to the addition of a sixteenth player, the young Jamaican Ken Rickards was added to the list. As it turned out, even 16 were insufficient for the task as the great Headley, nearing the age of 40, found the demands on his health and fitness too exacting and played only four matches in all.

On pitches which were simply too true to be good and against bowling which lacked the penetration of great pace or vicious spin, the batsmen prospered. The West Indies helped themselves to 11 centuries in the five Tests, four of them in succession to the rapacious Weekes to add to that he claimed in his previous innings against England. It was, and still is, a Test record and it would surely have been six in a row had he not suffered a questionable run-out decision when 90 in his fifth hand of the series at Madras. His 779 runs in only seven innings was a phenomenal return and he was joined in the feast of runs by Stollmeyer, Walcott, Rae, Christiani and Gomez of his own side and Vijay Hazare and Rusi Modi, who both exceeded 500 runs for the home team.

The effect of such predominance by the batsmen was that the first three Tests were drawn and it was not until some effort was made by the groundsmen to even the balance in the fourth and fifth that the contest became fairer. The West Indies won the fourth at Madras by an innings and the last, at Bombay's Brabourne Stadium, was drawn in a finish of pulsating excitement.

The first Test between the two countries, at New Delhi, was a delight for statisticians and batsmen. The West Indies lost Rae,

Stollmeyer and Headley to the outswing of Rangachari with only 27 scored yet amassed 631, their highest score in Test cricket at the time. Four men recorded centuries—Walcott, Gomez, Weekes and Christiani—to equal the same ratio England had achieved against Australia at The Oval in 1938. Walcott and Gomez, whose fourth-wicket partnership initially turned the tide, added 267, then the highest for any wicket for the West Indies in Test cricket.

India's batsmen also made use of the placid pitch but what would have been adequate in normal circumstances was not so in these. A total of 454, the highlight of which was Adhikari's undefeated 114, meant following on and when six were down for 152 with an hour and 20 minutes remaining in the second innings, a West Indian win was likely. However, Adhikari and Sarwate, inspired by a chanting crowd, pulled their team to safety.

The second Test, at the Brabourne Stadium, again saw India under pressure to save the match after another gigantic West Indian total—629 for six declared. This time, the home team earned the draw more comfortably than they had done at New Delhi.

Rae and Stollmeyer set the pattern with a stand of 134 for the first wicket and the left-hander continued to a sedate 104. Then Weekes, with 194, Christiani, 74, and Cameron, 75 not out, accelerated despite the steady, mostly negative spin of Mankad and Hazare. The innings lasted into the third day of the five-day match and when India were out for 273 midway through the fourth day, the West Indies were scenting victory, even more so as the openers fell quickly to the new ball when the follow-on was enforced. However, the chance was spoiled by catching errors, principally off Ferguson's leg-spin, which allowed Modi and Hazare to put on 156 for the third wicket and Hazare and Amarnath a further 144 unbroken for the fourth, and stumps were drawn at 333 for three.

If Calcutta's Eden Gardens did not witness the same heavy scoring from the West Indies as did New Delhi and Bombay, at least the huge crowds saw history created by Weekes, whose great form was reflected in scores of 162 in the first innings and 101 in the second, his fifth Test century in succession. Walcott's 54 and 108 were the only other West Indian innings of substance in totals of 366 and 336 for nine declared. India's position was formidable at the end of the second day when they were 201 for two in their first innings but they collapsed to 272 all out to Gomez's medium-pace, Ferguson's leg-spin and Goddard's off-breaks. Their second innings, in which every West Indian but Rae bowled, and which finished at 325 for three, was simply an exercise in defence after Goddard had set them 431 to win.

The Madras Test broke the stalemate. The ground had been used for the preceding match against a South Zone team and the West Indies had been heartened by the pace of the pitch on which Gomez took 9 for 24 in a first-innings total of 46. Consequently, both Jones and Trim, the only fast bowlers available, were chosen and this and Goddard's continuing luck with the toss were the major factors in the only decision in the series—by an innings and 193 runs.

The West Indian total of 582 was the third of more than 500 in five Test innings and was based on a first-wicket partnership of 239 between the consistent Rae (109) and the graceful Stoll-meyer (160), which has stood, since then, as a West Indian Test record. Weekes' 90, so cruelly ended by a run-out, and Gomez's even half-century helped keep India in the field two days, by which time the bounce of the ball was variable on a pitch which had lost none of its pace.

The outstanding Indian bowling feat was Datu Phadkar's 7 for 159 from 45½ overs but his persistent use of the bouncer was to prove an unwise tactic. Jones and Trim retaliated in kind—and were barracked for it—and India collapsed for 245 and 144. Trim took seven wickets, Jones six and Gomez four and the teams returned to Bombay for the decider.

For a change, the bowlers held their own, but this was hardly surprising on a surface which lacked the usual meticulous prepara-tion. The West Indies, batting first for the fifth successive occa-sion, were out for 286 and, following their earlier exploits, this was a collapse against a well-balanced Indian attack—Phadkar and Banerjee, fast-medium, Mankad, left-arm slow, and Ghulam Ahmed, off-spin. Stollmeyer top scored with 85 and Weekes "failed", caught off Ghulam for 56. India did even worse against the West Indian quick bowlers, surrendering a lead of 93 which the West Indies, thanks principally to Rae's 97, stretched to 360 in their second innings.

India, therefore, were left to make what was, by a long way, the highest score in the match to win. They were without the wicket-keeper, Sen, who had injured himself on the first day, and lost the openers cheaply. Yet this did not deter them in their bold quest for the runs. The pitch, if anything, had improved with wear and first Amarnath, up to No. 3 in the order, then Modi and Hazare, the two outstanding home batsmen, carried India's standard in brilliant fashion. The fourth wicket added 137, Hazare's 122 being his second century of the series, then Jones bowled him and the big fast bowler proceeded to chip away at the rest of the batting in a spell of sustained stamina.

When he started what was to be his final and 41st over, India needed 13 with the injured Sen, arm in sling, padded and ready to go in if necessary. Phadkar and Ghulam got seven of them so that six were required off the last ball with still a minute or so to go—or so everyone thought. As Jones walked back to bowl it, the standing umpire, Joshi, possibly caught up in the general excitement, suddenly removed the bails and called time. Of all the things, he had miscounted—to add a final touch of anti-climactic absurdity to a wonderful match.

It was the closest India would come to winning a Test against the West Indies before finally breaking the barrier in 1971.

India in the West Indies 1953

India's first tour of the West Indies, early in 1953, was an historic one. All cricketing visits hitherto had been by English teams and now the Indians, under the captaincy of Hazare, broke new ground. As was expected, they proved immensely popular, particularly in Trinidad, where record crowds turned out for the two Tests at Queen's Park, and in Guyana, despite the fact that rain played havoc with the cricket. In both territories, they played a two-day match against a local East Indian team.

As was the case in India four years earlier, only one Test decided the rubber, again in favour of the West Indies, who won the second at Kensington Oval. The abiding memory of the tour is of the little Indian leg-spinner Subhash Gupte flighting the ball temptingly, the West Indian batsmen, principally the vivacious Weekes, stepping out to drive him powerfully and the fielders, many bedecked in large pith helmets, swooping on the ball and throwing it back to the wicketkeeper with speed and precision. It was engrossing cricket and, even though Weekes again showed his passion for Indian bowling, Gupte finished with 27 wickets. Weekes' aggregate of 716 (average 102.28) included a double-century in the first Test and single centuries in the third and fifth and he also scored 253 for Barbados for good measure.

The West Indies introduced a new fast bowler to Test cricket and Frank King, a young Barbadian, performed creditably. Yet too much still depended on the spin of Ramadhin and Valentine and, even though they were principally responsible for the decisive victory at Kensington, they had to work long and hard for their successes. Valentine, as immaculate as ever, took 28 wickets, but Ramadhin was nowhere near his best form, possibly suffering the affects of his disappointments in Australia a season earlier.

The blueprint for the series was established in the first Test at the Queen's Park Oval. The Indians, badly shaken by a humiliating defeat in England in the summer, apparently considered holding the West Indies to be the limit of their ambitions and they batted with according care on the Queen's Park matting to accumulate 417. Polly Umrigar, a big man with power in his shots who was to score prolifically in later encounters, led the way with 130 which lasted five hours and there was consistent support for him.

The West Indies topped that by 21, two individuals on either side dominating the innings. For the West Indies, Weekes, 207, and Bruce Pairaudeau, a bespectacled, 22-year-old Guyanese who scored 115 in his first Test innings, added 219 for the fourth wicket; for India, Gupte bowled 66 overs and took 7 for 162, Mankad 63 overs, one for 129. For there to be a result, the West Indies needed to dismiss India quickly and cheaply a second time and, when four wickets were down for 106, it was on the cards. However, Umrigar and the all-rounder Phadkar stopped the rot and the West Indies were left just under three hours at the end to get 274, a proposition to which they gave no thought.

Heavy rain, which had allowed the Indians to escape defeat against Barbados, affected the preparation of the second Test pitch by the Kensington groundstaff, and throughout it became progressively more helpful to the bowlers. Gupte and Mankad put the West Indies in such trouble on the first day that they were 222 for eight before Walcott, who was given out leg-before-wicket for 98 by his uncle the umpire, Harold, and Ramadhin added a precious 58 for the ninth wicket. In reply, India passed 200 with only four men out but the last six wickets went down for only 49 to present the home team with a narrow but telling advantage of 43.

By now, the pitch was untrustworthy and batting required concentration, patience and luck. Stollmeyer played a captain's innings of 54 for the West Indies but against the accurate medium-pace of Phadkar and the spin of Gupte and Mankad they could total only 228. It was obvious, however, that victory would be theirs so long as their bowlers could exploit the conditions and Ramadhin and Valentine did not falter. Both turned the ball appreciably, the former's figures at the end being: 24.5-11-26-5. For the remainder of the series, he took only two more wickets and was dropped for the final Test.

Georgetown's equatorial climate caused the third Test to be shifted to Port-of-Spain because of the saturated state of the Bourda Oval and, except for brief periods, batsmen again had their way on the matting. That way, unfortunately, lacked much enterprise and another meaningless draw resulted.

There were so few exceptions, such as Ramchand, who played positively in India's first innings for 62, and Weekes, who gathered another century in fine style, this time 161 in 334 minutes. But the undefeated 163 by the opener Apte in India's second innings was a tortured effort lasting over eight hours and containing two actual and several near misses. In the circumstances, King's 5 for 74 represented fair return for honest work.

When the tour did eventually reach Georgetown, the public there, as has so often been the case over the years, was subjected to the disappointment of a rain-spoiled Test, only two and a half innings being completed. In that time, the crowds witnessed high-quality spin bowling from Valentine (5 for 127 and 3 for 71 from a combined total of 87.5 overs), Gupte (4 for 122) and Mankad (3 for 155) and fine batting by the three Ws, all of whom passed 50 with Walcott going on to 125, his first Test century in the West Indies. They also used their threatening influence to prompt the umpires to rescind a decision that there would be no play on the second day because of a heavy outfield. The umpires were, literally, bullied into allowing an hour's cricket at the end which prompted a sharp rebuke from the MCC at Lord's on the danger of yielding to mob rule!

For all the heavy scoring in the earlier Tests, nothing could match the final at Sabina Park for its abundance of runs. The Ws, who had provided forewarning of their form at Bourda, scored a century each for the first time in a single innings, Worrell's 237 being the highest score of the series. The Indians were not to be outdone and Umrigar in the first innings and Roy and Manjrekar in the second also carried on past three figures. It was all a long toil for the bowlers—for the West Indies, King bowled 34 overs in the first innings and 26 in the second, Gomez 28 and 47, Valentine 27.5 and 67 (with nine wickets for 213 to show for his labours). The Indian spinners were worked even harder as Worrell, Weekes and Walcott piled up the runs, Mankad taking 5 for 228 in 82 overs and Gupte 5 for 180 in 65.1.

The West Indian lead on first innings of 264 presented India with a real challenge but Roy and Manjrekar erased any worries with a second-wicket partnership of 237, a record which remains the highest for any wicket for India against the West Indies. There was something of a decline in the Indian batting when they were dismissed on the final day for 444 and the West Indies found themselves with just a chance of winning—181 in $2\frac{1}{4}$ hours. However, the loss of two cheap wickets settled the issue as a draw, Weekes just having enough time to pass Headley's previous record aggregate for a series in the West Indies.

West Indies in India 1958-59

The signs that the dismal days of the mid-50s were over for the West Indies were encouragingly clear in their 1958 home series against Pakistan and the lengthy tour of India and Pakistan the following season fashioned the nucleus of the team which progressed to such great deeds in the early 1960s. Sobers, Kanhai and Collie Smith had been on tour already and although all still in their early 20s formed the nucleus of the experienced players in a greatly revised side. Butcher and Solomon, two batsmen with a keen appetite for runs, and Gibbs, a slim off-spinner with long, powerful fingers, had been part of the remarkable revival of Guyanese fortunes under the tutorship of Clyde Walcott and all three were travelling overseas with the West Indies for the first time. Hall, who had been to England in 1957 when he was very much a young tearaway, had developed more co-ordination and control in the interim and was selected, if only as an afterthought when Worrell became unavailable because of university studies. None of the three Ws was present, the first time the West Indies had played without them since the War.

The exhaustion of playing 22 first-class matches, including eight Tests (five in India, three in Pakistan) in 20 different towns and cities in a period of five months, was well worth it for the West Indies. Under the captaincy of Alexander, whose first series had brought him a 3-1 triumph over Pakistan in the Caribbean, they swept all before them in India, where their batsmen and fast bowlers maintained consistent and devastating form. The only cloud to shadow the glory was the trouble which led to Gilchrist being sent home as a disciplinary measure. The reasons, even now, are not clear but are said to have involved a feud between the Jamaican fast bowler and his captain over the overuse of beamers. There was probably more to it than that but his banishment, the cause of heated speculation at the time, proved to be the end of a brief and turbulent Test career for a bowler as fast as any to have played for the West Indies.

From the first Test of the series to the last, India's batsmen held the pair of Gilchrist and Hall in awe and the administrators only contributed to the decline in morale by appointing four different captains who had as many as 24 different players under them. It was a sure formula for disaster—as the West Indies themselves knew from past experience.

In each of the first two Tests, Gupte renewed his battles with

West Indian batsmen and his clever leg-spin placed India in an early position of strength. But his work was undone by batsmen with neither the technique nor the pluck to cope with bowling of pace and hostility. At Bombay, in the first, Gupte brought about a late-order first-innings collapse which left the West Indies with a paltry 227 but India could reply with only 152 against Gilchrist and Hall, backed by the lesser pace of Eric Atkinson (elder brother of the former Test captain, Denis), who claimed all the wickets to fall to the bowlers. Sobers' 142 not out and his unbeaten fifth-wicket partnership of 134 with Butcher were the highlights of a declared West Indies second innings, which left India 399 to win in 9½ hours. The prospect did not interest them and they played safely for a draw, Roy, the little opener, spending almost 7½ hours over 90.

At Kanpur, Gupte's mystique proved even more baffling to the batsmen and he claimed 9 for 102 in a total of 222 out of which Solomon and Alexander added 100 for the seventh wicket. Again, however, the home batsmen faltered—even though the West Indies were without Gilchrist and even though the first four in the order had lifted the reply to 182 for two. Hall and his new partner, the loose-limbed Trinidadian Jaswick Taylor, then swept aside the last eight wickets for 40 and, after losing Hunte and Holt without a run scored, the West Indies finally laid low the bogey of Gupte. Sobers led the way as only he could by stroking 28 fours in 198 before he was run out and 443 for seven declared (in which Gupte took 1 for 121 from 23 overs) was the first of a string of even more gigantic efforts for the rest of the series—614 for five declared at Calcutta, 500 at Madras and 644 for eight declared at New Delhi.

The Kanpur Test ended in a 203-runs victory, with India folding for 240 in their second innings, Hall's 5 for 76 bringing his match analysis to 11 for 126.

At Calcutta, Kanhai achieved his first century in his 13th Test and, like Sobers before him, made it a big one, carrying on and on to 256 (6½ hours, 42 fours). He says he was goaded into it by the taunts of Gupte, who had gloated after dismissing him three times cheaply in the first four innings of the series. Now Kanhai laughed last and laughed longest. Butcher, 103, Sobers, 106 not out, and Solomon, 69 not out, left no scraps on the plate after their feast and a dispirited Indian team could reply only meekly with 124 and 154 again the fury of Hall and Gilchrist, pent up for two days while they watched their batsmen flay the opposing bowlers. The margin of victory—an innings and 336 runs—is the greatest ever achieved by the West Indies in a Test.

The fourth Test, at Madras, might well have been another

innings loss for the home team but for Alexander's decision to bat again after securing a lead of 278. India were making satisfactory progress when taking the first five West Indies wickets for 248, including Sobers and Kanhai, the latter run out for 99, but Butcher's 142 and the steadiness of the late order lifted the total to 500. India's 222 exposed them to a swift demise which was only delayed by Alexander's decision to bat a second time. When finally faced with nearly a day and a half's survival, Hall and Gilchrist, and illness which prevented Mankad from batting, India were in no mood for heroics and fell for 151.

For the final Test at New Delhi, India desperately recalled Adhikari, an army officer who had not played Test cricket for two years, to lead the side. He was 39 but he brought new fight into his team and India at least earned a draw and, even though the West Indies needed only 47 to win in their second innings when time ran out, some respect as well.

Chandu Borde, a young all-rounder of great potential, very nearly completed a century in each innings, falling—literally—four short in the second innings in a race against the clock, out hit-wicket bowled Gilchrist 96. Adhikari himself scored 63 and 40 and India's first-innings 415, in which the left-handed opener Contractor and Umrigar added 137 for the second wicket, was their best batting effort. However, it was dwarfed by the West Indian reply of 644 for eight declared in which Holt, Smith and Solomon all recorded their first centuries of the series and this left them, yet again, with the task of holding out for a draw. This time, they managed it—if only barely.

India in the West Indies 1962

According to the astrologers, who so abound in the orient, the portents for India's second tour of the West Indies were ominous. The stars, they said, were unfavourably placed on the day the team departed and ill-luck would dog them unceasingly. Such predictions proved uncannily correct for not only did India lose all five Tests but their captain, the left-handed opening batsman Nari Contractor, came perilously close to death after being struck on the head by fast bowler Charlie Griffith in the match against Barbados. From the time the squad arrived in Trinidad to the day it left Jamaica, it was stricken with a series of illnesses and injuries which simply added to its woes.

Yet, there was more than the influence of the planets to the unique West Indian record, the only time they have achieved the maximum number of victories in a single series. To begin with, under Worrell, they had developed into an exceedingly strong team which had shown glimpses of its true potential in Australia a year earlier and which was now ready to dominate international cricket. Neither were the Indian players done justice by the rigorous programme to which they were subjected. They arrived in the Caribbean having just completed their own season, an exacting five months during which they had played five Tests against England. They won that series, 2-0, but England, under Dexter, had not been at full strength and the result was hardly a true indication of India's worth. The absence for disciplinary reasons of Gupte, for years their most successful bowler, did not help India's cause any.

Entering the first Test at Port-of-Spain having played only a single first-class match in the Caribbean, India slumped on the first day against the three opposing fast bowlers (Hall and Watson having been joined by Charlie Stayers, a tall Guyanese with a useful turn of speed). Half-centuries from the left-handed all-rounder Durani and Surti spurred a recovery to 203 and when the West Indies were 150 for six at the end of the second day, with only Solomon of the main batsmen remaining, the match was nicely poised. From that point it slipped quickly away from India and they were beaten by 10 wickets with a day to spare.

The new wicketkeeper, Jackie Hendriks, ignored the pain of a fractured finger to topscore with 64 in his first Test innings and, as it turned out, his last for the series on account of the injury. Hall, in his own flamboyant way, hit 37 not out and the West Indian lead was 86, which Hall immediately turned into a winning one by brushing aside the first three Indian second-innings wickets for eight runs. There was no revival, the spin of Gibbs and Sobers later playing its part, and India's 98 was their lowest in a Test innings against the West Indies.

The West Indian superiority had been established and it was never in doubt for the rest of the series—innings victories in the second and third Tests and comfortable, if not as resounding, results in the fourth and fifth.

India, in fact, had some cause for satisfaction after their first innings of the second Test at Sabina when they batted with resolute consistency to total 395. That, however, paled into insignificance once the West Indies got going. McMorris, on his home ground, Kanhai and Sobers all scored centuries, the first two sharing a second-wicket stand of 255 and Sobers clouting four sixes and 11 fours in 153, his 12th Test century. Worrell and Hendriks' replacement as wicketkeeper, Ivor Mendonca of Guyana, stretched the lead to 236 before declaration.

Not for the first time, Hall's great speed devastated the Indian batsmen and his 6 for 49 (yielding a match return of 9 for 128) was the principal instrument in their second-innings collapse to 218.

The Barbados leg of the tour was depressingly overshadowed by Contractor's injury and the side had to endure several agonising hours, both on and off the field. Barbados, possessing a fast attack comparable to any of that era, beat them by an innings and 95 runs; the West Indies by an innings and 30.

In Contractor's absence, the Nawab of Pataudi, at the age of 21, became the youngest captain ever to lead a Test team. He had to do so in an unhappy situation and his initiation was not an auspicious one. He himself topscored with an attractive 48 but India could manage only 258 in their first innings, not in the least awe-inspiring. For some reason, however, it evinced a most tiresome response from the West Indies on the third day after Kanhai's brilliant 89 (three sixes, 13 fours in two hours) had already put them ahead. On that day, they added 164 off 131 overs while losing four wickets with Umrigar, despite his fibrositis and his 35 years, returning the remarkable figures of 49-27-48-2. It was a complete negation of all that the West Indies had achieved in Australia yet it earned a lead of 217.

For a long time, India held out surely, retiring to lunch on the final day 158 for two with Sardesai and Manjrekar seemingly entrenched and a draw on the cards. Kensington Oval had seen most things in its long history but it now witnessed a sensational spell of bowling from Gibbs who, after lunch, took eight wickets for six runs from 15.3 overs, 14 maidens. The batsmen were hypnotised by his guile and pushed catch after catch into the close field as defeat rapidly closed in on them. At the end, Gibbs' analysis was 53.3-37-38-8.

The series was now decided but this was no reason for the West Indies to slacken their grip. Worrell was not the skipper to play in that way and India found the West Indies as determined as ever in the last two Tests, the fifth shifted from Georgetown to Kingston because of serious political and racial strife at the time in Guyana.

The fourth Test at Port-of-Spain was notable for several individual efforts. Kanhai scored a glorious 139, Worrell and Hall added 98 for the last wicket, Hall skittled the first five Indian first-innings wickets for 20 and Durani, promoted to No. 3, justified the confidence placed in him, with India's first century of the series in the second innings. Yet nothing could surpass Umrigar's all-round excellence—5 for 107 from 56 overs with the ball in the West Indies first innings, 56 and 172 not out with the bat in a brave but vain attempt to save his side.

The second Sabina Test was one of low scoring in which a new partner emerged for Hall, if only temporarily. After Sobers had been the hub of a West Indian total of 253, there was an extraordinary start to the Indian first innings—five out for 26 in just over an hour, all to Lester King, a native of Kingston, a bustling, fast-medium right-hander who seemed to strike fire from the pitch. He took no other wicket for the innings but that was enough to leave India in a state of ruin from which there was no escape. Umrigar, in the last of his 59 Tests, could not bowl because his back was simply too stiff from his exertions at Port-of-Spain but scores of 32 and 60 were a satisfying way to end a distinguished career. It was, however, scant consolation for the disappointment of the team as a whole.

West Indies in India 1966–67

"One's immediate estimate at the end of this short tour was that the West Indies had declined in strength," wrote D. J. Rutnagur in *Wisden* after the third West Indian tour of India. It was an observation which could not be disputed, despite victory in two of the three Tests, and, as he had done in England in the summer, Sobers found himself having to handle an enormous workload.

He headed the batting averages, scoring nearly 100 runs more than anyone else in the three Tests, took 14 wickets in his three styles, held seven catches, figured prominently in the wins at Bombay and Calcutta and stood between India and their first defeat of the West Indies in the final Test at Madras. Kanhai, Lloyd and Hunte also averaged in excess of 50 per innings but the West Indian batting did not have the same prolific authority of previous visits to India. The most noticeable shift in balance was in the bowling, which was carried by the spin of Gibbs and Sobers rather than the pace of Hall and Griffith, neither of whom made any startling impression on the supposed Indian weakness against fast bowling. One new player did immediately establish himself—Clive Lloyd, a gangling, bespectacled left-hander from Guyana whose power off the back foot reminded Indians of Clyde Walcott before him and who was a spectacular saver of countless runs in the outfield.

For India, the series was most significant in that it marked the start of the association of a quartet of spin bowlers who were to prevail over their team's fortunes for the next decade. Chandrasekhar, delivering his mixture of leg-breaks, googlies and topspinners with a withered right arm at nearly medium pace, had already announced himself to the cricket world and now intro-

duced himself to the West Indies with 18 wickets in the series.
The off-spinners, Prasanna and Venkataraghavan, and the orthodox left-armer Bedi, a distinctive figure with beard and turban,
joined him in an almost unremitting diet of spin, a formula to
be used by India with good effect in the coming years.

Hall and Griffith enjoyed their best moments in the opening
exchanges of the series, in the first Test at Bombay's Brabourne
Stadium. Inside 40 minutes, they had India 14 for three but they
could not sustain the effort and, on an easy pitch, Borde put
together an unblemished 121 out of 296. Then, after a mere two
overs, the West Indies were confronted by the wiles of Chandrasekhar. For a time, he looked like keeping India in the match but
a disciplined 101 from Hunte, Lloyd's aggressive 82, Sobers' 50,
Holford's splendid 80, Hendriks' 48 and faulty catching stabilised
matters and the West Indian total of 421 put them in an excellent
position, despite Chandrasekhar's 7 for 157.

India succumbed in the second innings to the combined spin
of Gibbs, Sobers and Holford, and it was 217 for eight before
Kunderan breathed life into it again with an aggressive 79. The
West Indies, with 192 to win, lost four wickets to Chandrasekhar
for 90, and a close finish was in prospect until Lloyd and Sobers,
in a stand of left-handed aggression, saw them home without
further loss.

Holford, with 2 for 68 and 3 for 94 to embellish his batting,
enhanced the reputation he had made in England in the summer
but he soon afterwards fell ill with a serious bout of pleurisy
which kept him out for the remainder of the tour—a telling blow
for the team.

The second Test at Calcutta, won by the West Indies by an
innings and 45 runs, was the subject of international headlines—
but not on account of the cricket. On New Year's Day, 1967, the
second day of the match, a combination of a ticket racket which
swelled the crowd to several thousand more than the stadium's
capacity and strong-arm tactics by the police led to a riot of major
proportions which prevented any play on the second day. Stands
and furniture were put to the torch and the violence spilled over
into the streets of the city. For a time, the tour was in jeopardy
but the presence of Sir Frank Worrell in Calcutta, by happy
coincidence on university business, had considerable bearing on
subsequent deliberations and the match was continued without
further trouble.

The toss was the decisive factor in the result for the pitch was
underprepared, apparently deliberately so. Sobers won it and the
West Indies totalled 390; India collapsed for 167 and 178 with

seven wickets each to the captain in his slower style and Gibbs on a surface which bit sharply.

The final Test provided India with a golden opportunity to clinch their first victory over the West Indies but their fielders let it slip. Engineer set the mood for his team-mates when he began the match with a flurry of aggressive shots which carried him to 94 at lunch on the first day. He eventually made 109, Borde 125 and the total mounted to 404. Yet the West Indies, with Sobers topscoring with 95 at No. 7, bettered it by two.

By more bold tactics, principally from the left-handers Wadekar and Subramanya this time, India's batsmen gave their bowlers enough time and enough runs to make a match of it and, with the pitch turning, the West Indies were never on terms with an equation which required them to score 322 in 4½ hours.

In fact, they were 193 for seven with an hour and a half remaining but then Sobers was dropped twice before he was 10. The West Indies captain thereafter made no error, Griffith used every possible method to defend his wicket against Chandrasekhar, Prasanna and Bedi, and India were frustrated. It was a great disappointment to the large crowd but their time for finally turning the tables on the West Indies was soon to come.

India in West Indies 1971
India at last broke the long jinx, not only by winning their first Test ever against their old adversaries but also by securing the rubber on the 1971 tour.

It was highly-deserved triumph. The team under a new captain, Wadekar, arrived in the Caribbean underestimated by the public and possibly by the opposition as well. It left with the respect of all cricket-followers for its purposeful, dedicated performance under firm competent leadership.

The defeat had a disturbing effect at all levels of West Indian cricket from the ordinary supporter to the public media to the selectors who chose no fewer than 20 players for the five Tests. Every excuse was found for what was, after all, a narrow loss to an excellent team. Disturbing doubts had hung over the series because of the involvement of Sobers, still the West Indies captain, in a tournament in Rhodesia for which he was sharply criticised and for which he eventually conveyed his "sincere regrets" to the West Indies Board. If he had not done so, the Government of Guyana would not have allowed him to enter the country to lead the Test team, the implications of which would have been dire. However, the controversy was ended by Sobers' diplomatic statement and the great left-hander, as usual, played a principal part—597 runs and 12 wickets. Now, however, there were distinct signs that his interest in the game was waning and his captaincy lacked the flair of earlier years, a condition aggravated by a lack of penetration in the bowling at his disposal.

Gibbs' powers of spin and flight had temporarily gone into decline and he played only one Test. Although his replacement, the ageing Trinidadian, Jack Noreiga, did great things on his home pitch, he was not in the same class. More importantly, there was no genuine pace except for a fleeting period from Uton Dowe, a young Jamaican, in the fourth Test.

The Indians owed most of their success to six men—the batsmen Sunil Gavaskar, a 21-year-old opener from Bombay who broke record after record in his first series, and Dilip Sardesai, the plucky left-handed all-rounder Eknath Solkar, and the three spinners, Prasanna, Venkataraghavan and Bedi. Chandrasekhar, inexplicably, had been left at home. However, more than anything else, a wonderful team spirit evident both on and off the field was responsible for India's showing.

The entire course of the series was, in large measure, decided on the opening day of the first Test. Then, India, sent in to bat, were reeling at 75 for five. In the preceding matches against Jamaica and the President's XI, the visitors' batting had been suspect and this was further proof of it. If the progress had been as expected, India would have been all out for a total of less than 200 and their morale would have been shattered. Instead, Sardesai responded to the crisis in most courageous fashion, calling on his great experience to score the first double-century ever made by an Indian against the West Indies, an effort lasting eight hours seven minutes and including a six and 17 fours. With able support from Solkar and the No. 10, Prasanna, the Indian total was hoisted to 387 and confidence was restored. When the West Indies were forced to follow on in reply it could hardly have been higher. It was a commodity which was vital during the tour.

The circumstances of the West Indian follow-on make a strange story. Rain had completely washed out the first day, thus reducing the match to four days and the follow-on margin from 200 to 150, a fact of which the West Indies were unaware until they were bowled out for 217 in their first innings, 170 behind. Wadekar duly put them back in but the match was comfortably drawn through an undefeated 158 from Kanhai, 93 from Sobers and 57 from Lloyd, who was run out for the second time in the game.

It was, fittingly, at Port-of-Spain, where they had always received such wonderful support, that the Indians created history with their first Test victory over the West Indies. Again, the principals of their success were the same as those in Jamaica—the spinners took 17 of the 20 wickets to fall, this time the veteran left-hander Durani claiming two most important victims in the second innings; Sardesai, with 112, and Solkar again shared a crucial stand. Gavaskar, who had not played at Sabina because of an injured finger, scored 65 and 67 not out in his first Test.

Throughout, the cricket was gripping. The West Indies were out for 214, then their lowest total against India, and although Noreiga rewrote the record books with his off-spin by becoming the only West Indian bowler to claim nine wickets in a Test innings (9 for 96 were his figures), Sardesai scored another century and the West Indies were left to make up a deficit of 138. They came back into contention strongly and entered the fourth day 150 for one—12 ahead with a lot of batting to come. However, Fredericks was run out for 80 without addition, Durani dismissed Sobers and Lloyd in quick succession and only Charlie Davis, following his first-innings 71 with 74, both not-out, batted with any conviction thereafter. India, therefore, required only 124 and got them for three wickets with no alarms and a day to spare.

They and their local supporters were jubilant and Wadekar knew from that point that his best policy would be to play for draws. Perhaps he carried his defensive tactics too far and there were, frequently, meticulous and time-consuming field placements which reduced the over rate for spinners to 14 an hour. All the same, he achieved his objective.

The Bourda pitch, benignity itself, precluded any result. Gavaskar, Davis and Sobers made centuries on it and Desmond Lewis, a new wicketkeeper-batsman from Jamaica, compiled a diligent 81 in his first Test innings. The only other notable occurrence was the third run-out in five innings for Clive Lloyd after a mid-wicket collision with his partner, Sobers, which left both groggily prostrate on the pitch.

In Barbados, the West Indies held a commanding grip on the game more than once but could never convert their superiority into victory. They were sent in by Wadekar, lost a wicket with only four on the board and still could declare at 501 for five, thanks principally to Sobers' undefeated 178 and the contributions of Lewis (88), Kanhai (85) and Davis (79). Their best chance—perhaps only chance—was to force India into a follow-on and they came very close to it. Nevertheless, once India wriggled free and the West Indies had to bat a second time, a draw was virtually certain.

India reeled at first against Dowe, who bowled with great fire to leave them 70 for six, a precarious situation. As in Jamaica, however, Sardesai (150) and Solkar (65) rose to the occasion with another memorable stand of 186 and when the West Indies threatened to break through on the final day, Gavaskar was the man of the hour with an undefeated 117.

On a pitch which had obviously received careful preparation, India protected the narrow advantage in the series by batting their way to a draw in the final Test at the Queen's Park Oval over six days. In fact, in one hectic last bid to level the series, the West Indies very nearly threw away the match.

The sluggish pitch helped no bowler and the scoring was heavy. Gavaskar emulated Doug Walters' feat of 1969 with a century and a double-century in the same Test, his 124 and 220 carrying his aggregate to 774 in eight innings. Davis and Sobers each passed 500 in the series with centuries, Foster was only one short of his when he played on, and Lewis and Sardesai maintained their consistency with 70s.

The West Indies needed a virtually impossible 262 to square the rubber at a rate of better than six an over and, although they made a frantic attempt to get them, it just wasn't on. They were 165 for eight at the end, desperately holding out in the final overs to draw the game.

West Indies in India 1974–75

Before it started, the West Indies tour of India, Sri Lanka and Pakistan in late 1974 and early 1975 was, quite reasonably, regarded as crucial to the development of a comparatively new crop of players. Not only was the assignment itself an exacting one, with seven Tests in $4\frac{1}{2}$ months, but there was to be a new captain and vice-captain in charge of a talented but generally inexperienced young contingent. Additionally, for the first time in 17 years, the West Indies would be without their two most seasoned and successful Test cricketers, Sobers and Kanhai, on tour.

The results, at the end of it all, were greatly encouraging. An enthralling series against India was won 3-2 yet West Indian spirits lifted more by the individual performances, not least the captain's, and by the indisputable evidence that Lloyd had a team of enormous potential under him. There were some players whose statistical record was moderate but not one could have considered the tour an embarrassment. In the Tests, all the specialist batsmen recorded centuries and every bowler made his contribution.

India entered the series following a terrible beating in the three

Not quite the best position for a Wes Hall yorker: the Nawab of Pataudi is bowled for 40 in the first innings of the third Test of the 1966–67 series, at Madras.

Dilip Sardesai, a hero several times over for India during their successful **1971** series in the Caribbean, on the attack in the Bridgetown Test, where he made 150. Wicketkeeper is Desmond Lewis and Rohan Kanhai is at slip.

Willie Alleyn

A spectacular slip catch by Garry Sobers claims an early wicket in the first Test against India in the 71 series: Jayantilal caught off Grayson Shillingford for six.

Jamaica Gleaner

Jack Noreiga, the Trinidadian off-spinner who came from obscurity to take nine wickets in an innings in the second Test against India, Port-of-Spain, 1971.

Trinidad Guardian

West Indies on their way to victory at Bombay in the decisive Test match of the 1974-75 series: Gundappa Viswanath receives a beauty from Vanburn Holder and becomes one of the fast bowler's six victims in the innings. Gibbs and Kallicharran are at slip, Deryck Murray is wicketkeeper, and Viv Richards is exultant at short leg.

Bristol Photo

Tests in England the preceeding summer and their morale must have been exceedingly low after huge losses in the first two Tests. Pataudi had been recalled to replace the retired Wadekar as captain and every adversity seemed to confront him personally and his team in the early Tests. That they could have recovered their spirit to level the series going into the final match was an outstanding achievement.

The West Indies established what appeared an invincible position by comfortably winning the first two Tests, in which they were superior in every department. Bangalore was the scene of the opening match, the first time the garden city had hosted a Test and the West Indies won by 267 sums mainly on account of outstanding batting by three players and the consistency of their fast bowlers, of whom Andy Roberts, a young Antiguan on his first tour, was always the most dangerous.

Sent into bat on a pitch damp from overnight rain, the West Indies ended the first day 212 for two; they were all out next day for 289. With further rain during the night, the pitch became a vicious turner, fully exploited by the classy Indian spinners, but it was a masterful technical display by the left-handed Kallicharran which was the highlight of the exchanges. He carried his score from 64 to 124 before he was last out—in other words 60 out of the 77 added by his team on the second day.

India's reply was built around a succession of steady innings but they fell 29 short. At 75 for three in their second innings and the Indian spinners rampant, the West Indies were faced with a potential emergency. At this juncture, Lloyd, with able support from Gordon Greenidge, virtually settled the result with an explosive 163, compiled in only three hours 25 minutes and including two sixes and 22 fours. Greenidge, in his first Test, had been denied the satisfaction of a century in the first innings when run out for 93 but he reached it now, his 107 assisting in a fourth-wicket partnership of 207. India were beaten almost before they started the last innings of the game. Their two most experienced batsmen, Engineer and Pataudi, were unable to bat because of injury sustained while fielding and Gavaskar's dismissal for a duck was a further setback. The effect was a total of 118.

India's defeat at the Ferozsha Kotla ground in New Delhi, which gave West Indies a 2-0 lead, was even more devastating but this time West Indian spin played a more prevalent part than it had done at Bangalore. The home team were without Pataudi, still injured, and Venkataraghavan was named to replace him only on the morning of the match. He did his first duty by winning the toss but a paltry total of 220 was spectacularly overhauled by the West Indies, for whom Richards, Lloyd, Julien and Boyce were in exuberant mood. Richards, troubled by Chandrasekhar at Bangalore but now fully in command, and Lloyd, again in irrepressible form, added 120 for the fifth wicket; Richards and Boyce 124 in an hour and a quarter for the eighth. Richards clouted six huge sixes and 20 fours in six hours 20 minutes' batting which brought him 192, the signal of a great player in the making.

India, 273 behind, made a pugnacious effort to stave off defeat but the combination of Gibbs' off-spin and a rain-affected pitch on the fourth day betrayed them.

By now, there were thoughts of a clean sweep by the West Indies, so conclusive had been their dominance. It was their own complacency and carelessness and the Indian adroitness at capitalising on it which dramatically altered the picture.

The first day of the third Test at Calcutta gave no indication that an Indian renaissance was imminent. Roberts' 5 for 50 meant an Indian first-innings total of 233, and the vast crowd streamed out of the ground at the end of the first day resigned to another uphill struggle. The struggling, however, was done by the West Indies. Only Fredericks approached his task with the seriousness of a Test match when they replied and they were all out for 240, the medium pace of Madan Lal earning him 4 for 22. India were back in it and Viswanath ensured that, this time, there would be no surrender. A neat, compact player, he provided the foundation of a total of 316 and, on a pitch favouring the spin of Bedi, Chandrasekhar and Prasanna, India finalised a well-deserved victory by bowling the West Indies out for 224.

It was a tonic for them and, conversely, a depressant for the West Indies. For the fourth Test, the Madras pitch, dry and dusty, provided a stern test for the batsmen and the contest was really between West Indian pace and Indian spin, the latter eventually squaring the rubber for their team.

Roberts bowled magnificently throughout, never allowing the batsmen to relax with his speed and accuracy, taking 7 for 64 as India folded for 190 in their first innings and 5 for 57 in their second-innings 256. Viswanath, attacking boldly as he ran out of partners, was 97 not out when the first innings ended and he and the bespectacled Anshuman Gaekwad, son of a former Test player, held together the second innings with a stand of 93.

Small as India's scoring was, the West Indies' was smaller—192 in their first innings and 154 in the second, the first time they had ever been dismissed for under 200 in a Test against India. Prasanna had nine wickets, Bedi six and Chandrasekhar three, India finished victors with a day in hand and, on the crest of a wave, were favourites for the deciding Test, to be played on the new Bombay Cricket Association Stadium at the end of January.

The pitch was hosting its first first-class match but it behaved impeccably. Not so the police, whose overuse of violence against a lone spectator who had come onto the field to hail a double-century by Lloyd incited yet another riot. Play was abandoned at tea on the second day but there were no further incidents when it continued.

By then, the West Indies had secured an unassailable position. Fredericks' 104, Kallicharran's 98 and Lloyd's double saw them to 528 for five at that stage and Lloyd continued to extend it to 604 for six before closing. He himself was dropped when 8, a crucial miss, and went on to his highest Test innings—242 not out with four sixes and 19 fours; his vice-captain, Murray, with 91 was with him while 250 were added for the sixth wicket.

India responded capably. Gavaskar, who had not played since the first Test because of injury, contributed a solid 86, the left-handed Solkar reached his first Test century, Viswanath continued his consistency with 95 and Gaekwad had 51. Yet the follow-on was avoided by only two runs. Having to bat again, the West Indies pressed so hard to achieve the quick declaration they wanted that they scored 205 for three at over five runs an over and gave their bowlers four sessions of play to dismiss the opposition. They needed only two, Holder's 6 for 39 removing any hindrance, securing victory by 201 runs and clinching the series for the West Indies.

Lloyd's final aggregate of 636 was his highest in any Test series and it was significant that when he failed at Calcutta and Madras, the whole batting failed. Roberts' 32 wickets were more than any other West Indian had taken in a series in India.

India in West Indies 1976

Few teams have been subjected to as disastrous a start to a tour as the Indians in the West Indies in 1976. They were badly beaten by 10 wickets by Barbados and were totally outplayed by an innings and 97 runs in the first Test. Yet they rallied with real spirit to provide a close and hard-fought series.

The Indians arrived after three Tests in New Zealand which ended one match each with the other drawn. For the West Indies, the series immediately followed a most disappointing tour to Australia. The contest, therefore, provided both teams with an opportunity to re-establish themselves but the outcome proved decisive for neither.

India were unquestionably favoured by the fact that two Tests, the second and third, were played at the Queen's Park Oval, the latter hastily transferred after flooding ruled out any possibility of using Bourda as scheduled. The slow, turning pitch there suited their spinners and blunted the edge of the West Indian fast bowlers. They would almost certainly have won the second Test but for the loss of a full day through rain and a dropped catch; they won the third by scoring 406 in the fourth innings for the loss of only four wickets, an historic feat. Unfortunately, the fourth Test, played on a fast, bouncy pitch at Sabina, was decided amidst a highly unusual controversy with India batting five men short in their second innings, three of them injured while batting and two while fielding.

The Indian performance in the first Test was simply pathetic. They batted with no gumption whatever and were bowled out for 177 and 214. The West Indies' 488 for nine declared, in which Richards marked his first Test at home with 142, Kallicharran scored 93 and Lloyd 102, was more than ample.

In less than two weeks between that defeat and the start of the second Test some remarkable transformation took place in the Indian camp for which Bedi, on his first overseas assignment as captain, and Umrigar, the knowledgeable manager, must take great credit. The West Indies, sent in after the first day had been washed out, viewed the pitch and the bowling with such suspicion that they could muster no more than 241. The one shining exception was Richards, who scored 130 out of 212 while he was at the wicket in commanding fashion. Gavaskar, renewing acquaintances with the ground on which he had scored a single and a double-century in the fifth Test five years earlier, and the stylish Brijesh Patel were responsible for a fifth-wicket partnership of 204 which allowed Bedi to declare at 402 for five, Gavaskar 156, Patel 115 not out.

The West Indies were hard-pressed to hold out for a draw in the remaining $7\frac{1}{2}$ hours and only did so through the courtesy of a chance which allowed Lloyd to escape when 27 of an eventual 70. Bedi, Chandra and Venkataraghavan were like Bengal tigers stalking their prey on the final day but they could not complete the job in time.

Unexpectedly, it was not India's bowlers but the batsmen who gained their great victory in the third Test. The West Indies had the whip-hand for the first three and a half days; India, however, were in front when it mattered on the fifth. Richards' 177 showed no respect to any bowler and was the basis of a West Indian total of 359. Holding, bowling at great speed despite the lethargic pitch, took 6 for 65 from 26.4 overs to rout India for 228 and

Lloyd then allowed his lead to pass the 400 mark before he made his fateful declaration, Kallicharran's topscore of 103 not out being painfully made under the handicap of a right shoulder stricken with fibrositis.

The West Indian bowling was without Roberts, who was resting because of sheer exhaustion after his exertions in Australia, and Gibbs, pensioned off by the selectors. In addition, Holding had taken a lot out of himself in the first innings, which left the job in the hands of an inexperienced staff of spinners. India were convinced, from the start, that they could get the runs. They planned their strategy with precision. Their two most experienced batsmen, Gavaskar and Viswanath, showed the way with splendid centuries and Mohinder Amarnath, son of the former Indian captain, was no less influential with a steady 85. Two of the four wickets which fell were run out and India completed their famous triumph in convincing fashion.

All else in the Sabina Test was overshadowed by the accusations of the Indians against the West Indian fast bowlers, mainly Holding. Bedi termed the match "a war" and the manager called a press conference on the rest day to complain about what his teamed regarded as intimidatory bowling. There can be no doubt that Holding bowled with great pace and hostility before his home crowd and that three batsmen were forced to retire hurt after being struck, two by Holding and one by Holder. There could also be no doubt that the pitch, off which the ball frequently flew from a good length, was a contributory factor. Whatever else, neither umpire found it necessary to issue a caution.

Lloyd sent India in after winning the toss, but, despite the barrage, Gavaskar and Gaekwad put on a record 136 for the first wicket and they reached 306 with only six actual wickets down. However, Gaekwad and Patel had retired hurt and Bedi and Chandrasekhar were disinclined to risk injury so the declaration was made. The West Indies faltered to 217 for six in reply before Murray's cool 71 and Holding's swashbuckling 55 carried them ahead by 85 and, although there were very few short balls when India batted a second time, they had neither the heart nor the resources to do more than go through the motions.

Gaekwad, Viswanath and Patel all remained in the pavilion nursing their injuries of the first innings and Bedi and Chandrasekhar did not appear either on account of knocks they had received in the field. It was a bizarre ending to the match, compounded by the non-appearance of Bedi to lead his team through the final rites when the West Indies required 13 to win.

West Indies in India 1948–49

AT New Delhi. November 10 *to* 14. Match drawn. West Indies 631 (C. L. Walcott 152, E. D. Weekes 128, R. J. Christiani 107, G. E. Gomez 101, D. S. Atkinson 45, J. D. C. Goddard 44, C. R. Rangachari 5 for 107). India 454 (H. R. Adhikari 114 not out, K. C. Ibrahim 85, R. S. Modi 63, L. Amarnath 62, D. G. Phadkar 41) and 220 for six (Ibrahim 44).

AT Bombay. December 9 *to* 13. Match drawn. West Indies 629 for six declared (Weekes 194, A. F. Rae 104, F. J. Cameron 75 not out, Christiani 74, Walcott 68, J. B. Stollmeyer 66). India 273 (Phadkar 74, W. Ferguson 4 for 126) and 333 for three (V. S Hazare 134 not out, Modi 112, Amarnath 58 not out).

AT Calcutta. December 31 *to January* 4. Match drawn. West Indies 366 (Weekes 162, Walcott 54, Ghulam Ahmed 4 for 94, S. S. Banerjee 4 for 120) and 336 for nine declared (Walcott 108, Weekes 101). India 272 (Modi 80, Hazare 59, Mushtaq Ali 54) and 325 for three (Mushtaq Ali 106, Modi 87, Hazare 58 not out).

AT Madras. January 27 *to* 31. West Indies won by an innings and 193 runs. West Indies 582 (Stollmeyer 160, Rae 109, Weekes 90, Gomez 50, Cameron 48, Walcott 43, Phadkar 7 for 159). India 245 (Modi 56, Phadkar 48, J. Trim 4 for 48) and 144 (Hazare 52, P. E. Jones 4 for 30).

AT Bombay. February 4 *to* 8. Match drawn. West Indies 286 (Stollmeyer 85, Weekes 56, Goddard 41, Christiani 40, Phadkar 4 for 74) and 267 (Rae 97, Weekes 48, S. N. Banerjee 4 for 54). India 193 (Hazare 40) and 355 for eight (Hazare 122, Modi 86, Jones 5 for 85).

India in West Indies 1953

AT Queen's Park. January 21 *to* 28. Match drawn. India 417 (P. R. Umrigar 130, M. L. Apte 64, G. S. Ramchand 61, D. H. Shodhan 45, D. K. Gaekwad 43) and 294 (Umrigar 69, D. G. Phadkar 65, Apte 52). West Indies 438 (E. D. Weekes 207, B. H. Pairaudeau 115, C. L. Walcott 47, S. P. Gupte 7 for 162) and 142 for no wicket (J. B. Stollmeyer 76 not out, A. F. Rae 63 not out).

AT Kensington. February 7 *to* 12. West Indies won by 142 runs. West Indies 296 (Walcott 98, Weekes 47, Pairaudeau 43) and 228 (Stollmeyer 54, Phadkar 5 for 64). India 253 (Apte 64, V. S. Hazare 63, Umrigar 56, A. L. Valentine 4 for 58) and 129 (S. Ramadhin 5 for 26).

AT Queen's Park. February 19 *to* 25. Match drawn. India 279 (Ramchand 62, Umrigar 61, P. Roy 49, F. M. King 5 for 74) and 362 for seven declared (Apte 163 not out, V. Mankad 96, Umrigar

67). West Indies 315 (Weekes 161, Gupte 5 for 107) and 192 for two (Stollmeyer 104 not out, Weekes 55 not out).

AT Bourda. March 11 *to* 17. Match drawn. India 262 (Mankad 66, C. V. Gadkari 50 not out, Valentine 5 for 127) and 190 for five (Roy 48, Umrigar 40 not out). West Indies 364 (Walcott 125, Weekes 86, Worrell 56, Gupte 4 for 122).

AT Sabina Park. March 28 *to April* 4. Match drawn. India 312 (Umrigar 117, Roy 85, V. L. Manjrekar 43, Valentine 5 for 64) and 444 (Roy 150, Manjrekar 118, Gomez 4 for 72, Valentine 4 for 149). West Indies 576 (Worrell 237, Walcott 118, Weekes 109, Pairaudeau 58, Gupte 5 for 180, Mankad 5 for 228) and 92 for four.

West Indies in India 1958–59

AT Bombay (Brabourne Stadium). November 28 *to December* 3. Match drawn. West Indies 227 (R. B. Kanhai 66, O. G. Smith 63, S. P. Gupte 4 for 86) and 323 for four declared (G. S. Sobers 142 not out, B. F. Butcher 64 not out, Smith 58). India 152 (P. R. Umrigar 55, G. S. Ramchand 48, R. Gilchrist 4 for 39) and 289 for five (P. Roy 90, Ramchand 67 not out).

AT Kanpur. December 12 *to* 17. West Indies won by 203 runs West Indies 222 (F. C. M. Alexander 70, J. S. Solomon 45, Gupte 9 for 102) and 443 for seven declared (Sobers 198, Solomon 86, Butcher 60, Alexander 45 not out, Kanhai 41). India 222 (Umrigar 57, Roy 46, N. J. Contractor 41, W. W. Hall 6 for 50) and 240 (Contractor 50, Roy 45, Hall 5 for 76).

AT Calcutta. December 31 *to January* 4. West Indies won by an innings and 336 runs. West Indies 614 for five declared (Kanhai 256, Sobers 106 not out, Butcher 103, Solomon 69 not out). India 124 (Umrigar 44 not out) and 154 (V. L. Manjrekar 58 not out, Gilchrist 6 for 55).

AT Madras. January 21 *to* 26. West Indies won by 295 runs. West Indies 500 (Butcher 142, Kanhai 99, J. K. Holt 63, Solomon 43, V. Mankad 4 for 95) and 168 for five declared (Holt 81 not out, Gupte 4 for 78). India 222 (A. G. Kripal Singh 53, Roy 49, Sobers 4 for 26) and 151 (C. G. Borde 56).

AT New Delhi. February 6 *to* 11. Match drawn. India 415 (Borde 109, Contractor 92, Umrigar 76, H. R. Adhikari 63, Hall 4 for 66) and 275 (Borde 96, Roy 58, D. K. Gaekwad 52, Adhikari 40, Smith 5 for 90). West Indies 644 for eight declared (Holt 123, Smith 100, Solomon 100 not out, C. C. Hunte 92, Butcher 71, Sobers 44, Kanhai 40, R. B. Desai 4 for 169).

India in West Indies 1962

AT Queen's Park. February 16 *to* 20. West Indies won by 10 wickets.

India 203 (R. F. Surti 57, S. A. Durani 56) and 98 (G. S. Sobers 4 for 22). West Indies 289 (J. L. Hendriks 64, C. C. Hunte 58, J. S. Solomon 43, Sobers 40, Durani 4 for 82) and 15 for no wicket.,

AT Sabina Park. March 7 to 12. West Indies won by an innings and 18 runs. India 395 (C. G. Borde 93, R. G. Nadkarni 78 not out, F. M. Engineer 53, P. R. Umrigar 50, Sobers 4 for 75) and 218 (Engineer 40, W. W. Hall 6 for 49). West Indies 631 for eight declared (Sobers 153, R. B. Kanhai 138, E. D. A. McMorris 125, I. L. Mendonca 78, F. M. Worrell 58).

AT Kensington. March 23 to 28. West Indies won by an innings and 30 runs. India 258 (Nawab of Pataudi 48, Durani 48 not out, M. L. Jaisimha 41) and 187 (D. N. Sardesai 60, V. L. Manjrekar 51, L. R. Gibbs 8 for 38). West Indies 475 (Solomon 96, Kanhai 89, Worrell 77, Hunte 59, Sobers 42, D. W. Allan 40 not out).

AT Queen's Park. April 4 to 7. West Indies won by seven wickets. West Indies 444 for nine declared (Kanhai 139, Worrell 73 not out, McMorris 50, W. V. Rodriguez 50, Hall 50 not out, Umrigar 5 for 107) and 176 for three declared (McMorris 56, S. M. Nurse 46 not out). India 197 (Umrigar 56, Pataudi 47, Borde 42, Hall 5 for 20) and 422 (Umrigar 172 not out, Durani 104, V. L. Mehra 62, Gibbs 4 for 112).

AT Sabina Park. April 13 to 18. West Indies won by 123 runs. West Indies 253 (Sobers 104, Kanhai 44, V. B. Ranjane 4 for 72) and 283 (Worrell 98 not out, Sobers 50, McMorris 42, Kanhai 41). India 178 (Nadkarni 61, Surti 41, L. A. King 5 for 46) and 235 (Umrigar 60, Surti 42, Manjrekar 40, Sobers 5 for 63).

West Indies in India 1966–67

AT Bombay (Brabourne Stadium). December 13 to 18. West Indies won by six wickets. India 296 (C. G. Borde 121, S. A. Durani 55, Nawab of Pataudi 44) and 316 (B. K. Kunderan 79, Pataudi 51, M. L. Jaisimha 44, A. A. Baig 42, L. R. Gibbs 4 for 67). West Indies 421 (C. C. Hunte 101, C. H. Lloyd 82, D. A. J. Holford 80, G. S. Sobers 50, J. L. Hendriks 48, B. S. Chandrasekhar 7 for 157) and 192 for four (Lloyd 78 not out, Sobers 53 not out, Hunte 40). *AT Calcutta. December 31 to January 5.* West Indies won by an innings and 45 runs. West Indies 390 (R. B. Kanhai 90, Sobers 70, S. M. Nurse 56, Hunte 43). India 167 (Gibbs 5 for 51) and 178 (Sobers 4 for 56).

AT Madras. January 13 to 18. Match drawn. India 404 (Borde 125, F. M. Engineer 109, R. F. Surti 50 not out, Pataudi 40) and 323 (A. L. Wadekar 67, V. Subramanya 61, Hanumant Singh 50, Borde 49, C. C. Griffith 4 for 61, Gibbs 4 for 96). West Indies 406 (Sobers 95, Kanhai 77, Hunte 49, M. R. Bynoe 48, Chandrasekhar

4 for 130) and 270 for seven (Sobers 74 not out, Griffith 40 not out,
B. S. Bedi 4 for 81).

India in West Indies 1971

AT Sabina Park. February 18 *to* 23. Match drawn. India 387
(D. N. Sardesai 212, E. D. Solkar 61, V. A. Holder 4 for 60). West
Indies 217 (R. B. Kanhai 56, R. C. Fredericks 45, G. S. Sobers 44,
E. A. S. Prasanna 4 for 65) and 385 for five (Kanhai 158 not out,
Sobers 93, C. H. Lloyd 57).

AT Queen's Park. March 6 *to* 10. India won by seven wickets. West
Indies 214 (C. A. Davis 71 not out, Prasanna 4 for 54) and 261
(Fredericks 80, Davis 74 not out, S. Venkataraghavan 5 for 95).
India 352 (Sardesai 112, S. M. Gavaskar 65, Solkar 55, A. V.
Mankad 44, J. M. Noreiga 9 for 95) and 125 for three (Gavaskar
67 not out).

AT Bourda. March 19 *to* 24. Match drawn. West Indies 363
(D. M. Lewis 81 not out, Lloyd 60, Fredericks 47, M. C. Carew 41)
and 307 for three declared (Davis 125 not out, Sobers 108 not out,
Carew 45). India 376 (Gavaskar 116, G. R. Viswanath 50, S. Abid
Ali 50 not out, Sardesai 45, Mankad 40) and 123 for no wicket
(Gavaskar 64 not out, Mankad 53 not out).

AT Kensington. April 1 *to* 6. Match drawn. West Indies 501 for five
declared (Sobers 178 not out, Lewis 88, Kanhai 85, Davis 79) and
180 for six declared (Fredericks 48, Lloyd 43). India 347 (Sardesai
150, Solkar 65, U. G. Dowe 4 for 69) and 221 for five (Gavaskar
117 not out).

AT Queen's Park. April 13 *to* 19. Match drawn. India 360 (Gavaskar
124, Sardesai 75, Venkataraghavan 51) and 427 (Gavaskar 220,
A. L. Wadekar 54, Noreiga 5 for 129). West Indies 526 (Sobers 132,
Davis 105, M. L. C. Foster 99, Lewis 72, D. A. J. Holford 44,
Venkataraghavan 4 for 100) and 165 for eight (Lloyd 64).

West Indies in India 1974–75

AT Bangalore. November 22 *to* 27. West Indies won by 267 runs.
West Indies 289 (A. I. Kallicharran 124, C. G. Greenidge 93, S.
Venkataraghavan 4 for 75, B. S. Chandrasekhar 4 for 112) and
356 for six declared (C. H. Lloyd 163, Greenidge 107). India 260
(H. S. Kanitkar 65, S. Abid Ali 49) and 118.

AT New Delhi. December 11 *to* 15. West Indies won by an innings
and 17 runs. India 220 (P. S. Sharma 54, S. S. Naik 48) and 256
(F. M. Engineer 75, Sharma 49, L. R. Gibbs 6 for 76). West Indies
493 (I. V. A. Richards 192 not out, Lloyd 71, K. D. Boyce 68,
B. D. Julien 45, Kallicharran 44, E. A. S. Prasanna 4 for 147).

AT Calcutta. December 27 *to January* 1. India won by 85 runs.

India 233 (G. R. Viswanath 52, S. Madan Lal 48, A. M. E. Roberts
5 for 50) and 316 (Viswanath 139, Engineer 61). West Indies 240
(R. C. Fredericks 100, Madan Lal 4 for 22) and 224 (Kallicharran
57, Richards 47, B. S. Bedi 4 for 52).

AT Madras. January 11 *to* 15. India won by 100 runs. India 190
(Viswanath 97 not out, Roberts 7 for 64) and 256 (A. D. Gaekwad
80, Viswanath 46, Roberts 5 for 57). West Indies 192 (Richards 50,
Prasanna 5 for 70) and 154 (Kallicharran 51, Prasanna 4 for 41).

AT Bombay (*Wankhede Stadium*). *January* 23 *to* 29. West Indies
won by 201 runs. West Indies 604 for six declared (Lloyd 242 not
out, Fredericks 104, Kallicharran 98, D. L. Murray 91, K. Ghavri
4 for 140) and 205 for three declared (Greenidge 54). India 406
(E. D. Solkar 102, Viswanath 95, S. M. Gavaskar 86, Gaekwad 51,
Gibbs 7 for 98) and 202 (B. P. Patel 73 not out, Gaekwad 42, V.
A. Holder 6 for 39).

India in West Indies 1976

AT Kensington. March 10 *to* 13. West Indies won by an innings
and 97 runs. India 177 (S. Madan Lal 45, D. A. J. Holford 5 for 23)
and 214 (G. R. Viswanath 62, Madan Lal 55 not out). West Indies
488 for nine declared (I. V. A. Richards 142, C. H. Lloyd 102, A. I.
Kallicharran 93, R. C. Fredericks 54, B. S. Chandrasekhar 4 for 163).

AT Queen's Park. March 24 *to* 29. Match drawn. West Indies 241
(Richards 130, D. L. Murray 46, B. S. Bedi 5 for 82) and 215 for
eight (Lloyd 70, L. G. Rowe 47). India 402 for five declared (S. M.
Gavaskar 156, B. P. Patel 115 not out).

AT Queen's Park. April 7 *to* 12. India won by six wickets. West
Indies 359 (Richards 177, Lloyd 68, B. D. Julien 47, Chandrasekhar 6 for 120, Bedi 4 for 73) and 271 for six declared (Kallicharran 103 not out). India 228 (Madan Lal 42, Viswanath 41,
M. A. Holding 6 for 65) and 406 for four (Viswanath 112, Gavaskar
102, M. Amarnath 85, Patel 49 not out).

AT Sabina Park. April 21 *to* 25. West Indies won by 10 wickets.
India 306 for six declared (A. D. Gaekwad 81 retired hurt,
Gavaskar 66, Holding 4 for 82) and 97 (five men absent injured)
(Amarnath 59). West Indies 391 (Fredericks 82, Murray 71,
Richards 64, Holding 55, Rowe 47, Chandrasekhar 5 for 153) and
13 for no wicket.

PARTNERSHIP RECORDS

West Indies:

1st	239	J. B. Stollmeyer and A. F. Rae	Madras	1948-49
2nd	255	E. D. A. McMorris and R. B. Kanhai	Kingston	1962
3rd	220	I. V. A. Richards and A. I. Kallicharran	Bridgetown	1976
4th	267	C. L. Walcott and G. E. Gomez	N. Delhi	1948-49
5th	219	E. D. Weekes and B. H. Pairaudeau	Port-of-Spain	1953
6th	250	C. H. Lloyd and D. L. Murray	Bombay	1974-75
7th	127	G. S. Sobers and I. Mendonca	Kingston	1962
8th	124	I. V. A. Richards and K. D. Boyce	N. Delhi	1974-75
9th	106	R. J. Christiani and D. S. Atkinson	N. Delhi	1948-49
10th	98*	F. M. Worrell and W. W. Hall	Port-of-Spain	1962

India:

1st	136	S. M. Gavaskar and A. D. Gaekwad	Kingston	1976
2nd	237	P. Roy and V. L. Manjrekar	Kingston	1953
3rd	159	M. Amarnath and G. R. Viswanath	Port-of-Spain	1976
4th	150	P. Roy and P. R. Umrigar	Kingston	1953
5th	204	S. M. Gavaskar and B. P. Patel	Port-of-Spain	1976
6th	137	D. N. Sardesai and E. D. Solkar	Kingston	1971
7th	186	D. N. Sardesai and E. D. Solkar	Bridgetown	1971
8th	94	R. G. Nadkarni and F. M. Engineer	Kingston	1962
9th	122	D. N. Sardesai and E. A. S. Prasanna	Kingston	1971
10th	62	D. N. Sardesai and B. S. Bedi	Bridgetown	1971

West Indies
v.
Pakistan

OVERALL RECORD

	Tests	Won by W. Indies	Won by Pakistan	Drawn
In West Indies	10	5	2	3
In Pakistan	5	1	2	2
TOTAL	15	6	4	5

HIGHEST TOTALS
West Indies in Pakistan:

493	Karachi	1975

Pakistan in Pakistan:

406	Karachi	1975

West Indies in West Indies:

790 for 3 declared	Kingston	1958

Pakistan in West Indies:

657 for 8 declared	Bridgetown	1958

LOWEST TOTALS
West Indies in Pakistan

76*	Dacca	1959

(*Lowest total by West Indies in all Tests)
Pakistan in Pakistan:

104	Lahore	1959

West Indies in West Indies:

154	Port-of-Spain	1977

Pakistan in West Indies:

106	Bridgetown	1958

MOST RUNS IN A SERIES

West Indies in West Indies:	824	G. S. Sobers	1958
Pakistan in West Indies:	628	Hanif Mohammad	1958
West Indies in Pakistan:	274	R. B. Kanhai	1959
Pakistan in Pakistan:	199	Saeed Ahmed	1959

MOST WICKETS IN A SERIES

West Indies in West Indies:	33	C. E. H. Croft	1977
Pakistan in West Indies:	25	Imran Khan	1977
West Indies in Pakistan:	16	W. W. Hall	1959
Pakistan in Pakistan:	21	Fazal Mahmood	1959

West Indies v. Pakistan

PAKISTAN'S first representative match after the new nation was born out of the partition of India in 1947 was played against the West Indies. It was not an official Test, merely one of the first-class fixtures on the West Indies tour of India in 1948–49, but the Pakistanis did themselves proud in a drawn match. After that initial contact, however, interchange between the two has been spasmodic and there have been only 15 Tests spread over four series—two in the Caribbean and two in Pakistan.

Pakistan in West Indies 1958
Only in the first, in the West Indies early in 1958, did either team establish any clear superiority, the West Indies winning three of the first four Tests before Pakistan gained the satisfaction of an innings triumph in the fifth and final.

Two monumental batting achievements, one on each side, made that initial series unique. In the first Test, at Kensington Oval, Hanif Mohammad, Pakistan's opener, batted longer than anyone has done before or since in a single first-class innings—970 minutes while collecting 337 match-saving runs for his team. In the third at Sabina Park, Sobers, the 21-year-old, left-handed West Indian all-rounder, not only reached the century which had eluded him in the 16 Tests he had played to then but continued on to the highest score ever recorded in a single Test innings, 365 not out.

These were, naturally, the highlights of a keen series, full of good cricket and more evenly contested than the results suggest. Pakistan, except for their first innings, batted consistently yet were still outscored time and again. For the first time, Sobers revealed his capacity for big scores and his 824 runs left him only three short of Walcott's overall record for the West Indies. Walcott himself and Weekes, each in their last full series, batted with their old authority and Conrad Hunte, a stylish new opening batsman who had only missed the 1957 tour to England because the West Indies Board had no knowledge of his whereabouts, scored 622 in his first appearance.

Two opening bowlers of vastly differing styles and speed spearheaded the respective attacks. For the West Indies, Gilchrist, relying on pure pace, took 21 wickets and so shattered Hanif's confidence that the opener eventually reverted to the middle of the order after the third Test. For Pakistan, Fazal Mahmood, the master of medium-pace swing, took 20 wickets and bowled 122 overs more than anyone else on his team. But spinners also made their presence felt, Nasimul Ghani, aged 16½ (then the youngest in a Test), and Lance Gibbs, a 23-year-old off-spinner from Guyana, topping their team's bowling averages.

Worrell, because of university studies, had to decline the captaincy and the West Indies were led, for the first time, by Alexander, the wicketkeeper from Jamaica and former Cambridge University Blue. The results he and his team achieved were most satisfying, following, as they did, the debacle in England in 1957.

West Indian crowds had seen no Test cricket since the Australian tour of 1955 and they turned out in large numbers for all the Tests. Those who watched the Kensington opener were treated to a great match, filled with great deeds. Two local batsmen, Weekes with 197 and Hunte with a debut 142, led a huge West Indian first-innings total of 579 for nine declared and, on the third morning, after the declaration, the ground was bursting at its seams in anticipation of watching Gilchrist in action. There had been no outstanding fast bowler in the West Indies since the war and, through his exploits in England the previous summer, Gilchrist had stirred the imagination of an island with a long tradition for fast bowling. The Jamaican cut an unlikely figure, small-framed with long arms, but he did not disappoint.

Spurred by the excitement of the crowd, he bowled at great pace and Pakistan folded for 106. He took 4 for 32 and Collie Smith's off-spin 3 for 23. The lead was 473 and the follow-on was enforced in expectation of a quick kill. It never came.

Hanif, with purposeful and determined concentration, set his mind to batting for as long as was necessary to stave off defeat. For hour after hour he presented a broad bat—through the third day, through the fourth, through the fifth and into the sixth and final. Seven West Indian bowlers tried for more than 300 overs to dislodge him but he faltered only when he knew the match was safe, caught behind off Denis Atkinson for 337 after 16 hours 10 minutes. He would not have been able to do it alone and Imtiaz Ahmed, Alim-ud-Din, Saeed Ahmed and Haniff's elder brother, Wazir, each stayed with him more than two hours while century partnerships were recorded. It was, to be sure, one of the finest rearguard actions in Test cricket history.

Hanif went straight into the match against Trinidad and scored a century but the exertions took their toll for he contributed no other major innings on the tour, frequently falling to

Gilchrist. In the second Test, at the Queen's Park Oval, the West Indies won a match in which the highest total was 325 by 120 runs. Their batting revolved around Sobers, with 52 and 80, Weekes 78 run out, and Kanhai, whose 96 was his highest Test score at the time. In each Pakistan innings, only two batsmen overcame the speed of Gilchrist (seven wickets in the match) and the off-spin of Smith, 4 for 71 in the first innings, and Gibbs, 3 for 32 in the second. Wallis Mathias, with 73, and Fazal, with 60, saw to it that a precarious 155 for eight was lifted to 282 all out in the first innings; in the second, Hanif's 81 and Saeed's 64 were the basis of a second-wicket partnership of 130 but there followed a total collapse to 235 all out.

The third Test at Sabina brought misfortune and an innings defeat for Pakistan—and the eclipse by Sobers of Len Hutton's 364 as the highest individual Test score. Pakistan made an excellent start with 122 by Imtiaz and half-centuries by Saeed and Mathias pushing them past 200 with only two wickets down, but, on a pitch freshened by rain, they collapsed to 328 all out on the second day, Eric Atkinson's movement off the pitch bringing him five wickets for 42.

Pakistan's woes began in the very first over of the West Indian innings when Mahmood Hussain pulled a hamstring muscle so badly that he could not bowl another ball for the rest of the tour. Later, Nasim fractured his thumb after only 14 overs and, since the Pakistan captain Kardar had ignored the doctor's orders and entered the match with a cracked finger on his left hand, the team was down to two fit bowlers—Fazal and Khan Mohammad.

So Sobers had things pretty much his own way, a fact which he undoubtedly appreciated. So too did Hunte, who added 446 for the second wicket with him, before being run out for 260 at 533 for two, only the fourth of his 78 Test innings for the West Indies and his highest. Sobers, however, kept on going, past 250, past 300 and, minutes before the end of the fourth day, past Hutton's score. The sell-out crowd at Sabina, always Sobers' favourite ground, could not contain their emotions and streamed onto the field to mark the event in joyous fashion, pummelling Sobers with congratulatory back-slaps and, finally, lifting him shoulder-high. Unrestrained in their delight, they also badly damaged the pitch so that play was abandoned for the day and the umpires ordered that repairs be carried out on the rest day.

There was nothing wrong with the surface when play resumed but Pakistan batted without Nasim and Mahmood and, in spite of Wazir's 106, were beaten early on the final day.

The West Indies made sure of the rubber in the fourth Test at

Bourda, which again was dominated by Sobers, who followed his Sabina marathon with centuries in each innings—125 in the first when he opened and 109 not out in the second. In three successive innings, therefore, he had aggregated 599 runs for once out. The West Indies won by eight wickets, a straightforward enough margin, but Pakistan were again handicapped by injury.

They totalled 408 in their first innings, with Saeed (150) and Hanif (79) adding 136 for the third wicket, and 318 in their second, with Wazir running out of partners at 97 not out, five of those partners snared by Gibbs' off-spin. In spite of a second-wicket association between Sobers and Walcott which yielded 269, 145 of them to Walcott, the West Indies led by only two on first innings and found themselves having to get 317. However, Pakistan lost Fazal with a leg injury after he had bowled only four overs and, with no other quck bowler, the West Indies were not tested, Hunte joining Sobers in passing three figures.

Pakistan hardly deserved the ill-luck which thwarted them all tour and their victory by an innings and one run in the final Test at Port-of-Spain was just reward for the tenacity. They owed it to the bowling of Fazal, who took six wickets in the first innings, and the teenaged Nasim, who had Hunte, Sobers, Walcott and Smith among his six in the second, and the batting of Wazir, Saeed and Hanif, who saw them to a sizable total of 496. Wazir batted $6\frac{3}{4}$ hours for 189 and added 169 with Saeed and 154 with his brother against a West Indian attack for which Taylor, a Trinidadian fast bowler in his first Test, took 5 for 109, and Gibbs 4 for 108.

The Pakistanis left having created a most favourable impression but it was fully 19 years before they were to be seen in the Caribbean again.

West Indies in Pakistan 1959

The West Indies' first series in Pakistan in 1959, involving three Tests, was an appendage to their protracted tour of India which had lasted three months by itself and which had brought them considerable success. Pakistan, however, was to be a different proposition altogether and they came forewarned. Watch Fazal Mahmood on the matting, they were told. Watch the umpires. Don't let Hanif stick. The statistics revealed that Pakistan had lost none of the nine Tests previously played there and the West Indians soon discovered why.

In the first Test at Karachi and the second at Dacca, Fazal's devastation on the jute matting surfaces was manifest. At his brisk medium pace he would swing into the bat in the air and then cut sharply away off the mat. To the left-hander, of course, the theory was reversed and, in his first three innings, Sobers was a cheap lbw victim. The West Indians were prepared to argue that the wicket, each time, was the umpire's but, whether there was any justification for such a claim or not, the fact was that they were dismissed for 146 (Fazal 4 for 35) and 245 (Fazal 3 for 89) at Karachi, where they lost by 10 wickets, and 76 (Fazal 6 for 34) and 172 (Fazal 6 for 66) at Dacca, where the defeat was by 41 runs. The Dacca first innings remains their lowest ever in Tests.

Hanif, in the only complete innings he played for the series, scored 103 in Pakistan's first-innings total of 304 at Karachi, obstructing their bowlers for 6½ hours and adding 178 with Saeed Ahmed for the second wicket. Without Gilchrist, sent home from India on disciplinary charges, the West Indies bowling was weakened and, even though Pakistan's last seven wickets succumbed for 41, a lead of 158 was quite enough. Butcher and Solomon batted responsibly to reach the 60s but Pakistan needed a mere 88 to win, the West Indies' only consolation being an injury to Hanif in that time which kept him out of the final two Tests.

After travelling 1000 miles across the sub-continent to get to Dacca, the capital of Pakistan's east wing, the West Indies gained spectacular successes after Alexander had sent Pakistan in in the second Test. Five were down for 22, four of them to Hall, but this was only presaging the low scoring which followed. Pakistan, through Wallis Mathias' 64, rallied to carry their first-innings total to 145 and then Fazal went to work with Nasim, the 16-year-old left-arm spinner of the 1958 series in the Caribbean, as his accomplice. After passing 50 with only two wickets down the West Indies went into a flat spin and were all out for 76. Their last six batsmen failed to score and extras contributed 14 to the effort.

Batting became no easier and, in Pakistan's second innings, Eric Atkinson found the mat to his liking and claimed four of the first six wickets. Hall then returned to clean bowl the last four batsmen so that Pakistan, all out for 144, set the West Indies 214 to win—or more than any previous total in the game. Sobers and Smith were the most assured of the batsmen but they were never on terms with the target.

At Lahore, the West Indies were finally rid of the dreaded mat and they made the most of that and the weather which favoured them in the later stages to inflict on Pakistan their first defeat at home, by an innings and 156 runs. Batting first, they lost their makeshift openers, Alexander and the 18-year-old schoolboy Robin Bynoe, cheaply to Fazal but the feared medium-pacer, captaining Pakistan in the series for the first time, held no further terror for the rest of the innings and the West Indies mounted a total of 469. Kanhai dominated all else with a sparkling exhibition for 217, lasting seven hours and decorated with 32 fours. With Sobers, dropped first ball off Fazal, he added 162, with Solomon 100.

Pakistan's chances were hindered by a number of factors. Imtiaz and Wazir were both run out, opener Ijaz Butt had to retire after being struck by a Hall bouncer, Hall's fury was such on the third morning that he included the only hat-trick of his Test career in a five-wickets analysis, and rain intervened to add some devil to the pitch. After following on 260 in arrears, Pakistan could not cope with Atkinson, Ramadhin and Gibbs second time around and were all out for 104. In fact, the only item of cheer for the home crowd in the match was the debut appearance of Mushtaq, a younger brother of Hanif and Wazir, at the age of 15 years 124 days, by a long way the tenderest age at which any player has joined the hurly-burly of Test cricket. It was the start of a great career for the young man.

West Indies in Pakistan 1975

It was another 16 years before the teams met again and, once more, the brief series was tacked onto the end of a full tour of India. This time, only two Tests were played and, although both were drawn, it was not until the closing stages that the results were clear. There were only two survivors of the 1959 encounter, Mushtaq and Gibbs, both then young men with no particular standing in international cricket, both now among the game's outstanding individuals.

In the intervening years, Pakistan had gathered a reputation for ideal batting pitches and unruly crowds and the West Indies experienced both. Initially, however, conditions at the Gaddafi Stadium in Lahore encouraged the bowlers since rain preceding the match dampened the pitch and affected its preparation. Consequently, there was an unexpected spate of low scoring on the first two days by two teams exceptionally powerful in batting.

Pakistan faltered badly against the fast bowling of Roberts and Boyce after Lloyd sent them in to bat and were 111 for five at the end of a shortened first day. They owed a fine total of 199 to a magnificent last-wicket stand of 57 between their captain, Intikhab, who had to shake off the effects of a blow on the head

ne of the 32 wickets taken by fast
owler Andy Roberts in the 1974–75
ries in India was off the opening
elivery of the Calcutta Test, when
udhir Naik was caught by
icketkeeper Murray. *Indian Express*

unil Gavaskar, India's diminutive
ut high-scoring opening batsman
ho was the scourge of West
dian bowlers on two successive
urs, on the way to a century in
e third Test, at Queen's Park
val, in 1976—a century which
as the foundation on which India's
eat victory was built.

Trinidad Guardian

Looking remarkably fresh, Hanif Mohammad returns to the pavilion after his marathon innings for Pakistan at Bridgetown in 1958: 337 in 970 minutes, the longest-ever first-class innings. *Barbados Advocate*

Garry Sobers acknowledges the applause from the Kingston crowd as he reaches 300 against Pakistan in 1958. He went on to 365 not out, a new world Test record.

Crown Caribbean Publications

West Indies on top at Bridgetown, 1958: Pakistan's Saeed Ahmed is stumped by **Gerry** Alexander off Collie Smith as the visitors slide to a disastrous 106 all out. *Barbados Advocate*

One of Colin Croft's record number of 33 wickets in the 1977 series against Pakistan: Asif Iqbal caught-and-bowled for 15 at Bourda. *Vernon Fung*

West Indies cricket touched new heights when the Prudential World Cup was won
Lord's in 1975. In the thrilling final as many as five batsmen were run out in the Australi
innings. Here Alan Turner fails to beat Viv Richards' throw. *Ken K*

Having proudly received the World Cup trophy, captain Clive Lloyd steps forward aga
to receive the Man of the Match award from HRH Prince Philip. *Patrick Ea*

from a Roberts bouncer, and Asif Masood.

Kallicharran's mastery of the problems which troubled all the other batsmen was almost completely responsible for a West Indian reply of 214. Sarfraz, a well-built fast-medium bowler with county cricket experience, took 6 for 89 for Pakistan but the left-handed Kallicharran was seldom bothered and finished 92 not out, denied a well-deserved century by a lack of adequate support

Four Pakistan wickets went down for 153 by the end of the third day and a result then appeared a probability rather than a possibility. However, the pitch had improved after the rest day and the bowlers could not gain the ascendancy again. Mushtaq took seven hours to compile his seventh Test century and young Aftab Baloch was 60 not out when Intikhab declared at 373 for seven with six and a quarter hours remaining. When the West Indies were 89 for three just after lunch on the last day, the tension was high but Leonard Baichan, an obstinate left-hander from Guyana in his first Test, and Lloyd, also a Guyanese left-hander but with no other similarity, saw them safely through the choppy waters. Baichan eked out a century in his debut Test just before the end, having added 164 for the fourth wicket with Lloyd, and the match was drawn.

The second Test, at the National Stadium in Karachi, was marred by a crowd disturbance which caused play on the second day to be abandoned for $2\frac{1}{2}$ hours, time which could well have been enough for the West Indies to have won the match in the end. As was the case in India, an invasion of the field to congratulate a player on reaching a landmark (this time, the left-handed Wasim Raja had passed his first Test hundred) sparked the trouble and violent police reaction only fanned it. The West Indies would not agree to make up the lost time on subsequent days and this was to their detriment.

Both teams batted so positively in their first innings that, despite totals of over 400, ample time remained for a result to be achieved. A magnificent century by the opener, Majid Khan, filled with majestic strokes, was the feature of the first day, but, even with it, Pakistan's 246 for six at close was insecure. It was lifted from this modest level by Raja and the wicketkeeper, Wasim Bari, who added 128 for the seventh wicket and caused such elation among a crowd of 60,000 that the riot ensued. Intikhab was able to declare at the end of the shortened second day at 406 for eight.

The West Indies comfortably passed this. Kallicharran's sixth Test century (115 with 16 fours) was their best innings but

Julien's second, a heavy-handed and lucky 101, Fredericks' 77 and Lloyd's 73 were equally important to a lead of 87. When Pakistan entered the last day 90 for four and Sadiq Mohammad and Wasim Raja both injured and severely handicapped, the West Indies were positively placed more particularly when the fifth wicket fell in the first over.

Pakistan's adversity, however, produced a hero—the left-handed Sadiq, youngest of the four Mohammad brothers. Struck on the jaw while fielding close to Julien, his head movement was severely restricted as a result yet for five and a quarter hours he held the West Indies bowlers at bay. It was a cruel twist of fate that he was two short of a meritorious century when the last wicket fell. Raja, his foot in plaster after wrenching an ankle, even hobbled to the wicket to bat at No. 11 in the interest of Sadiq's landmark but it was a sacrifice that proved in vain. Nevertheless, Sadiq's main satisfaction was in saving the match for his team, an accomplishment in which Sarfraz's long defiance for 15 was also significant.

The West Indies batted only an over in their second innings before agreeing to calling the match off—so two evenly-matched sides had failed to gain a decision for the second time.

Pakistan in West Indies 1977
Pakistan returned to the Caribbean in 1977 after a long and inexplicable absence of 19 years. They brought with them a well-established reputation as an immensely strong batting team, perhaps a little weak in bowling, but at all times aggressive in intent and attractive in manner.

Mushtaq was their captain but they came amidst some strife between the players and the administration. Six of their leading lights, Mushtaq among them, adamantly refused to undertake the tour (which also included three preceding Tests in Australia) unless their fees were increased. At first the Board refused to budge to the demands and, when it finally did acquiesce, it removed Mushtaq from the captaincy and replaced him with Intikhab. When this action also caused a fuss, the Government stepped in, reconstituted the Board and reinstated Mushtaq.

The West Indian public, anxious to see the Pakistanis in their entirety, watched the drama unfold with great interest. For its own part, the home team was charged with immense confidence after a marvellous performance in England the previous summer. Local optimism, however, was greatly tempered when injury to two of the leading fast bowlers, the Jamaican Holding and the Barbadian Daniel, robbed Lloyd of a major portion of his striking force, and when a fractured wrist eliminated Rowe, the stylish Jamaican batsman, from contention.

As it happened, two entirely new fast bowlers, Colin Croft of Guyana and Joel Garner of Barbados, filled the gaps created by Holding and Daniel and were primarily responsible for a 2-1 advantage to the West Indies in a keenly-contested series. Massively built, with the advantage of youth, strength, speed and enthusiasm, Croft and Garner took 58 wickets between them, Croft's 33 equalling Valentine's overall record for a West Indian bowler in a single series.

Since the Pakistanis also possessed surprisingly penetrative bowling, the Tests did not provide the extravaganza of runs that had been anticipated. There were eight different individual centuries, four per side, one total in excess of 500 and three more over 400, yet the tempo of the cricket was always urgent and entertaining.

No match contained more fluctuations of fortune and more feverish excitement than the first Test, at Kensington Oval, which the West Indies drew with the last pair occupying the wicket for the final eight and a half overs. The first three days appeared to confirm what everyone had expected, with first-innings totals of over 400. Pakistan reached 435 in which the left-handed Raja stroked a thrilling 117 not out and Majid a more sober 88; West Indies replied with 421, dominated by Lloyd's 157 (three sixes, 21 fours) and his sixth-wicket partnership of 151 with Murray, 52.

There was a succession of startling developments on the fourth day. Pakistan, 32 without loss on resumption, slipped to 158 for nine and their cause appeared lost, only for Raja and the wicket-keeper, Bari, to swing the match once more with Pakistan's best last-wicket stand in Tests, 133. Bari, rescued from drowning the day before by a lifeguard at his hotel, turned lifesaver himself for his team while Raja simply carried on from where he had left off in the first innings. Raja made 71, Bari 60 not out and the extras were a healthy 68, a world Test record.

The West Indies needed 306 with plenty of time to get them and a second-wicket stand of 130 between Fredericks (52) and Richards (92) suggested that they would. Once they had been separated, however, a collapse set in against the medium-pace of Sarfraz Nawaz, Imran Khan and Saleem Altaf and it took the fast bowlers, Roberts, Holder and Croft, batting an hour and 35 minutes between them, to deny the Pakistanis victory.

The West Indies recovered their composure in the second Test and won easily by six wickets. Pakistan's fate was sealed on the first day by Croft, who bowled magnificently to capture 8 for 29 in two separate spells. His pace, bounce and movement off the pitch were countered by no batsman and Pakistan were all out for 180 just after tea. An accomplished 120 by Fredericks gave the West Indies a lead of 136 and, even though the left-handers Sadiq (81) and Raja (84) batted with real purpose in a Pakistan second innings of 340, the West Indies were set only 205 to win. Once Fredericks and Greenidge had started by adding 97 for the first wicket the issue was seldom in doubt—even though Pakistan did not give up until the last ball was bowled.

For the second successive Test, Pakistan fell cheaply in the first innings at Bourda. This time they were sent in by Lloyd and the four West Indian fast bowlers—Roberts, Croft, Garner and Julien—reduced them to 194. The West Indies consolidated through a string of consistent scores, the highest, 120, made by Irvine Shillingford, a right-hander from Dominica who had been Test material as far back as 1966 but who was playing only his second Test. Greenidge got to 91 and was then bowled, Richards scored an even 50 and Kallicharran, at last showing glimpses of his best form, 72. When he was ruled leg-before-wicket to Imran on the second afternoon, his actions as he returned to the pavilion revealed his disgust and inflamed his adoring home crowd, who hurled bottles onto the field and delayed play for 20 minutes.

A West Indian total of 448 gave them a lead of 254 runs and left Pakistan with no alternative but to play for a draw with nearly $2\frac{1}{2}$ days remaining. The character of the Bourda pitch, however, matched its reputation and the absence of a practising spinner from their attack proved a severe obstacle to the West Indies. Pakistan not only earned a draw but did so in style, with a total of 540 and an unforgettable display of the art of batsmanship from Majid, who made 167, and Zaheer, 80. The final stages were notable for the dismissal of Greenidge for 96 off the last ball of the match, only the third batsman to fall twice in the 90s in the same Test.

At this stage, the form of the Pakistan captain, Mushtaq, had been so sketchy that he had voluntarily stood down from the team in the one-day international. His best he reserved for the vital match, the fourth Test at the Queen's Park Oval, where his all-round skill was the prime factor in his team's 266-runs triumph. He scored 121 out of 341 in the first innings and 56 out of 301 in the second and claimed 5 for 28 and 3 for 69 with his leg-spin.

The West Indies lost because they batted poorly in both innings. In the first, they folded to 154 after Fredericks and Greenidge gave them a rousing start of 73; in the second, they totalled as much as 222 only through an obdurate eighth-wicket association between Murray and Roberts. Only briefly were they in anything but a difficult position.

It was not, of course, all Mushtaq. Majid contributed a polished 92 in the first innings, Raja (70) and Sarfraz (51) put together a solid 73 for the eighth wicket in the second, and Imran, Sarfraz and Raja all chipped in with good wickets. But no-one did half as much as the skipper.

It left the final Test at Sabina Park to decide the rubber and a fast, true pitch contributed towards an excellent match. Fast and leg-spin bowling held sway and no fewer than 22 of the 40 wickets went by way of catches off the outside edge to 'keeper or slips. When the West Indies were dismissed for 280 on the opening day, Pakistan appeared to have gained an early and decisive advantage. It would have been disastrous for the home team but for Greenidge's perfect 100. There was not a false shot in his 3½ hours, only sure and confident strokeplay which gathered three sixes and 15 fours to his account. Imran was Pakistan's best bowler with 6 for 90 but his success should have been a forewarning for his team that the West Indian fast bowlers would also be in their element on such a pitch. So it was and Croft and Roberts, well supported by the veteran leg-spinner Holford, checked Pakistan's advance and dismissed them for 198.

Greenidge and Fredericks exactly doubled the lead of 182 in the second innings before they were dismissed in successive overs, Greenidge passing 500 runs for the second successive series with 82 and Fredericks scoring 83. Even though there was no other score of any substance, a total of 359 presented Pakistan with a nigh impossible 442 to make the match and rubber theirs.

Once Pakistan had lost their first three wickets for 32 to Croft, the result was as good as finalised. Asif Iqbal, with a stirring 135 including a six and 20 fours, and Raja, as effervescent as ever, counter-attacked boldly in a partnership of 115 in only 95 minutes but the cause was a lost one and the West Indies won by 140 runs within half an hour of the fifth day.

Pakistan in West Indies 1958

AT Kensington. January 17 *to* 23. Match drawn. West Indies 579 for nine declared (E. D. Weekes 197, C. C. Hunte 142, O. G. Smith 78, G. S. Sobers 52, C. L. Walcott 43, Mahmood Hussain 4 for 153) and 28 for no wicket. Pakistan 106 (R. Gilchrist 4 for 32) and 657 for eight declared (Hanif Mohammad 337, Imtiaz Ahmed 91, Saeed Ahmed 65).

AT Queen's Park. February 5 *to* 11. West Indies won by 120 runs. West Indies 325 (R. B. Kanhai 96, Weekes 78, Sobers 52, Smith 41) and 312 (Sobers 80, F. C. M. Alexander 57, Smith 51, Fazal Mahmood 4 for 89). Pakistan 282 (Wallis Mathias 73, Fazal 60, Smith 4 for 71) and 235 (Hanif 81, Saeed 64, Gilchrist 4 for 61).

AT Sabina Park. February 26 *to March* 4. West Indies won by an innings and 174 runs. Pakistan 328 (Imtiaz 122, Mathias 77, Saeed 52, E. S. Atkinson 5 for 42) and 288 (Wazir Mohammad 106, A. H. Kardar 57, Saeed 44). West Indies 790 for three declared (Sobers 365 not out, Hunte 260, Walcott 88 not out).

AT Bourda. March 13 *to* 19. West Indies won by eight wickets. Pakistan 408 (Saeed 150, Hanif 79, Gilchrist 4 for 102) and 318 (Wazir 97 not out, Kardar 56, Alim-ud-Din 41, Gibbs 5 for 80). West Indies 410 (Walcott 145, Sobers 125, Weekes 41, Nasimul Ghani 5 for 116) and 317 for two (Hunte 114, Sobers 109 not out, Kanhai 62).

AT Queen's Park. March 26 *to* 31. Pakistan won by an innings and one run. West Indies 268 (Smith 86, Weekes 51, Walcott 47, Fazal 6 for 83) and 227 (Walcott 62, Hunte 45, Kanhai 43, Nasimul 6 for 67). Pakistan 496 (Wazir 189, Saeed 97, Hanif 54, Kardar 44, J. Taylor 5 for 109, Gibbs 4 for 108).

West Indies in Pakistan 1958–59

AT Karachi. February 20 *to* 25. Pakistan won by 10 wickets. West Indies 146 (B. F. Butcher 45 not out, Fazal Mahmood 4 for 35, Nasimul Ghani 4 for 35) and 245 (J. S. Solomon 66, Butcher 61). Pakistan 304 (Hanif Mohammad 103, Saeed Ahmed 78) and 88 for no wicket (Ajiz Butt 41 not out).

AT Dacca. March 6 *to* 8. Pakistan won by 41 runs. Pakistan 145 (Wallis Mathias 64, W. W. Hall 4 for 28) and 144 (Mathias 45, E. S. Atkinson 4 for 42, Hall 4 for 49). West Indies 76 (Fazal 6 for 34) and 172 (G. S. Sobers 45, Fazal 6 for 66, Mahmood Hussain 4 for 48).

AT Lahore. March 26 *to* 31. West Indies won by an innings and 156 runs. West Indies 469 (R. B. Kanhai 217, Sobers 72, Solomon 56). Pakistan 209 (Ajiz 47, Waqar Hassan 41, Imtiaz Ahmed 40, Hall 5 for 87) and 104 (S. Ramadhin 4 for 25).

West Indies in Pakistan 1974–75

AT Lahore. February 15 *to* 20. Match drawn. Pakistan 199 (A. M. E. Roberts 5 for 66) and 373 for seven declared (Mushtaq Mohammad 123, Aftab Baloch 60 not out, Asif Iqbal 52, Roberts 4 for 121). West Indies 214 (A. I. Kallicharran 92 not out, R. C. Fredericks 44, Sarfraz Nawaz 6 for 89) and 258 for four (L. Baichan 105 not out, C. H. Lloyd 83, Kallicharran 44).

AT Karachi. March 1 *to* 6. Match drawn. Pakistan 406 for eight declared (Wasim Raja 107 not out, Majid Khan 100, Wasim Bari 58) and 256 (Sadiq Mohammad 98 not out, Asif Iqbal 77). West Indies 493 (Kallicharran 115, B. D. Julien 101, Fredericks 77, Lloyd 73) and one for no wicket.

Pakistan in West Indies 1977

AT Kensington. February 18 *to* 23. Match drawn. Pakistan 435 (Wasim Raja 117 not out, Majid Khan 88, J. Garner 4 for 130) and 291 (Raja 71, Wasim Bari 60 not out, C. E. H. Croft 4 for 47). West Indies 421 (C. H. Lloyd 157, D. L. Murray 52, C. G. Greenidge 47, Garner 43) and 251 for nine (I. V. A. Richards 92, R. C. Fredericks 52, Sarfraz Nawaz 4 for 79).

AT Queen's Park. March 4 *to* 9. West Indies won by six wickets. Pakistan 180 (Raja 65, Majid 47, Croft 8 for 29) and 340 (Raja 84, Sadiq Mohammad 81, Majid 54, A.M.E. Roberts 4 for 85). West Indies 316 (Fredericks 120, Mushtaq Mohammad 4 for 50) and 206 for four (C. G. Greenidge 70, Fredericks 57).

AT Bourda. March 18 *to* 23. Match drawn. Pakistan 194 (Imran Khan 47, Mushtaq 41, Garner 4 for 48) and 540 (Majid 167, Zaheer Abbas 80, Haroon Rashid 60, Sadiq 48, Garner 4 for 100). West Indies 448 (I. T. Shillingford 120, Greenidge 91, A. I. Kallicharran 72, Richards 50, Murray 42, Majid 4 for 45) and 154 for one (Greenidge 96, Fredericks 52 not out).

AT Queen's Park. April 1 *to* 6. Pakistan won by 266 runs. Pakistan 341 (Mushtaq 121, Majid 92) and 301 for nine declared (Raja 70, Mushtaq 56, Sarfraz 51). West Indies 154 (Fredericks 41, Mushtaq 5 for 28, Imran 4 for 64) and 222 (Kallicharran 45).

AT Sabina Park. April 16 *to* 21. West Indies won by 140 runs. West Indies 280 (Greenidge 100, C. L. King 41, Imran 6 for 90) and 359 (Fredericks 83, Greenidge 82, Lloyd 48). Pakistan 198 (Haroon 72, Croft 4 for 49) and 301 (Asif Iqbal 135, Raja 64).

PARTNERSHIP RECORDS

West Indies:

1st	182	R. C. Fredericks and C. G. Greenidge	Kingston	1977
2nd	446	C. C. Hunte and G. S. Sobers	Kingston	1958
3rd	162	R. B. Kanhai and G. S. Sobers	Lahore	1959
4th	182*	G. S. Sobers and C. L. Walcott	Kingston	1958
5th	185	E. D. Weekes and O. G. Smith	Bridgetown	1958
6th	151	C. H. Lloyd and D. L. Murray	Bridgetown	1977

7th	70	C. H. Lloyd and J. Garner	Bridgetown	1977
8th	58	B. D. Julien and V. A. Holder	Karachi	1975
9th	46	J. Garner and C. E. H. Croft	Port-of-Spain	1977
10th	26	A. M. E. Roberts and C. E. H. Croft	Georgetown	1977

Pakistan:

1st	219	Majid Khan, Sadiq Mohammad and Zaheer Abbas (Sadiq retired hurt at 60)	Georgetown	1977
	152	Hanif Mohammad and Imtiaz Ahmed	Bridgetown	1958
2nd	178	Hanif Mohammad and Saeed Ahmed	Karachi	1959
3rd	169	Saeed Ahmed and Wazir Mohammed	Port-of-Spain	1958
4th	154	Wazir Mohammad and Hanif Mohammad	Port-of-Spain	1958
5th	87	Haroon Rashid and Mushtaq Mohammad	Kingston	1977
6th	166	Wazir Mohammad and A. H. Kardar	Kingston	1958
7th	128	Wasim Raja and Wasim Bari	Lahore	1975
8th	68	Mushtaq Mohammad and Sarfraz Nawaz	Port-of-Spain	1977
9th	73	Wasim Raja and Sarfraz Nawaz	Bridgetown	1977
10th	133	Wasim Raja and Wasim Bari	Bridgetown	1977

Prudential
World Cup
1975

Prudential World Cup 1975

A WORLD championship for cricket, because of the way the Test game is constituted, could not have been a reality but for the development of the limited-overs, single-innings matches in the 1960s. While it was simply not practical to organise the major cricket-playing countries into a single tournament for a round-robin series of full, five-day Tests, it was for "instant" cricket, the variety which could be completed with a definite decision within a day.

So England was the venue for cricket's first World Cup tournament in the summer of 1975. It was England which had pioneered the introduction of limited-overs cricket to the first-class level of the game and there that it had proved a great success. It was England that found a sponsor for this bold innovation, the Prudential Assurance Company.

Eight teams—Australia, East Africa, England, India, Pakistan, New Zealand, Sri Lanka and the West Indies—took part and it was a hit beyond even the greatest expectations of the most optimistic organisers.

For two weeks, cricket captured the sporting imagination as it had seldom done before. The crowds flocked to the 15 matches, with nearly 200,000 spectators watching an enthralling tournament. There was an overall profit of approximately £200,000. The entire venture was blessed by extraordinary luck. One of the principal ingredients for its triumphant run was the weather, which remained magnificent throughout, warm and sunny for most days. Being matches of a single innings per team, their flow could so easily have been interrupted by rain and bad light, the frequent twin pestilences of English cricket. Instead, not a ball was lost because of the elements and the final, a match of wonderful cricket with a dramatic ending, lasted until 8.42 pm.

Obviously, not the weather alone could have been responsible for the satisfaction the Cup provided. It needed to be supplemented by the quality of the cricket and there was little lacking in this regard. It is true that the teams with no experience of international cricket, East Africa and Sri Lanka, were out of their depths and that it was clear from the start that the eventual champions would be either England, Australia, Pakistan or the West Indies. Yet every round of the tournament produced its fascination, culminating in a final which was a most fitting climax.

The champions, as had been widely predicted, were the West Indies. They came through a tough first round in a zone also containing Australia and Pakistan to beat New Zealand in the semi-final and Australia in the final, played at Lord's before a capacity crowd. They had to endure the palpitations of a near-calamity in their first-round engagement against a talented Pakistan team but otherwise played superbly. It could not be denied that their players, all of whom were county professionals, had benefited greatly by the experience of limited-overs cricket they had gained in England. Yet it is the type of cricket ideally suited to the West Indian style and attitude. Learie Constantine, for instance, would have been a veritable god at it.

The West Indies coasted through their first match against Sri Lanka and won by nine wickets but their real challenge was against Pakistan and Australia. Only two teams would advance into the semi-finals from each group and defeat in any match could have meant elimination. The amazing match against Pakistan at Edgbaston almost proved the West Indies' undoing. Pakistan's powerful batting mounted an excellent total of 266 for seven from the 60 allotted overs and Sarfraz Nawaz, their huge fast-medium bowler, then pinned the West Indies into a corner by taking three quick and cheap wickets at the start of the innings. At 166 for eight all appeared lost, with 100 to make and only Deryck Murray, Vanburn Holder and Andy Roberts to do it. Yet, by dint of cool-headed application, it was done. The Pakistanis panicked, Murray was 61 not out at the end, Holder made 16 and Roberts 24 not out and the match was won, with two balls to go, by one wicket.

The first confrontation between the West Indies and Australia attracted a large crowd at The Oval, in south London, and in the heart of a West Indian immigrant community the West Indies were strongly backed. They were never pressed while winning by seven wickets. Australia's fast bowlers, Dennis Lillee and Jeff Thomson, brought a fearful reputation to England with them as a result of their exploits in the Ashes series in Australia a few months earlier but, on a slow pitch, they were put to the sword, particularly by Alvin Kallicharran, one of the smallest men among the 122 in the competition, who hooked, cut and drove in sparkling manner for 78.

The semi-finals were England and Australia in one match at Headingley and the West Indies and New Zealand in the other at The Oval. Australia won through in a low-scoring match in which 16 wickets fell for 187 runs and the West Indies overcame a spirited but limited New Zealand side by five wickets. So, it was generally agreed, the two best and most attractive teams had qualified for the final—and what a performance they served up.

One innings alone, a peerless 102 by the West Indian captain, Clive Lloyd, during which he battered the ball to all parts of the field and, twice, into the stands as well, would have made the match a memorable one. He came in when the West Indies were in dire straits at 50 for three, he left at 199 for four having stripped the Australians of their self-confidence. If the Australians didn't, the crowd, and especially the West Indians in it, loved the entire scintillating exhibition. The steady presence through it all of the greying veteran Rohan Kanhai, only in the team because of the withdrawal of the injured Sir Garry Sobers, was vital to a 60-overs total of 291 for eight.

It was, surely, beyond Australia's reach. Yet all through their innings the Australians kept in touch. Everyone contributed to the cause, captain Ian Chappell's 62 being the best, but they were always committed to taking risks, not least in running between the wickets, and this created problems. The left-handed opener Alan Turner, Chappell and his brother, Greg, were all run out at vital stages—and each time the fielder was Vivian Richards, whose speed, anticipation and accuracy of throw were almost as important to the West Indian triumph as Lloyd's bludgeoning bat.

At 233 for nine, with Lillee and Thomson, the Nos. 10 and 11, together, only the final rites remained. Yet, with a combination of typical tail-end slogging, commendable common sense and luck, the Australian fast bowlers built the excitement again with a partnership which raised Australian hopes. Once, when Thomson was caught at cover off a Holder no-ball, thousands of spectators, thinking the match was over, swarmed the outfield, only to be turned back after some minutes. Their second invasion, however, was no false alarm as Murray, standing back, took the ball when Thomson missed a swing at Holder and threw the wicket down with the Australian out of his ground. It was the fifth run-out of the innings, a tribute to the excellence of the West Indian fielding. Seventeen runs separated the teams and eight balls of the match remained.

Lloyd, who also produced a stint of accurate medium-paced bowling to supplement his batting, was presented with both the Man of the Match medal and the Cup by Prince Philip. The almost unanimous demand that the competition become a regular feature on the international cricket calendar has been heeded and it appears here to stay. Those that follow will have much to live up to.

	Territory	Tests	Type	Born/Died	Debut*
ACHONG, Ellis "Puss"	T	6	LHB/SLA	16.2.1904	v E, 1930
ALEXANDER, Franz Copeland Murray "Gerry" (Captain for 18 Tests, 1958–59)	J	25	RHB/WK	2.11.1928	v E, 1957
ALI, Inshan	T	12	LHB/SLC	25.9.1949	v I, 1971
ALI, Imtiaz	T	1	RHB/LBG	28.7.1954	v I, 1976
ALLAN, David Walter	B	5	RHB/WK	5.11.1939	v I, 1962
ASGARALI, Nyron	T	2	RHB	28.12.1922	v E, 1957
ATKINSON, Denis St Eval (Captain for seven Tests, 1955–56)	B/T	22	RHB/RM or OB	9.8.1926	v I, 1949
ATKINSON, Eric St Eval	B	8	RHB/RM	6.11.1925	v P, 1958
BAICHAN, Leonard	G	3	LHB	12.5.1946	v P, 1975
BARRETT, Arthur George	J	6	RHB/LBG	4.4.1944	v I, 1971
BARROW, Ivan	J	11	RHB/WK	6.1.1911	v E, 1930
BARTLETT, Edward Lawson "Barto"	B	5	RHB	18.3.1906 21.12.1976	v E, 1928
BETANCOURT, Nelson (Captain for one Test, 1930)	T	1	RHB/WK	4.6.1887 12.10.1947	v E, 1930
BINNS, Alfred Phillip	J	5	RHB/WK	24.7.1949	v I, 1953
BIRKETT, Lionel Sydney	B/G/T	4	RHB/RM	14.4.1905	v A, 1931
BOYCE, Keith David	B	21	RHB/RFM	11.10.1943	v I, 1971
BROWNE, Cyril Rutherford "Snuffy"	B/G	4	RHB/RM or LBG	8.10.1890 12.1.1964	v E, 1928
BUTCHER, Basil Fitzherbert	G	44	RHB/LBG	3.9.1933	v I, 1959
BUTLER, Lennox Stephen "Bunny"	T	1	RHB/RM	9.2.1929	v A, 1955
BYNOE, Michael Robin	B	4	RHB/LM	21.2.1941	v P, 1959
CAMACHO, George Stephen	G	11	RHB/LBG	15.10.1945	v E, 1968
CAMERON, Francis James	J	5	RHB/OB	22.6.1923	v I, 1949

CAMERON, John H.	J	2	RHB/OB	8.4.1914	v E, 1939
CAREW, George McDonald	B	4	RHB	1910 9.12.1974	v E, 1935
CAREW, Michael Conrad "Joey"	T	19	LHB/OB	15.9.1937	v E, 1963
CHALLENOR, George	B	3	RHB/RM	28.6.1888 30.7.1947	v E, 1928
CHRISTIANI, Cyril Marcel	G	4	RHB/WK	28.10.1913 4.4.1938	v E, 1935
CHRISTIANI, Robert Julien	G	22	RHB/WK/ OB	19.7.1920	v E, 1948
CLARKE, Carlos Bertram "Bertie"	B	3	RHB/LBG	7.4.1918	v E, 1939
CONSTANTINE, Learie Nicholas Lord, Baron of Maraval and Nelson	T	18	RHB/RF/ RM	21.9.1902 1.7.1971	v E, 1928
CROFT, Colin Everton Hunte	G	5	RHB/RF	15.3.1953	v P, 1977
DaCOSTA, Oscar C.	J	5	RHB/RM	11.9.1907	v E, 1930
DANIEL, Wayne Wendell	B	5	RHB/RF	15.1.1956	v I, 1976
DAVIS, Bryan Alan	T	4	RHB	2.5.1940	v A, 1965
DAVIS, Charles Alan	T	15	RHB/RM	1.1.1944	v A, 1969
deCAIRES, Frank I.	G	3	RHB	12.5.1909	v E, 1930
dePEIZA, Clairemonte	B	5	RHB/WK/ RM	10.10.1927	v A, 1955
DEWDNEY, Thomas	J	9	RHB/RFM	23.10.1933	v A, 1955
DOWE, Uton George	J	4	RHB/RF	29.3.1949	v I, 1971
EDWARDS, Richard Martin "Prof"	B	5	RHB/RF or RM	3.6.1940	v A, 1969
FERGUSON, Wilfred	T	8	RHB/LBG	14.12.1917 23.2.1961	v E, 1948
FERNANDES, Marius Pacheco "Maurice" (Captain for one Test, 1930)	G	2	RHB	12.8.1898	v E, 1928
FINDLAY, Thaddeus Michael	WI	10	RHB/WK	19.10.1943	v E, 1969
FOSTER, Maurice Linton Churchill	J	13	RHB/OB	9.5.1943	v E, 1969
FRANCIS, George Nathaniel	B	10	RHB/RF	7.12.1897 12.1.1942	v E, 1928
FREDERICK, Michael Campbell	B/J	1	RHB	6.5.1927	v E, 1954
FREDERICKS, Roy Clifton	G	59	LHB	11.11.1942	v A, 1969

FULLER, Richard L. "Dickie"	J	1	RHB/RFM		v E, 1935
FURLONGE, Hammond A.	T	3	RHB	19.7.1934	v A, 1955
GANTEAUME, Andrew George	T	1	RHB	22.1.1921	v E, 1948
GARNER, Joel	B	5	RHB/RFM	12.12.1952	v P, 1977
GASKIN, Berkeley McGarrell	G	2	RHB/RM	23.3.1908	v E, 1948
GIBBS, Glendon R.	G	1	LHB/SLA	27.12.1925	v A, 1955
GIBBS, Lancelot Richard "Lance"	G	79	RHB/OB	29.9.1934	v P, 1958
GILCHRIST, Roy	J	13	RHB/RF	28.6.1934	v E, 1957
GLADSTONE, George	J	1	LHB/SLA		v E, 1930
GODDARD, John Douglas Claude (Captain for 25 Tests, 1948–57)	B	27	LHB/RM or OB	21.4.1919	v E, 1948
GOMES, Hilary Angelo "Larry"	T	2	LHB/RM	13.7.1953	v E, 1976
GOMEZ, Gerald Ethridge "Gerry" (Captain for one Test, 1948)	T	29	RHB/RM	10.10.1919	v E, 1948
GRANT, George Copeland "Jackie" (Captain for 12 Tests, 1930–35)	T	12	RHB	9.5.1907	v A, 1931
GRANT, Rolph Stewart (Captain for 3 Tests, 1939)	T	7	RHB/OB	15.12.1909 18.10.1977	v E, 1935
GREENIDGE, Cuthbert **Gordon**	B	17	RHB/RM	2.5.1951	v I, 1975
GREENIDGE, Geoffrey Alan	B	5	RHB/LBG	26.5.1948	v NZ, 1972
GRELL, Mervyn George	T	1	RHB/RM	18.12.1899 11.1.1976	v E, 1930
GRIFFITH, Charles Christopher	B	28	RHB/RF	14.12.1938	v E, 1960
GRIFFITH, Herman C.	B	13	RHB/RF	1.12.1893	v E, 1928
GUILLEN, Simpson Clement "Sammy" (Also played 3 Tests for NZ)	T	5	RHB/WK	24.9.1924	v A, 1952
HALL, Wesley Winfield "Wes"	B/T	48	RHB/RF	12.9.1937	v I, 1959
HEADLEY, George Alphonso (Captain for one Test, 1948)	J	22	RHB/OB	30.5.1909	v E, 1928
HEADLEY, Ronald George Alphonso	J	2	LHB	29.6.1939	v E, 1973

HENDRIKS, John Leslie "Jackie"	J	20	RHB/WK	21.12.1933	v I, 1962
HOAD, Edward Lisle Goldsworthy (Captain for one Test, 1930)	B	4	RHB/LBG	29.1.1896	v E, 1928
HOLDER, Vanburn Alonza	B	30	RHB/RFM	8.10.1945	v E, 1969
HOLDING, Michael Anthony	J	13	RHB/RF	16.2.1954	v A, 1976
HOLFORD, David Anthony Jerome	B	24	RHB/LBG	16.4.1940	v E, 1966
HOLT, John Kenneth Jnr	J	17	RHB	12.8.1923	v E, 1954
HOWARD, Anthony Bourne	B	1	LHB/OB	27.8.1946	v NZ, 1972
HUNTE, Conrad Cleophas	B	44	RHB/RM	8.5.1932	v P, 1958
HUNTE, Errol A. C.	T	3	RHB/WK	3.10.1905 .8.1967	v E, 1930
HYLTON, Leslie George	J	6	RHB/RFM	29.3.1905 17.5.1955	v E, 1935

JOHNSON, Hines Hophine	J	3	RHB/RF	17.7.1910	v E, 1948
JOHNSON, Tyrell Francis	T	1	LHB/LFM	10.1.1917	v E, 1939
JONES, Charles M.	G	4	RHB/WK/ SLA		v E, 1930
JONES, Prior E.	T	9	RHB/RFM	6.6.1917	v E, 1948
JULIEN, Bernard Denis	T	24	RHB/LFM, SLA, SLC	13.3.1950	v E, 1973
JUMADEEN, Raphick Rasif	T	8	RHB/SLA	12.4.1948	v NZ, 1972

KALLICHARRAN, Alvin Isaac	G	40	LHB/LBG	21.3.1949	v NZ, 1972
KANHAI, Rohan Babulal (Captain for 13 Tests, 1973–74)	G/T	79	RHB/OB	26.12.1935	v E, 1957
KENTISH, Esmond Seymour Maurice	J	2	RHB/RF	21.11.1916	v E, 1948
KING, Collis Llewellyn	B	4	RHB/RM	11.6.1951	v E, 1976

KING, Frank McDonald	B	14	RHB/RFM	14.12.1926	v I, 1953
KING, Lester Anthony	J	2	RHB/RFM	27.2.1939	v I, 1962
LASHLEY, Patrick Douglas "Peter"	B	4	LHB/RM	11.2.1937	v A, 1961
LEGALL, Ralph	B/T	4	RHB/WK	25.2.1926	v I, 1962
LEWIS, Desmond Michael	J	3	RHB/WK	21.2.1946	v I, 1971
LLOYD, Clive Hubert (Captain for 27 Tests, 1974–77)	G	63	LHB/RM or LBG	31.8.1944	v I, 1967
McMORRIS, Easton Dudley Ashton	J	13	RHB	4.4.1935	v E, 1960
McWATT, Clifford Aubrey	G	6	LHB/WK	1.2.1922	v E, 1954
MADRAY, Ivan Samuel	G	2	RHB/LBG	2.7.1934	v P, 1958
MARSHALL, Norman Edgar	B/T	1	RHB/OB	27.2.1924	v A, 1955
MARSHALL, Roy Edwin	B	4	RHB/OB	25.4.1930	v A, 1952
MARTIN, Frank Rginalnd "Freddie"	J	9	LHB/SLA	12.10.1893 23.11.1967	v E, 1928
MARTINDALE, Emmanuel Alfred "Manny"	B	10	RHB/RF	25.11.1909 17.3.1972	v E, 1933
MENDONCA, Ivor Leon	G	2	RHB/WK	13.7.1934	v I, 1962
MERRY, Cyril Arthur	T	2	RHB	20.1.1911 19.4.1964	v E, 1933
MILLER, Roy C.	J	1	RHB/RFM		v. I 1953
MOODIE, George H.	J	1	RHB/SLA	26.11.1915	v E, 1935
MURRAY, Deryck Lance	T	49	RHB/WK	20.5.1943	v E, 1963
NEBLETT, James M.	B/G	1	RHB/LBG	13.11.1901	v E, 1935
NOREIGA, Jack Mollison	T	4	RHB/OB	15.4.1936	v I, 1971

NUNES, Robert Karl (Captain for 4 Tests, 1928–29)	J	4	RHB/WK	7.6.1894 22.7.1958	v E, 1928
NURSE, Seymour McDonald	B	29	RHB	11.11.1933	v E, 1960
PADMORE, Albert Leroy	B	2	RHB/OB	17.12.1946	v I, 1976
PAIRAUDEAU, Bruce H.	G	13	RHB	14.4.1931	v I, 1953
PASSAILAIGUE, Clarence C.	J	1	RHB	.8.1902 7.1.1972	v E, 1930
PIERRE, Lance Richard	T	1	RHB/RFM	5.6.1921	v E, 1948
RAE, Allan Fitzgerald	J	15	LHB	30.9.1922	v I, 1949
RAMADHIN, Sonny	T	43	RHB/OB, LBG	1.5.1930	v E, 1950
RICHARDS, Isaac Vivian Alexander "Viv"	LI	26	RHB/OB	7.3.1952	v I, 1975
RICKARDS, Kenneth R.	J	2	RHB	23.8.1923	v E, 1948
ROACH, Clifford Archibald	T	16	RHB	13.3.1904	v E, 1928
ROBERTS, Anderson Montgomery Everton "Andy"	LI	25	RHB/RF	29.1.1951	v E, 1974
ROBERTS, Alphonso T.	WI	1	RHB	18.9.1937	v NZ, 1956
RODRIGUEZ, William Vincente "Willie"	T	5	RHB/LBG	25.6.1934	v I, 1962
ROWE, Lawrence George	J	24	RHB/RM	8.1.1949	v NZ, 1972
ST HILL, Edwin Lloyd	T	2	RHB/RM	9.3.1904 21.5.1957	v E, 1930
ST HILL, Wilton H.	T	3	RHB	6.7.1893 Deceased	v E, 1928
SCARLETT, Reginald O.	J	3	RHB/OB	15.8.1934	v E, 1960
SCOTT, Alfred P. H.	J	1	RHB/LBG		v I, 1953
SCOTT, O. C. "Tommy"	J	8	RHB/LBG	25.8.1893 16.6.1961	v E, 1928

SEALEY, Benjamin James	T	1	RHB/RFM	12.8.1899	v E, 1933
SEALY, James Edward **Derek**	B/T	11	RHB/RFM/ WK	11.9.1912	v E, 1930
SHEPHERD, John Neil	B	5	RHB/RM	9.11.1943	v E, 1969
SHILLINGFORD, Grayson Cleophas	WI	7	LHB/RFM	25.9.1946	v E, 1969
SHILLINGFORD, Irvine Theodore	WI	3	RHB	18.4.1944	v P, 1977
SINGH, Charran K.	T	2	RHB/SLA		v E, 1960
SMALL, Joseph A.	T	3	RHB/OB	3.11.1892 26.4.1958	v E, 1928
SMITH, Cameron Wilberforce "Cammie"	B	5	RHB/WK	29.7.1933	v A, 1961
SMITH, O'Neil Gordon "Collie"	J	26	RHB/OB	5.5.1933 9.9.1959	v A, 1955
SOBERS, Sir Garfield St Aubrun "Garry" (Captain for 39 Tests, 1965–72)	B	93	LHB/LFM, SLA or SLC	28.7.1936	v E, 1954
SOLOMON, Joseph Stanislaus	G	27	RHB/LBG	26.8.1930	v I, 1959
STAYERS, Sven Conrad "Charlie"	G	4	RHB/RFM	9.6.1937	v I, 1962
STOLLMEYER Jeffrey Baxter (Captain for 14 Tests, 1951–55)	T	32	RHB/LBG	11.3.1921	v E, 1939
STOLLMEYER, Victor Humphrey	T	1	RHB/LBG	24.1.1916	v E, 1939
TAYLOR, Jaswick	T	3	RHB/RFM	3.1.1932	v P, 1958
TRIM, John	G	4	RHB/RFM	24.1.1915 12.11.1960	v E, 1948
VALENTINE, Alfred Lewis	J	36	RHB/SLA	29.4.1930	v E, 1950
VALENTINE, Vincent A.	J	2	RHB/RFM	4.4.1908	v E, 1933
WALCOTT, Clyde Leopold	B/G	44	RHB/RM/ WK	17.1.1926	v E, 1948

WALCOTT, Leslie Arthur	B	1	RHB/LBG	19.1.1894	v E, 1930
WATSON, Chester	J	7	RHB/RF	1.7.1939	v E. 1960
WEEKES, Everton deCourcey	B	48	RHB/LBG	26.2.1925	v E, 1948
WEEKES, Kenneth H. "Bam Bam"	J	2	LHB	24.1.1912	v E, 1939
WHITE, Winston Anthony	B	2	RHB/RM/ OB	20.11.1938	v A, 1965
WIGHT, Claude Vibart	G	2	RHB	28.7.1902 Deceased	v E, 1928
WIGHT, George Leslie	G	1	RHB	28.5.1929	v I, 1953
WILES, C. Archibald	B/T	1	RHB	11.8.1892	v E, 1933
WILLETT, Elquemedo Tonito	LI	5	LHB/SLA	1.5.1953	v A, 1973
WILLIAMS, Edward Albert Vivian "Foffie"	B	4	RHB/RFM	10.4.1914	v E, 1939
WISHART, Kenneth Leslie	G	1	LHB	28.11.1908 18.10.1972	v E, 1935
WORRELL, Sir Frank Mortimore Maglinne (Captain for 15 Tests, 1960–63)	B/J	51	RHB/LM or SLA	1.8.1924 13.3.1967	v E, 1948

*(1929-30 series referred to as 1930, 1930-31 as 1931, etc.)

B—Barbados; G—Guyana; J—Jamaica; LI—Leeward Islands; T—
Trinidad; WI—Windward Islands; RHB—right-hand batsman; LHB—
left-hand batsman; RF—right-arm fast bowler; RFM—right-arm fast-
medium bowler; RM—right-arm medium-pace bowler; OB—right-arm off-
spin bowler; LBG—right-arm leg-spin bowler; LF—left-arm fast bowler;
LFM—left-arm fast-medium bowler; LM—left-arm medium-pace bowler;
SLA—orthodox left-arm spin bowler; SLC—left-arm chinaman and googly
bowler; A—Australia; E—England; I—India; NZ—New Zealand; P—
Pakistan.

Index